MY LIFE, MY LOVES
by
KING ERRISSON

Copyright 2016
King Errisson

ALL RIGHTS RESERVED

No portion of this publication may be reproduced, stored in any electronic system, or transmitted in any form or by any means, electronic, mechanical, photocopy, recording, or otherwise, without written permission from the author. Brief quotations may be used in literary reviews.

ISBN-13:
978-1537579115

ISBN-10:
1537579118

Errisson Publishing - kingerrisson@yahoo.com
Year of publication 2016

Dedicated to my mother

Josephine Brice Johnson

TABLE OF CONTENTS

Introduction	4
Chapter 1 -- Island Boy	6
Chapter 2 -- A Childhood in Paradise	17
Chapter 3 -- Storm Clouds	26
Chapter 4 -- Hoof Beats and Drum Beats: My Early Years in the Spotlight	37
Chapter 5 -- Love, Heartbreak and a Taste of Success	50
Chapter 6 -- On Tour as a Limbo Dancer	61
Chapter 7 – Fame in the Land of the Rising Sun	74
Chapter 8 – Adventures in America	84
Chapter 9 – Becoming "That *Thunderball* Drummer"	95
Chapter 10 -- Success and Forbidden Love	106
Chapter 11 -- Loss and New Beginnings	115
Chapter 12 -- Leader of the Band	126
Chapter 13 -- Becoming "Mr. Bermuda" -- and Losing My Shirt	136
Chapter 14 -- L.A. Bound and Rebound	145
Chapter 15 -- Women & Song	157
Chapter 16 – The Music Fixer	166
Chapter 17 – The Unsung Hero of Motown	175
Chapter 18 – The Ties that Bind	186
Chapter 19 – Milestones and the Incredible Bongo Band	195
Chapter 20 – Making Music with the Stars	207
Chapter 21 – Headed for the Future	217
Afterword	227
Appendix I -- Timeline	230
Appendix II -- Album Credits	233
Appendix III -- Solo Albums	235
Appendix IV -- The Motown West Coast Studio Band	236
Appendix V -- King Errisson Contact Information	237

Introduction

Many of my fans know me as the flamboyant percussionist in Neil Diamond's touring band. Since I have been with the band for 40 years now, they probably assume that I have always performed in arenas and stadiums across the world, stayed in luxury hotels, eaten at the best restaurants, and been surrounded by adoring fans. Most of them do not know that my life started off far differently – they may know that I am from the Bahamas, but I think they would be very surprised to learn about my humble beginnings and the struggles I overcame to become a world-class musician.

Over the years, I have told a few stories of my early days. When I do interviews, I am usually asked about my musical background or some of the recording artists I have backed. When I talk face-to-face with fans, they are usually more interested in my personal experiences (they seem to be the most surprised that my first success came not as a musician but as a jockey). This is the first time that I am telling the entire story, beginning with my childhood in the Bahamas to the start of my first world tour with Neil Diamond.

Although I started writing this book many years ago (I covered literally hundreds of sheets of lined paper with handwritten notes and later made tape recordings of some of my experiences and impressions), I wasn't too sure about writing about my entire life. I didn't know if people would be interested in my childhood and early career, but fans have repeatedly told me that they did, indeed, want to hear my story from the beginning.

I have tried to write this book in a conversational style – as if the reader and I were sitting down together enjoying a cup of coffee or a drink. I enjoy sharing my stories face-to-face, so I wanted to keep that kind of tone in this book. It is especially gratifying to be able to share the entire story – not just a snippet here and there.

To the best of my knowledge, this book is a factual account of my first 35-plus years. It was my goal to have this book be THE source for information about me and my early career; I have seen a lot of misinformation on the Internet – I am NOT Jamaican, for example – so this book is my opportunity to set the record straight. Since my 75th birthday is approaching, however, my memory may have gotten a little foggy, so I have relied on extensive research to ensure the accuracy of the book's content.

I also want to mention that I have toned down the language in my original scribblings and refrained from including graphic sexual material to avoid offending sensitive fans. But there are times when the "original" language brings the point home – and, as far as the content about women goes, I have been in more than my share of "adult situations" and this wouldn't really be the story of my life if I didn't mention some of my experiences in the romance department.

    In conclusion, I want to advise everyone that this is NOT a book about Neil Diamond. I have included mentions of recording, performing, and touring with him (those incidents are part of my career and it would be remiss to omit them), but this book was written to tell the story of King Errisson. I hope that you will enjoy reading it, and that it whets your appetite to learn more about my life and later career. Happy reading and hugs to all.

Chapter One

Island Boy

Although I was born and grew up in an island paradise, from a very early age I would look out over the sparkling blue ocean and dream of faraway places -- and of being "somebody." Fortunately, I would be one of the lucky ones whose dreams would come true -- I would, indeed, leave my island home to travel the world, creating and performing my own music and backing some of the best solo performers and groups in the business.

I have never stopped being thankful for the God-given talent that made my dreams come true. Even today, it sometimes seems hard to believe that I can be heard on the recordings of acclaimed giants -- Cannonball Adderley, Neil Diamond, the Jackson Five, Johnny Mathis, Diana Ross, Barry White, and a long list of others. Not to mention that I performed before thousands of enthusiastic fans who filled arenas and stadiums in places that I only used to dream about. And my story is all the more amazing when you consider my humble beginnings.

I made my debut as Errisson Pallaman Johnson in a modest three-bedroom clapboard house on a little street called Liza Malcolm Corner in Nassau, on the island of New Providence, in the Bahamas on October 29, 1941. Born to Pallaman "Stewie" Johnson and Josephine Brice-Johnson, I weighed in at eight and a half pounds. After I was born, my mother started to get up, but the midwife pushed her back down and said,

"There's going to be one more."

Sure enough, my twin sister, Aries, who weighed nine pounds, saw the light of day about 30 minutes later. My father, who was there when my mother gave birth, took one look at his two newborn babies and joked (or was he joking?) to my mother,

"I know the boy is mine, but who does the girl belong to?"

Both Aries and I were dark-skinned and very striking in appearance, but we were so different looking that if we had been born at a hospital, someone might have thought the babies had somehow been switched. There was no doubt she belonged to my father, though -- she was the spitting image of my dad's sister, Aunt Maud, who was the daughter of my father's mother, Petrona Darling Johnson, and her first husband, dad's father, Edward "Eddie" Johnson.

Since my parents were such great influences on my early life -- and, indeed, I wouldn't have a story without them -- an introduction is in order. My father, who was from Acklins, one of the out islands of the Bahamas, was a striking man. In fact, when the future Queen Elizabeth II visited the Bahamas with her father, King George VI, when she was a young princess, she declared that my dad was the most handsome man in the world! Dad was dark-skinned like his mother, who was the most beautiful woman in all of Acklins, and he had thick, wavy hair. He was a short guy, about 5'7½", but he had very thick shoulders and big hands and feet. Looking at those hands and feet, you would think he would have been at least six feet tall (his father and my dad's younger brother were six-footers, and dad's mother and sisters were all big gals).

My dad had only one physical flaw – the bad water on Acklins had rotted his teeth, but dad would later remedy that problem, using part of the money that he earned while working on contract in the United States to get all of his teeth capped with gold. Those were some beautiful gold teeth.

My dad was from a very large family. His mother, Petrona (everyone called her "Pet"), gave birth to 11 children with dad's father, including my Uncle Eddie, who was born after my granddad died in the hurricane of 1926. Pet later married a cousin of my dad's father, and she had another 11 children with him before she bled to death while giving birth to my beautiful Aunt Stella.

It doesn't surprise me that my mother found my father so attractive, but she was a beauty, too. My mother, who was called "Jo" or "Big Ma" by everyone who knew her, had been born in the settlement of Mt. Thompson, on the out island of Great Exuma, in 1919. One of 14 children, she was a happy, curious child with a beautiful singing voice. And she was a real "hottie" when my father met her.

Before he met my mother, my dad had been dating a girl from the settlement of Lovely Bay on Acklins. He later found out that the girl was a second cousin, so dad vowed that he would not take the chance of dating another woman from Acklins. Instead, he would load his homemade boats and rafts with fish, bottles and other merchandise to sell on other islands, sometimes sailing as far away as Haiti.

At the time dad met my mother, he was already a high school teacher, which was a great honor for someone who was only in his teens. He was also a boat builder, fisherman and salesman. One of the hardest workers I have ever known, dad was always doing something to make money. Little did he know that he would work even harder after he and mom got together.

Pallaman and Josephine met in Georgetown on Great Exuma during one of dad's trips there to sell his wares. It was love at first sight for him, but my mother always told her family and us children that she did not love him -- that dad threw some magic dust into her face and she could not help herself...she had to fall in love with him.

My father, the magic man, told the story a little differently (he said it was love at first sight for both of them). But, no matter how it all started, my mom and dad fell so much in love that they spent every moment that they could together – in fact, dad would make the trip to Georgetown on his boat twice a month to see her.

One fateful day (a day that I'm sure he later regretted), my dad picked up my mother in Georgetown and they sailed back to Pestell Beach on Acklins to meet Pet. My father was so in love with my mom that he wanted to get his mother's blessing, even though he wasn't sure he was ready for marriage.

I've heard it said that my parents' union had something to do with my mom being pregnant (she would later give birth to a son who lived just a few hours). Ironically, my grandmother had also lost her first son, so maybe that was part of the bond between them. Whatever the reason, the two women were crazy about each other, and it was my grandmother who insisted that mom and dad get married – and right away.

"You brought her to me, and I love her. You have to marry her," Pet insisted.

Well, Pet's word was law. And Pet was so eager to have my mother join the family that she planned the entire wedding, which took place in June of 1937.

Aries and I, the first of mom and dad's four children together, came along a little over four years later. My grandmother, Petrona, saw that there was something special about me, and she immediately dubbed me "King." If there was any doubt that I would become known as King, it was dispelled when I was just an infant.

One fateful day, my uncle, John Alfred Brice (we called him Uncle Fred), was walking down Bay Street, pushing the carriage that held Aries and me. On that day, someone else was also strolling down Bay Street. It was His Royal Highness Edward, the Duke of Windsor, who had been appointed Governor of the Bahamas in 1940, the year before I was born.

The new governor had previously reigned as King Edward VIII from June 22, 1936 to December 11, 1937, when he abdicated the throne to marry an American divorcee, Wallis Simpson. After Edward's brother (the father of Queen Elizabeth II and Princess Margaret) succeeded him as King George VI, the new king created the title of the Duke of Windsor for Edward. Edward and Wallis, who would become the darlings of

American society, were married a few months later and settled into a self-imposed exile in France. As World War II began sweeping across Europe, the Duke infuriated Winston Churchill when he expressed admiration for the Nazis. Determined to silence the popular ex-King, Churchill dispatched the Duke to the Bahamas on a British warship.

Installed as Governor and Commander in Chief of the Bahamas, where he served from 1940-1945, the Duke was said to have described the Bahamas as a "third-rate British colony." But if Edward had any disdain for our island paradise, the former King didn't show it on this particular day. He and a small entourage were enjoying walking down Bay Street, Nassau's bustling shopping district, soaking up the sunshine, the exotic culture and the smells of food and fish that hung in the fresh air wafting in from the velvet blue bay. News of the Duke's presence had traveled quickly, and more people than usual crowded Bay Street in the hopes of getting a glimpse of Edward and the local officials who were accompanying him. One of those expectant people was my Uncle Fred, who was convinced that there would be a blessing for his nephew and niece if they were presented to the former King.

My uncle was not disappointed. Attracted to the smiling black man who was pushing a baby carriage in his direction, Edward walked over to Uncle Fred and gazed down at the two infants who occupied the carriage. As my uncle was expressing his admiration for the former King, the Duke picked me up.

He held me in his arms for a few moments and looked warmly into my sparkling black eyes before handing me back to Uncle Fred, saying,

"You have your own King right here."

From that day on, I officially became known as King, and my mother would never permit a word of criticism about our new governor in her home. Her loyalty to the Duke may have had something to do with his remarkable -- and truly kingly -- gesture.

Edward must have discovered that fresh milk was not available on the island at that time, so a case of Carnation condensed milk was delivered to our door every week for an entire year. That milk, a gift from the Duke himself, was most welcomed and appreciated, even though my father owned a small grocery store and an ice cream shop on East Street and Farm Road at the time (those old clapboard buildings can still be seen there today).

Of course, I don't remember that incident or that Aries and I had spent time in Forbes Hill on the out island of Little Exuma when we were infants. I do remember playing on Pestell Beach on Acklins as I got a little older -- in fact, my Grandmother Pet thought so highly of me that I think she would have raised me herself if she hadn't passed away.

My earliest memories go back to when I was about two or three years old. During that time, my family moved into a new, four-bedroom house on Fleming Street. It was a big house, and it was situated on more land than I could run around on back then. Since it was such a large block of land, my father – with the help of two of my mother's brothers, Uncle Fred and Uncle Salvanis – built six houses (one-, two- and three-bedroom homes) on the property so that he could make money by renting them out.

At that time, my dad worked two other jobs, so my mother helped run my dad's store when he was away. My mother was famous for her cooking, especially for her baked crab, crab and rice, and conch chowder, which were extremely popular at Nassau's Goombay Festivals. Everyone loved "Big Ma's" cooking, and they would flock to the store, especially on Saturday mornings, to buy her pigs' feet and lambs' tongue sauces.

Although her cooking was extremely popular, my mother was best known for her baking. She baked the best bread on the island, and she could not keep up with the demand for it. I can remember that it seemed like her hands were always covered with flour.

When my mother made her bread, including her famous potato bread, she used lard. When the lard cans were empty, she would wash them out, put cellophane over the open ends and secure the cellophane with rubber bands to make drums for me. I loved to beat on the homemade drums that she made from those lard cans and empty coffee cans, and I became fascinated with music and rhythm at a very early age.

By the time I was three, I was also expanding my world -- beginning my childhood-long pursuits of catching birds and fishing with my friends. We younger boys would go along with two older guys, Leo and Selathel, in their boats to the cays (they are called keys in America), where we would get pigeons. You were only allowed to get the young birds, as it was against the law to kill the big ones, but we used to have bags and bags of birds when we came home. We would put them in one place and pick out what we wanted and share the rest with people who had no boats to get to the cays. We did the same thing when we went fishing – we would put all the fish on the beach, take what we wanted and share the rest.

I also got my first "swimming lesson" from Leo and Selathel. One day they took their boat out so far that you could hardly see land -- and then they threw us young kids off the boat and began to row away, laughing at the sight of us splashing desperately in the deep water!

You talk about sink or swim! Of course, if the older boys saw that someone was really in trouble, they would go back and pull the kid back into the boat. They didn't need to do that for me, though – I had no trouble swimming back to the boat, and, despite my rather unnerving introduction to swimming, I instantly loved being in the ocean. I would continue to swim and dive for the rest of my life, and I have been fearless around the ocean to this day (which has come in handy on more than one occasion).

In September of 1946, the month before I turned five years old, my brother, Rodney was born. By the time I was six, I was more than a big brother to Rodney – I took on the role of being a father figure to him when my mother went back to America to work on contract. Both of my parents worked on contract at various times in their lives -- signing up to work for a year or two in mostly farm jobs, such as picking crops or harvesting sugar cane. It was hard, menial labor, but Bahamians were able to make good money working on contract -- far more than what they could earn in the Bahamas -- so it was an attractive proposition for them.

Since dad was so busy with his store and other jobs, we kids were sent to live with my Aunt Edith, who lived in Forbes Hill on the island of Little Exuma. Aunt Edith, who was a pretty woman (she looked a lot like Jennifer Beals, the girl from *Flashdance*) whose husband was Uncle Frank Clarke (we called them "Mama Edith" and "Daddy Frank" when we stayed with them), They had three boys – my cousins, Audnell, who was the oldest, and Raja and Nigel, who were twins. Cousin Audnell suffered from asthma, and his family had a very unique way of treating it. They would catch a cockroach, mash it up, cook it in some butter and a tiny bit of kerosene oil and squeeze some lemon into the mixture. After they made him drink the concoction, they took Audnell outside, put him against a tree and had someone hammer a nail into the tree just above his head. The secret was that the taller the tree grew, the sooner he would grow out of the asthma. And, by damn, that worked!

Unfortunately, our Bahamian folk remedies weren't as effective for the twins. A few months after they were born, Raja took sick, and a priest came to tie a black ribbon on each boy's hand. The priest said that they had to cut the ties between the two boys; if they didn't, Raja would return for Nigel. I watched as Raja died and the priest cut the ribbon at the very time the breath left that baby's body.

Speaking of priests, I'll always remember Sunday mornings on Exuma – we had some great breakfasts on Sundays. Aunt Edith would always cook a pot of fish and make some kind of bread and some soft grits. She wasn't much of a cook, though, and, unfortunately, Daddy

Frank liked his grits a certain way. He wanted only two-minute grits, so if the grits were too hard, he would slap Aunt Edith upside the head with the pan and make her cook them over and over again until she got them right. Maybe that was why she was so mean – her husband was always slapping her.

Yes, despite being willing to take care of us when my mother was away, Aunt Edith was the meanest (and stingiest) one in the family to us kids – even though my parents had let her and Daddy Frank stay rent-free in one of their houses in Nassau for an entire year. When she cooked for all of us, Aunt Edith would make only one pot of fish or cook just one chicken. Even when a cow was killed for the people in the settlement, she only cooked a little bit for us kids.

I should mention something about those cows. There was a big pasture full of cows, sheep and goats on the island. And, ownership didn't seem to matter -- when an animal was butchered, the meat was shared among everyone. It was a beautiful thing to see, the way those people shared. Each animal had a mark, and people would take turns slaughtering them – one month, it would be my aunt's turn to choose an animal; the next month, another family would slaughter an animal for food. No matter whose turn it was, they always chose the biggest and fattest of the animals so they could share the meat with everyone else. My Aunt Edith participated in this, of course, but she hated the sight of meat -- she wouldn't eat any flesh, not even chicken. Aunt Edith only ate fish -- and I sure suffered for that.

One day, we kids went fishing and brought back loads of fish, so Aunt Edith fried up a fine dinner of jacks and snapper for us. That night, I woke up hungry for more of that snapper, so I went to get a piece of fish out of the safe (we had no refrigeration in those days on the out islands; in fact, we knew nothing about ice, so everything was put in the safe). The safe was just like a china cabinet, but with no glass – there was a screen instead so that food could get air. Unfortunately, Aunt Edith heard me getting some fish from the safe, and she came into the kitchen, grabbed my hand, put it on the table and slammed it with a Coke bottle – not once, but several times, and told me never to steal again.

I can't remember if I cried, but I do remember being more furious than I had ever been in my life – after all, I had helped to catch some of those fish! But you can bet that I never took another morsel of food in that house without asking.

And those fish were not the only thing that Aunt Edith was stingy about. While my mom was away, she kept a running tab with our cousin, Jeffrey Ferguson, who had a food store. Food for us would arrive like clockwork on the "Captain Roberts" mail boat, and my mother also sent money for clothing for her kids, but Aunt Edith always favored her own children over us. When she opened a can of peaches or fruit cocktail (from the food that my mom had sent for us!), for instance, she would only give some of the fruit to her boys; Rodney and I would just get some juice in a glass (Aunt Edith swore that the peaches would make me and Rodney men before our time).

My mom would also send money to buy clothes for us, but auntie used that money to buy clothes for her two boys – my mother's kids had to settle for clothes made from the bags that sugar, flour, rice, oats and beans came in! It was as if we were living the story of Cinderella! We only got to wear shoes on Sundays, and that was because we were going to church -- we looked like orphans the rest of the time, including when I went to school.

I began my school days while I was there in Forbes Hill. One day when I was sitting in the classroom, we heard a big explosion and everyone ran out of the schoolhouse to see what was wrong. It turned out that explosion was caused by a man by the name of Mr. Rolle, who loved to fish with dynamite. That day, he had dropped his dynamite into the sea to blow up a school of jack fish. When the cap did not go off right away, Mr. Rolle picked it up to check it. Well, it went off then, blowing off both of his hands. I had never seen so much blood, and I was afraid that the Coast Guard plane would not get there in time to save him. But that plane got there in no time, and Mr. Rolle was flown to Nassau. Although he lived, he never saw those hands again – he only had two stubs, and one of them was longer than the other. That was a day to remember, but Mr. Rolle went on to live to a ripe old age – and he never stopped fishing with dynamite.

I also had another frightening experience during that time. From the time he was a baby, my little brother, Rodney, would follow me around. To keep an eye on him, I would take him to school with me. I always got a desk next to the window so I could watch him, but one day, Rodney managed to put a piece of stick in his ear when I wasn't looking (he later explained that he was just trying to clean wax out of his ear).

That stick had gotten away from him, and the more he tried to pull it out, the farther down into his ear it went. When he started to cry, I knew that something was wrong, so I asked the teacher, Mr. Ferguson, to let me take a look. By this time, Rodney was screaming, and everybody came out of the school to see what was happening.

The stick had gone in so far that you could barely see the tip of it, so we had to send for the plane. By the time the plane arrived, though,

Leon Bowe, a man who lived nearby, had come from his house with a big sewing needle, which he used to pry the stick out. Thankfully, Rodney was okay, although his ears bled for a while, and he promised that he would never do such a dumb thing again.

Another frightening memory involved the pond behind Aunt Edith's house. A mysterious creature that we called the Devil lived in that pond. It looked somewhat like a goat, but to us kids it was more of a monster with big horns. Every day at about noon, the kids who were not in school would go to the pond and wait to see the source of our fear swim by. It wasn't difficult to know when it was coming -- someone must have put a bell on it because you could hear the sound of a bell ringing just before it came into sight.

We younger kids had to cross that pond in our little skiffs to get wood every couple of weeks, and we were scared to death! But it was something we had to do, and we always went in a group. We would throw stones and bottles at the creature, and it would dive beneath the water.

Although the Devil never bothered anyone, we knew that it loved cows and sheep. Every so often, we would find animals shredded to pieces and half eaten in the pasture. I had no idea what the Devil actually was when I was a boy – and I still don't know what kind of animal had terrified us so.

Despite having a few unpleasant experiences, I also have some wonderful memories of that stay on Exuma. One that stands out was when my great-grandfather, my mother's grandfather, was very ill, and just my Aunt Edith and I went to see him. Aunt Edith wanted to see her granddad before he died, and she chose me to walk with her to where my great-grandfather lived -- The Forest on the island of Great Exuma.

I sure walked when I was a boy. It was almost an entire day's journey from Forbes Hill to where we had to board the boat to Great Exuma, so we set out early in the morning to catch the ferry that took us across the great body of water between the two islands. Once we got to the other side, we had another three- to four-days' walk in front of us, and all we had to eat was bread, lard and some grits, which we cooked on the side of the track road (we got water for both cooking and drinking from potholes in the brush).

By the time we got to The Forest, my great-granddad, whose name was Hackless Ferguson, was very, very bad off – in fact, he would live less than a day after our arrival. Great-granddad had what they called stoppage in the water back then – he wasn't able to pee. I believe that his ailment is what we now call prostate cancer.

It was a shock to see my great-grandfather in such frail condition. He was a great big man, about seven feet tall, and his feet were so enormous that he had to wear shoes made from car tires. The older folks often wore that type of shoes, but don't ask me where they got the tires; I suppose they floated up onto the beach because in those days I never even saw a bicycle, much less a car. We didn't even have cars in Nassau when I was a young boy, so those tires must have floated up on the beach from some faraway place.

The evening of the day that my great-grandfather died, they held a wake for him, and he was buried the next day. Today, they would hold someone until all the family could be there for the funeral. Back then, however, it would have taken six months or more to get everyone together. In fact, sometimes it used to take the mail boat more than three days to get to Great Exuma – and that was one with a motor; the sailboats would take up to three weeks or even longer, depending on the weather.

After my great-grandfather's funeral, Aunt Edith and I got ready for the long walk back to Forbes Hill. Before we left, my aunt took me to Mt. Thompson, where she, my mother and their family were from. Aunt Edith showed me the house where they had been born and the hundreds of acres of land they owned (my family still owns a lot of that land). I have family who never left Great Exuma, and, although they took up all of the beachfront property, there was still a lot of black land (land furthest from the sea) for the taking.

After visiting my mom's family, we started our long journey to Forbes Hill, but now we were going back heavier than when we came. Everyone had shared something with us – sugar cane, apples, sappa jelly, and different kinds of baked bread. You name it, and we had it.

On the way back, we stopped in Georgetown for the night and met more family members. My mother had family from as far away as England. In fact, my mother's father's father, Papa John Hilton Brice, was a white man from England, and I was sure that he was a slave master's son – or even the slave master himself.

John Hilton Brice, who was a carpenter, was married to my great-grandmother, Margaret, who was a real peach. They lived happily together until she died in childbirth after having 14 children for her husband. Since John was a builder by trade, all of his sons followed in his footsteps. In fact, as soon as I was old enough, my uncles used to take me on jobs with them in Nassau. I became so good at building that they would wake me hours before school to go with them, and after school I had to head straight to the job site. My hard work paid off -- not only did I have the opportunity to earn a little money, but the skills that I learned would also prove to be invaluable later in my life.

Our stay in Exuma went by quickly. When mom returned from America, we kids went back home to Nassau to be with our parents, and I continued with my schooling there. Because my father had been a high school teacher while still in his teens, he was determined that his children were going to be educated.

Chapter 2

A Childhood in Paradise

It was wonderful being back home with my family, which would soon welcome a new addition -- my baby sister, Maddie -- in December of 1948. Maddie has always been my princess, but she did give me quite a scare once. Like me, Maddie loved the ocean, and she was just as fearless around it as I was. One day, she decided to go for a swim and I looked up just in time to see a wave washing her out to sea. Fortunately, Aries and I were able to pull Maddie to safety, but we didn't let her out of our sight from that day on.

Shortly after we returned to Nassau, Aries and I returned to school, and I must say that I was very smart as a youngster. I got good grades, and I was the number one speller and math person in my early classes. In fact, at one point I had made up my mind to be a lawyer – I was that sharp. But, as the years went by, I seemed to go backward instead of forward. I don't know where all my "smarts" went, but maybe it had something to do with all the distractions around me.

Some of those distractions involved school activities. I loved doing plays and singing in the choir. In fact, from the time I was six years old, I was singing and playing drums in school choruses. And it wasn't long before I was as passionate about drumming as I was about the ocean.

I practiced drumming on every object I could find in the hopes of making a satisfactory sound. I learned that wood, tin, paper boxes and everything else with a flat or round surface had its own resonance. And, it wasn't long before I joined two Folger's coffee cans together to make my first crude set of bongos.

During my childhood, I would spend hours in a coconut grove on the island, practicing different patterns of beating my hands on my coffee can bongos. The sounds that came from them were always different – false and untrue – from the sounds I heard in my head. The two would never match until I later acquired real bongos, but I was smart enough to realize, as young as I was, that I could manipulate the resonance of my homemade instruments by the pressure, speed and the way I shaped the surface of my hands when I struck their heads.

My mother was convinced that music was my "calling," and she did what she could to encourage me. I'm sure that my "calling" tried her patience more than once -- especially on the days when I went for water.

We didn't have indoor plumbing in those days, so we had to fetch water for drinking and bathing as well as doing laundry. Since I drummed on everything I could get my hands on, the tin pails that we used to get water literally took a beating. I beat on the bottoms of those buckets until I put holes in them, so there were countless times when I didn't make it home with much water -- most of it had dripped out long before I could get the water back to mom.

Although my constant drumming caused some problems, my practice paid off.
As I grew older people started paying attention to my music. As time went on, they were increasingly asking me,

"What was that beat? What was that sound you just made?"

I didn't know how to answer them. I was ignorant of musical terms, so I didn't understand the sounds I was making. I had never had a real music lesson, but there was music in my heart that I had to express through my hands. The sounds just seemed to emerge from them when I banged on a resonant surface, and I would continue to experiment and learn until I had some real instruction during my teenage years.

Besides enjoying drumming, I also loved to fight during my school days. Maybe I got my fighting spirit from my dad, because I remember one time when he took matters into his own hands after I got injured. When I was about seven or eight years old, I was struck by a bicycle as I was running to my father's shop after school. I was pretty bruised up, but I picked myself up and began walking (very slowly) toward the shop. Some of the kids who had seen what happened ran ahead of me and told dad what had happened.

Dad was really angry -- not only because I had gotten injured, but because the guy who had hit me hadn't even stopped to see how badly I was hurt. Unfortunately for that guy, the kids pointed out the hit-and-run bike rider to my father, and when that guy passed by dad's store, dad yanked him off his bike and gave him a good thrashing. Dad was tough for a little guy -- in fact, the only people who got the best of him were mom's brothers and sisters (I'll tell you about that in the next chapter).

Anyway, I became quite good at fighting -- and I was always looking for an excuse to fight. For some reason, I had this belief that if I drank a glass of milk in the morning before I went to school, I could beat anyone up. Besides, when I got biggety, I had a "secret weapon" -- my sister, Aries. Aries was a very good fighter, and she would beat up whoever had hit me the hardest. Aries would take the flack – and then she'd hit my opponents back.

Well, one day -- I was about nine years old, I think -- I went to school without drinking my milk. And, unfortunately, I didn't have my secret weapon with me either -- Aries didn't go to school that day. Forgetting that I hadn't had my milk, I picked a fight with a boy named Boba on the way home. Boba, who was a friend of my family's (his mother's sister was dating my Uncle Fred), was a fat little boy. But, that fat little boy beat me to a pulp – every time I got up, he'd knock me back down. And a crowd of school kids was all around him, screaming,

"Yeah, Boba, kill him. Kill him, Boba. He's too biggety. He's too biggety. Kill him, Boba."

It was only after I found myself on the losing end of that fight that I realized that I hadn't drank my milk, so I told Boba,

"O.K., stop. You're only winning this fight because I didn't drink my milk today. I don't want to fight any more."

After that, Boba left me alone – but I can't say that I stopped fighting. I loved to fight, and I can only remember one or two other times when someone got the best of me. One of these occasions wasn't exactly a real fight, either. I usually got along really well with my cousins -- especially my cousin, Henry (he was the son of my Aunt Susie, whom we called Tettie). Henry was six years older than me, and almost like a big brother, but one day he hit me in the stomach for no reason -- and with no warning. I bent over like a ball and cried like hell, even though I didn't want to seem like a cry baby (if there was one thing we kids hated, it was a cry baby). Aunt Tettie beat him for hitting me, of course, but I promised Henry that I would get even, and I lived for the day that I would settle the score with him.

Speaking of cousins, it was only natural that I would spend a lot of my time with my aunties, uncles and cousins, since I came from such a large extended family. I could fill an entire book with stories of the things that we did together while I was growing up, so I'll just share a couple of fond memories here.

My Aunt Rennie was the sweetest of all my mom's sisters. She and her husband, Herbie, who was a gardener, had a daughter named Sylvia. I had a great time with both Sylvia and Aunt Rennie, who were both funny and good sports.

I enjoyed going to the movies on weekends, and I got most of my money for them from Aunt Rennie. Both she and Sylvia were afraid of frogs (that surprised me about Sylvia because she was fearless around snakes), so anytime I wanted to get money from Aunt Rennie, I would threaten to show a frog to her. Aunt Rennie would sometimes protest that I was kidding her, but there were times when I would actually bring a frog or two to her house – and sometimes I would even chase her around the yard with them. It really didn't matter whether I had a frog or not -- Aunt Rennie would always provide the money for me to go to the movies (I used to ask for four shillings if I wanted to go to the show alone, or for ten shillings if I was taking a friend).

I also loved to accompany my Aunt Rennie when she did her shopping on Saturday mornings, and our trips were always eventful. One Saturday, we had a particularly memorable day while we were walking up Market Street, where beggars always gathered at the top of the hill. That day, there was a new guy there who said that he was blind, and he asked Auntie Rennie for a four-shilling paper note. I was lagging a little behind as Auntie gave the money to him and continued on her way. When I reached the beggar, he pulled out a gin bottle and held it toward me, inviting me to take a drink.

"Auntie, this man's a fake" I shouted, "And he offered me a drink of gin."

Wow, did that make auntie mad! She came running and demanded her money back.

"Here's your money. I don't need it," the beggar replied, as Auntie snatched that money out of his hand.

It greatly saddened me when Aunt Rennie was one of the first of my aunties to die. One of my mother's brothers, George, had already died from tuberculosis when I was a teenager. He had contracted the disease from smoking cigarettes, and maybe Auntie Rennie had gotten sick from tobacco, too. She used to send me into the bush to get wild tobacco for the pipe that she always smoked. That was some powerful stuff – it used to make her so high that everyone thought she was drunk, although I knew better.

Besides the good times I had with Henry, Sylvia and my other cousins, who included another cousin named Sylvia who claimed she could see spirits, I had also had some great friends when I was growing up. In fact, when I was a teenager, I had friends who were like a second family to me.

My closest boyhood friends were Wendell Stuart, who was one of my very best friends (Wendell was one of the greatest people who ever lived), and Francis Campbell. If Francis had a pound, I got half of it; if he had a shirt or a pair of pants made for himself, he would have one made for me. You couldn't get between us.

Another of my good friends was George Murray, one hell of a nice guy, who became a weight lifter. One day, George and I got into a big fight after school. I don't know who actually won that fight, but I beat George badly enough that he went into body building. George, who taught me how to lift weights, would go on to win the Mr. Bahamas title six times -- and he was Mr. World twice!

George had an older brother named James, who was bigger than most of us kids. One Sunday morning, when James went to Mass, the priest tried to molest him. Well, James beat that priest so bad that he ran out of the back door with his robes flying…with a screaming James hot on his heels. Needless to say, that priest was sent back to England that very week.

Wendell, Francis, George and I were like the Four Musketeers – we were that close -- and all of my friends grew up to be decent people. I am still friends with George, who drove a taxi after he retired from body building. Wendell, who is dead now, became a fantastic singer and guitar player. Francis, who has also died, went into law enforcement and became a police chief.

During my childhood, my friends and I spent most of our time swimming, fishing, catching birds and playing games. We didn't have a lot of toys back in those days, but I had some of the best spinning tops on the island. My Uncle Leroy, who was a finish carpenter man, made the best tops in the world. Sometimes, he would make my tops out of mahogany or ebony wood, but when he made them out of what we called neglom whittie – the hardest wood in the Caribbean – I was the envy of my peers. Those tops were indestructible; they could split every other top in half, so I had no problem selling some of them to make some cash.

I also enjoyed playing marbles with my friends (I had some beautiful marbles in those days). I suppose that our game was much like the one that boys played in the States -- we used our marbles to try to shoot our opponents' marbles out of a circle that we had drawn in the sand -- and I got so good at it that I sometimes made money playing against the other boys. One day, however, my love of the game got me into very serious trouble.

On Saturdays and Sundays, dad would work at the store, and mom would make up nice satchels of food for him. It was my job to deliver them to my dad, and, unfortunately, dad caught me in a lie when I was running one of those errands.

One Saturday, as I was on my way to the store with dad's meal, I saw some boys shooting marbles. I got so excited that I stopped to play with the other kids, forgetting that dad's food was in the satchel, which I had dropped to the ground. I spent about 20 minutes playing before I finally picked up that satchel and headed to the store.

Of course, the plate with dad's food was broken and cold by then, so when dad opened the satchel, he asked,

"Why is this plate broken?" What happened to my food?

"I don't know, sir," I answered.

"And, why is there sand on the satchel?"

Again, I replied, "I don't know, sir."

"The food is cold. You never brought cold food before."

"Daddy, I don't know," I repeated.

"You know. Come here," he ordered.

My daddy then strapped me to a pole, grabbed a piece of electrical cord and beat the living daylights out of me.

"Don't you ever lie to me again," he bellowed.

I sure learned my lesson that day -- I never lied to him again. In fact, I haven't told an outright lie in my life since then. I haven't always told the exact truth – but if I am caught in something, I admit to it.

Today, if you beat a child in America the way that my dad beat me that day, you'd go to jail. Hell, people can't even chastise their kids. Then, when kids lie, steal, cheat and get into trouble, you are accused of being a bad. Well, you can't take care of your child if you're worried that your child will go to the police station and say,

"Mommy just spanked me."

The beating wasn't pleasant, but it sure wasn't traumatic for me -- unlike a couple of other incidents from my childhood. One of them involved seeing a dead woman on a bicycle! Late one day, just as the sun was going down, I was standing in the door of my dad's shop when I saw a man we called "Po' Boy" ride by on his bicycle.

Po' Boy was a friend of the family -- or maybe even one of mom's relatives, as they were both from the same town on Great Exuma. He was a small guy, but a no-nonsense type of man, and he was always fighting with the woman he lived with. On this particular day, that woman was on the crossbar of his bike, and, as he rode by, Po' Boy was yelling at her,

"Sit up, you drunken bitch!"

I was only about seven or eight years old at the time, but I was convinced that the woman was dead -- she wasn't moving, and her head hung limply on the handlebars. When I ran to my mom to tell her what I had seen, she didn't seem too concerned -- Po' Boy and the woman were always fighting, so no one paid them any mind. Mom's attitude changed some days later, when the woman was found dead in a ditch; mom then warned me not to tell anyone what I had seen.

Amazingly, it took a long time for the police to arrest her murderer. I was surprised at that -- Po' Boy had sure been shouting, so I'm sure that other people had heard him and seen him ride by with the dead woman on his bicycle. But maybe it took so long because the police felt the same way that mom did at first; they knew that Po' Boy and the woman were always fighting. But their fights had never been violent -- they usually just involved a lot of shouting.

I was too young to remember all the details of the case, but the police finally arrested Po' Boy and put him in jail for murder. I know that my mom asked Po' Boy why he had killed the woman, but I don't know if she talked to him before he was arrested or while he was in jail. Although Po' Boy told her -- and the cops -- that he had not meant to kill the woman, he was sentenced to death by hanging (in those days, people were hung in the park on East Street and Wolf Road).

Despite these few unpleasant memories, I had a very happy childhood -- even though I became acquainted with hard work at a very early age. My daddy eventually owned three grocery stores as well as an ice cream shop (he was one of the first black men in the Bahamas to own so many businesses), so he never stopped working. I tried to make my father's burden a little lighter by doing what I could for him. I'd have hot coffee ready when he rose at three or four in the morning to head down to the bay to be the first on hand when the fisherman brought in their catches.

I would be dead asleep again before my dad loaded his fresh fish into the rectangular wooden box mounted on the rack over the rear fender of his bicycle. As dawn broke, my father would strike out on the circuit he had established around the island, which is 21 miles long and seven miles wide. Every morning, he would make his rounds to local restaurants and homes. The natives would eagerly look forward to his cry,

"Fish man's here! Fish man's here! Come and get your fresh fish."

The money that my father made from selling fish went into his store to purchase more merchandise. Not content with the combined income from the fish sales and the stores, he would then start preparations for his next task.

We didn't have a modern bathroom in our house, so we had to make do with a four-holer (an outhouse with four openings) in the outhouse and a big galvanized tub for bathing. It was my job to build a fire in the yard, set the tub on the flames and fill it with water. By the time my father got home, the water was hot enough for his bath.

Before he took his bath, however, my father would unbuckle the fish box from the back of his bike and I would help him scrub it out with a harsh cleanser that the islanders depended on. Called Detol, it was composed of ingredients as strong as lye salt, which burned like sin if it came into contact with an unhealed wound. Detol's main virtue was that it destroyed bacteria and banished objectionable odors.

My father, who believed that family privacy was overrated, would then take off his clothes, step into the tub, and sit on the wooden plank that was placed across the tub and wash himself. It was my job to scrub his back.

Dad then got dressed, and when the fish box was dry, he filled a briefcase with perfumes, skin conditioners, facial rinses and other ladies' toiletries, including sweet soaps. They were similar to the Avon products of today, but these carried the romantic "Lucky Heart" label. On his bicycle again, with the case of sweet-smelling cosmetics tucked away in the box that had previously held fish, my father would retrace his route of the early morning, singing out to the same customers in his baritone voice,

"Lucky Heart man calling!"

After he finished his second job, my father would return to work at his store, which my mother managed during the day (my Aunt Curlina ran the ice cream shop for him). He would work late into the night before coming home to get a few hours of sleep before repeating his routine.

Helping my dad was one of the most important jobs that I did without compensation, but, because my parents were both workaholics, I became interested in doing "real work" at an early age. Not only did I help my uncles in the construction trade, but I also cooked for a living. When I was about nine years old, I began helping my mom and my Aunt Tettie cook barbecue for The Conch Shell Club, never dreaming that I would later perform at the club, own a stake in the business and be "discovered" there many years later. I continued to cook for The Conch Shell until I was 12 years old, and my most memorable experience during that time was chasing off a guy named Herbie Musgrove, who would steal slabs of ribs right off the grill!

Sometimes I found fun ways to make money, too -- besides winning at marbles, I also collected bottles that I found in the streets or discarded in the bushes (and sometimes I would also steal bottles). I enjoyed having my own money, and I would sometimes take the money I had made -- maybe ten to 20 shillings -- to school to buy lunch for my friends (I was young and stupid back then).

It amazes me sometimes that I was able to cram so much into my days and nights, but we kids lived an active lifestyle back then. We always ate natural foods, so we were rarely sick, and when we did have a minor ailment, we didn't rush off to a doctor -- we fixed ourselves up.

One time, when I was about seven or eight years old, I was swinging from the limb of an almond tree when I fell flat on my face, knocking out nearly all of my bottom teeth. Being the smart boy that I was, I pushed those teeth back into my gums with my right hand and went home to pack my mouth with salt. I must have done a pretty good job, because my mouth healed completely in a couple of weeks and I didn't have any trouble with those teeth until one came loose -- when I was 55 years old! It was only after all those years that I had to get any dental work done on those teeth that I had taken care of myself!

We also took care of little things like burns and scrapes. If we burned ourselves, we cut off a piece of an aloe vera plant and rubbed the juice on the burn. That was a far more pleasant remedy than some of the other "cures" that our families swore by, so we did everything we could to avoid becoming sick.

If mom thought we were coming down with a cold, for example, she would make us piss in a cup. Then she added a little lemon juice to our pee and made us drink up. The alternative was even worse – drinking our mother's pee! Mom also had another treatment to pull a cold and fever out of our bodies. She would make us wash our heads with our pee! Most whites wouldn't know about these things -- and would probably be disgusted by some of the methods we used, but I later learned that American Indians understood these types of cures. And those home remedies worked -- our colds would be gone in one day, and we were usually healthy.

So it was a great beginning to my life -- how could I not be happy growing up on an island paradise, surrounded by family and friends who loved me? I thought that life would go on that way forever, but little did I know that things were about to change -- and that change would not be for the better.

Chapter 3

Storm Clouds

Money was very important to my father -- he wanted to be rich so that his family would have the best. But, unfortunately, daddy was not able to keep us from sliding into poverty. No matter how hard he worked, everything that dad brought in the front door was distributed out the back door by my mother.

Since dad's work day started at 4:00 a.m. and didn't end until eight or nine at night, my father trusted my mother to manage our family's finances. But every week, it seemed, she would pack up boxes of groceries and other goods from the store to send to her sisters and brothers who lived on other islands in the Bahamas. But she didn't make a distinction about what side of the family benefited from her generosity. Mom also sent boxes to my father's relatives on Acklins, who were just as poor and "no-account" (according to my father) as my mom's relatives.

I was about eight or nine years old when my father started raising hell with my mother about her acts of "charity" -- and the fact that she was heedless of the cost of them.

"How can you keep giving away what I work three jobs to bring in?" he roared.

My mother stubbornly refused to listen to my father's criticism. She either held her hands over her ears until he stopped shouting or she ran out of the house. God only knows how my dad lasted as long as he did.

The truth was that neither my mother nor her family had any respect for my father. Even though we helped everyone when they were down and out, my mom's family had no problem turning on my dad. If mom and dad had an argument, her whole family – and she had some pretty big brothers -- would jump on my dad like he'd just insulted the Queen. Even my little Aunt Susie (Tettie), who wasn't even five feet tall, got into the act. One time, when mom and dad were arguing in his ice cream parlor, Aunt Tettie, who was behind dad, grabbed the new signboard that he had just gotten made for the shop. That slab of wood was huge, but that little woman grabbed it out of the corner, jumped up on a chair and hit dad on the back of the head with it. Dad spent about six weeks in the hospital for that, but something even worse happened to him just a few weeks later -- my Uncle Fred, who was a carpenter, almost killed dad.

Uncle Fred had gotten mad at dad for arguing with mom, so he went to our house, where he destroyed thousands of dollars worth of mom's mahogany furniture with a hatchet. When dad went to confront him, Uncle Fred, who was sitting in a chair on his porch, got up and stabbed dad in the chest with a chisel. The stabbing put dad in the Bahamas General Hospital (later called the Princess Margaret Hospital after the princess visited the islands in 1955) for six months, and Uncle Fred spent six years in jail. Dad sure took some hell from my mother's family.

Unfortunately, mom's charity wasn't the only thing that affected our livelihood. I remember one time when my Uncle Jethro (we called him "Jet"), whom I loved very much, came into the store while my mother was in the outdoor toilet. While I was minding the shop for her during that brief time, my uncle took all the money from the cash box and left.

Since the store was suffering, my old man had to scrape by primarily from the sales of his fish and Lucky Heart products. You would think he would have had some income from the houses he rented out, but my mother would let her sisters and brothers live in those houses every time they came to Nassau from Exuma. They would "forget" to pay the rent every month -- and, as soon as a family got on their feet, they would move out, not paying a dime. And, ironically, when we fell on hard times, not one of the people that mom had helped came around to help us.

Within a year, all six of the small houses that my father had built to rent out were repossessed by the bank. I'll never forget watching those big trucks coming into the yard and hauling those houses away one by one. And I guess that made a big impression on my dad as well; he finally woke up to the fact that my mother was responsible for what had happened-- and that she was not going to change. I'll never forget the look of futility and shock that came over my father's face. Everything he had worked for was gone. Unable to stop our family's decline into debt, my father's absences grew longer and longer – until he rarely came home at all, and he trusted me enough to explain why.

A few months after my tenth birthday, my father took me aside and told me that he was seeing a woman by the name of Hilda, who was one of his Lucky Heart customers.

"Don't tell your mom, but if you need me for anything, this is where I'll be."

I was old enough by then to know that Hilda, the new woman in my father's life, offered a warm shoulder for him to cry on -- he sure wasn't getting any sympathy from my mother. If mom suspected that there was another woman occupying my father's nights, she kept quiet about it for about a year – until she had to do something about it.

One day when I was walking home from school, I was accosted by an older boy. That boy, whose name was George, was Hilda's son.

"I know who you are," George said, before slapping me in the face.

In response, I picked up a piece of wood and hit George with it – hit him hard enough to make him cry and run. I knew why he attacked me, though. George was ashamed of his helplessness. He was offended and frustrated that he could not confront my father about seeing his mother, so he had decided to punish me instead.

Hilda was angered over my assault on her son, of course, so the next day she marched over to my father's store and screamed for him to come out and apologize about George's injuries. In those days, that was how things were settled – no one thought about filing lawsuits, they just wanted apologies.

My father did not dare face Hilda, knowing that their relationship would certainly be revealed if he tried to reason with her. When dad refused to come out, Hilda was infuriated, and she screamed even louder,

"Pallaman Johnson, you come out here right this minute, you son of a bitch! Your son beat up my boy and you'd better do something about it."

Well, it wasn't my dad who responded to Hilda's demand – it was my mother. I took one look at her and knew that there was trouble coming. There was anger in mom's eyes and grim determination on her face – and her mouth was set in that straight, flat line that we only saw when she was angry. Then I heard her mutter one word, "Bitch," in a low, guttural voice.

Nobody -- not my dad, not my Aunt Curlina, not my sister, not a customer who was in the store and certainly not me – dared to try to stop my mom as she ran through the open door that led to the shop's kitchen. There, she grabbed the long, razor-sharp cane knife that she took to the sugar cane fields when she worked on contract on farms in America. It always hung on a rawhide loop on a hook behind the door, so it took her no time at all to grab that knife – and put it to use.

I was tongue-tied when mother, the long blade in her right hand, flung the back door open and headed straight for her enemy. Hilda was confused for a moment by the way my mother came at her in a fury, but then she started to scream. Her scream was cut short when my mother swiped the blade across her throat.

From the open door, I saw the blood spurt through Hilda's fingers, which she had reached up, too late, to protect her throat. Neighbors who had been attracted by Hilda's screaming also saw the attack, and someone called an ambulance. The police showed up at about the same time as the ambulance arrived, and they confiscated my mother's knife and jailed her for the night.

The charge against my mother came up before a judge several weeks later. I was afraid that my mom might be sentenced to a long term in jail for her attack on Hilda, especially since Hilda would have been dead had the blade gone another inch, but, thankfully, mom got a judge who was known as a fair man.

First, Hilda, her throat still bandaged over the stitches required to close her wound, gave her version of the attack to the judge. When my mother's turn came, she stood up and said in a precise, steady voice,

"Your Honor, this woman came to our store, shouting and screaming for my husband. She lured my husband away from his family with sweet promises. Then she showed up threatening us for my son's defense of himself after her boy had tried to beat him. I just got mad at this home wrecker and went after her."

When my mother sat down, the judge didn't hesitate. He looked fiercely at Hilda and said,

"This woman should have killed you for going to her husband's store the way you did. Case dismissed. Get out of my court."

Although the court case went well (although mother never got her cane knife back), the relationship between my mother and father continued to deteriorate steadily after his affair with Hilda was out in the open. Their arguments became more frequent, bitter and lasting -- and my father increasingly left home to spend time with Hilda.

It wasn't long before our house -- the house that my family had lived in for years -- was taken away by the bank. We had to pack up and leave, of course, and my mother, father and all four of us kids ended up in a two-room shack on a street that was ironically named Lucky Heart Corner.

What a change that was for us – going from a six-room house filled with beautiful furniture to that shack that was hardly big enough for two people, much less a family of six. We were crowded together with the few pieces of furniture that would fit into the small space; the overflow sat outside in the yard.

When we lost everything, my mother blamed it on my father.

Blind to the financial wreckage she caused during her marriage and the ruin of her relationship with the man who loved and trusted her, my mother blamed my father for her own failures.

I was so happy when I became a man and was able to talk to my dad and let him know that I saw everything and knew that he was not at fault. When I told dad that I loved him and always would, he started to cry. I loved my mom too, of course, but I could see that she was wrong.

I would get angry when my mom would talk bad about my dad to her friends, and I would shut her up by telling her that she was the one who was to blame for our troubles. Mom didn't like that too much (she could not stand to hear the truth), and she would tell me,

"You're just like your dad. No good."

For the remainder of her life – long after she and my father separated (they were never divorced by law) and even as she lay on her death bed -- my mother refused to admit that she was at fault for driving our family into debt.

Bitter over her change in circumstances, mom stayed in that little shack with us for only two months. One morning, after dad had gotten up to go to the fish market, she took my two sisters to my Aunt Tettie's house, leaving Rodney and I alone in the little shack. After dropping the girls off, she returned, gave Rodney three pence and told him that she was going downtown and that he was to stay with me and be a good boy until she returned.

Well, she went to town, all right – to a town in the United States! We didn't see mom for over a year. And every day for that year, Rodney would get up and cry,

"When is mommy coming home?"

I knew what had happened, but I would lie to Rodney and tell him that mom was coming home soon. I became like a father figure to Rodney – I looked after him as well as myself both at home and at school. He was old enough to go to his own classes by that time, so he didn't have to sit under my window, but you better believe I kept a close eye on him.

We hardly ever saw dad, who continued to work hard after mom left, selling his fish and his Lucky Heart products. After he sold all his fish and conch and all of the other seafood from his crate, he'd bring home what he couldn't sell -- the fish heads and tails and the conch slop – and he would fix the most fantastic pot of stew for Rodney and me. Sometimes, we had dumplings, sometimes okra soup with those waste parts of the fish. I guess that's why I like those "rejects" so much – I grew up eating them so much that you can't get me to eat the body of the fish today...all I want is the fish head or tail.

After dad fixed the meal for Rodney and me, he would leave us again to go sell his Lucky Heart products. In the evenings, he stayed with his sweetheart. Although Rodney and I were by ourselves a lot, we did have neighbors who lived nearby, and they watched out for us.

I remember living next door to a family, the Browns, who were poorer than we were. Isaiah, the son, was the same age as I was and we went to school together, but I especially remember his mother, Estelle. One day, Estelle was cooking a pot of black beans and rice, and she decided to add a bit of fish that she had bought from my father. Unfortunately, she had run out of fat – she had no cooking oil or lard to cook the fish -- so she substituted kerosene oil. Well, that meal was excellent, but every time I belched, that kerosene oil came up with it. I'll never forget that meal because it stayed with me for weeks. No matter what I ate, I couldn't get that oil off my chest.

On the weekends, Rodney and I would go to Aunt Tettie's house, where the girls were living. We walked there, of course, since we walked everywhere in those days, and we always looked forward to being together.

When mom came home at the end of the year, it was not to return to her husband. She moved us kids into a small house that she rented from a man named Mr. Carey in Cocoanut Grove (we just called it the Grove). Mr. Carey was one lucky man. One day, a plane had crashed into his house (the plane missed Uncle Cecil's house by inches), and Pan Am had to pay a big settlement to him because of the accident. Mr. Carey used the money to buy several acres of land, on which he built about 20 houses – pretty much in the same way that my dad had done when I was younger.

After mom and dad separated, all of us suffered. My dad walked the streets as a drunk after mom didn't come back to him. In fact, he was drunk every day of his life -- but he became a real fighter. We started calling him "Bully" or "the Bully Man" because he would get really pissed off and want to fight everyone when he was drunk. Dad had hands of steel. As a matter of fact, people used to say that his fists were fixed with voodoo -- whenever he hit anyone, their skin would burst open and bleed. Once, a man said something about God that upset dad, and dad punched the man so hard that he nearly killed the guy with one blow (he had to go to court over that one).

My mom and we kids also went through some tough times. Our two-bedroom house rented for two pounds a week (a pound was about three dollars back then), which was a lot of money to come up with every week. My mother was good with white people, though, so she got a job in a place called Orange Hill. The American spinsters who hired her had a chicken farm on their property (they didn't own the farm – it belonged to a private company), so on Friday nights, after the farm had closed, I would go there and steal chickens to sell over the weekend.

I learned how to steal from my mother's uncle, my great-uncle Sam, who was the youngest brother of my grandfather, John Hilton Brice. Uncle Sam, who was a 6'5" giant of a man and black as tar, came from the Forest on Great Exuma, and it seemed that he and my Uncle Jet were the ones who cared the most about my mother and her kids.

One day, Uncle Sam, who was about 60 years old at the time, came to visit mom, as he did a couple of times a week. When he arrived, we were sitting around eating grits and lard.

"Josephine, how do you expect these children to grow on dry grits?" he asked.

"I don't have any money for meat," my mother replied.

"O.K.," my Uncle Sam said, "I'll be right back."

Well, there was a goat and sheep farm just down the street from us, and some other folks had chickens running around. Uncle Sam was back in a half hour with a goat on his shoulders – and some advice for me,

"Young man, from now on, don't you let your sisters and brother go hungry. There are plenty of people who have more than they can use. Go and take what you need."

From that day on, we always had fresh meat – even if it was only a chicken. Uncle Sam always brought a piece of meat when he visited, and I kept the family supplied by stealing the rest of the meat we needed.

I was now the "man of the house," so by the time I was 11 or 12, I felt like I was a slave for my family. On laundry day, for example, I had to get enough water to fill at least five tubs for washing and rinsing our clothes. And, it seemed like I was always running for water for drinking and bathing. I was usually a pretty good sport about it – I loved my brother and I knew that Rodney would have helped if I had asked him (which I never did), and I loved my sisters, so I usually didn't mind doing things for them -- but I sure paid for being born 30 minutes before Aries.

One fateful day, though, I was in the mood for some fun -- not chores -- and that resulted in the one spanking that my mother gave me -- and what a spanking it was! That day, I was tired of being Cinderfella (a male Cinderella), so when my mother asked me to go for water again, I got hopping mad and told her that I would not do it.

"What did you say?" she asked.

"You heard me...I'm not going for any damned water," I replied.

"Everyone is thirsty, so you have to go for water right now," my mom insisted.

"Why me all the time?"

"Because you are the oldest and that's your job."

"Not today! If someone else can't help, then drink your piss!" I retorted before leaving the house.

Well, from the look on mom's face, I knew that I was dead, but I didn't give a crap – it was time to have some fun. I wandered about a mile down the road to a place where they were digging a ditch near some houses that were being built. A tractor had dug a big hole that filled with water when it rained, and we kids would swim in that makeshift pond before and after school and on weekends and holidays. As I usually did, I took off all my clothes and began to swim.

Well, there had been many times in my eleven or twelve years on earth that my mother had threatened to kick my butt, but I had never paid attention (especially since that never happened). On this day, however, mom made good on her promise. When she told my Cousin Henry, my Aunt Tettie's son, what had happened, he not only told mom where I was (he had seen me on his way home), he brought her to me.

I had been swimming for about an hour when Henry, who was fully clothed, came into the pond, grabbed me and held me for mom, who began to beat me with a tamarind switch. That woman beat me with that switch for almost the entire mile back home. And, not only did mom beat me, but every time she hit me, she also reminded me of something I had done wrong – whether it was a week, a month or even a year before!

"Mom, don't you forget anything?"

"I told you I would give you a long rope for a short catch," she replied.

My punishment was witnessed by all of the other kids, who were following and teasing me as my naked butt was being whipped all the way home. And, as if that wasn't enough, I still had to go and get the water!

Some of those taunting kids were my cousins. A lot of my family lived in the Grove. Besides my Uncle Cecil, who had the best house of any member of my mother's family at the time, my Aunt Tettie and my cousin, Henry, also lived there. I missed having dad around, but we had some good times while living on Market Street in the Grove. And one of my activities would lead to an encounter that I would remember many years later, when I had realized my dream of being a professional musician and performed before royalty in Europe.

I have already told you that Princess Margaret made her first visit to the Bahamas in 1955. Her visit caused a big stir, of course, and the people of the Bahamas did everything they could to ensure that her visit was a memorable one. At the time, I belonged to the Brigades, which was a boys' group organized along the same principles as the Boy Scouts. But our uniforms were totally different from the ones that American Boy Scouts wore. Ours were very English, and we looked quite splendid in our black pants with a red stripe down the side, a white tunic and a "bonnet" that was modeled after the type of cap that the English bobbies (police) wore in London.

I can't tell you how proud and handsome I felt as I stood with the Brigades on Bay Street, awaiting our inspection by Princess Margaret. Since I was a sergeant, I was in the front row, and I was thrilled when the smiling princess stopped in front of me. Not only did she shake my hand, but Princess Margaret also asked me what my name was and where I went to school -- and she wanted to know about my family.

The princess was gracious, sweet, and sincerely interested, and, amazingly, she looked just as beautiful as I remembered from that day in Nassau when I next saw her over two decades later, when I was playing with Neil Diamond at the London Palladium in June of 1977. When I looked up and saw Princess Margaret and her entourage sitting in the royal box, I felt honored that I had met her in my youth.

At the time I met her, of course, I was far from being ready to become a professional conga drummer. But it wasn't long after I met Princess Margaret that I had the opportunity to embark on my first "real" career and be able to do more to provide for my family.

My cousin Henry, who had been in the same school that I attended, had gone on to become the best jockey in the Bahamas -- Henry was earning money every time he sat on a horse. I was determined to be just as successful, and I was ecstatic when Henry agreed to help me.

I had my first riding lesson on the back of a hard-headed donkey. The animal threw me twice, so, after being thrown the first time, I was holding the rope halter fastened to the donkey's head when he threw me the second time. Well, that animal trotted about a hundred yards down a rocky road, pulling me over lumps, bumps and holes before colliding with an old fire engine. I had cuts, scratches and bruises for almost two weeks, but I learned how to mount and dismount properly.

Henry then took me to the Hobby Horse Hall Rack Track on Cable Beach, where I studied the actions of the jockeys until I was ready to ride "companion" horses – those trained to trot along next to nervous thoroughbreds and quiet them with their steadiness.

It wasn't long before I met a man named Alonzo Taylor, who saw real promise in me. But the first lesson I learned from him was a harsh one – Alonzo beat me thoroughly (for the first and only time) with his whip when the horse I was riding threw me and the horse got away because I had not held the reins tightly. I had welts all over my body, and I was sore for two weeks, but I never forgot the lesson that Alonzo taught me:

"I beat you," Alonzo said, "so you'll never forget that when you're thrown you always hold on to your horse. He's worth a hell of a lot more than you are. If that horse runs into the street and gets hit by a car and is crippled, that's the end of the horse and the money invested in him."

I was a quick learner, and I became so adept at handling and riding crazy or temperamental horses that I was hired to break them. I could size up a horse in a minute and sense the way the animal was going to break – and it paid off. I was pretty daring – I would jump up on the horse and stick on its back like a fly in honey. Bucking horses learned quickly about my sticking ability, and they soon just gave up and lay down.

I was earning a fee of $15 or $20 to break a horse, and during that time I also earned a nickname, "Fool." "Let Fool ride him if he's dumb enough!" the trainers used to wisecrack. But they knew that I was dependable, and that I had a way with horses -- I could ride any nag until she stopped in her tracks, her chest heaving for air.

Pleased with my success, I gave up my idea of becoming a lawyer and was determined to become a jockey. My mother tried to talk me out of that, of course -- she wanted me to stay in school, even though I would be able to make money to help our family if I became a jockey.

By this time, I was getting nowhere with my schooling anyway. Part of the reason was that I would be at the track every day before school, exercising my horses, and I can't count how many classes -- and even days (especially race days) -- that I missed so I could be at the track. I could exercise the horses in the early morning before school on most days, but on race days (which were usually Fridays and sometimes Fridays and Saturdays), I had to stay at the track all day, so I missed all my classes on Fridays.

By the time school closed for summer in 1957, I was studying with Alonzo full time. At age 13, I had just passed grade four, which is the equivalent of eighth grade in America, and, although I returned to school that fall, my education was about over.

In those days, you had to finish school by the age of 14 or get put out, so, since I had neglected my studies and had not finished, I was put out. My formal schooling ended, I threw my energy into my new career, determined to make something of myself despite my lack of education.

As Henry warned me, it wasn't going to be easy, and it was, indeed, a long and difficult road to the top. I consider myself fortunate to have made it through that phase of my life without serious consequences to life and limb.

Chapter 4

Hoof Beats and Drum Beats: My Early Years in the Spotlight

I was only 14 years old when I started my career as a jockey, and there were a couple of older guys, including a guy named "Uncle" Clinton and another guy who was nicknamed Saddle, who liked to take advantage of us youngsters. Both of them worked for the same stable, and they were always looking for an opportunity to gang up on me or any other newcomer to the game.

I should mention that the stable was owned by a man named Cordy Basterand. Unfortunately, Cordy's life would take a very tragic turn many years after I quit racing. Cordy had a big insurance policy on his mansion (he called the home "Chippenham"), and one day he decided to set the place on fire to collect the insurance money. Cordy, however, did not know that his oldest son was sleeping in the home at the time. The young man burned to death, and a devastated Cordy would never be the same again.

During those early days of racing for Basterand, opportunity soon came knocking for Uncle and Saddle to "get" me. In an eight-horse race of four furlongs, I was riding a horse named Raw Edge; Uncle's horse was named Chippaur, and Saddle was riding Morning Star. When the gate opened, I was the first one out, but Uncle and Saddle sandwiched me in with their horses with such vicious blows that I went flying over my horse's head -- and I landed so far ahead of the pack that I was run over by four or five of the horses!

My head was pretty busted up, and my horse's flank had been split so bad that they had to tow him off the track. My mother, who was there and witnessed the accident, immediately ran out on the track. I could hear her screaming, but I couldn't move, so they put me on a stretcher and I was taken to the hospital, my mother at my side.

Even though I was in incredible pain, I promised myself right then and there that I would kill those two guys. Saddle retired the next year, but Uncle stayed in the game, and I would one day face him again and get my revenge.

Before I tell you about that, I'd like to say that I did extremely well as a jockey – I was so good that I got all the horses that would throw an ordinary jockey. Other than that time that I was the victim of the cruel prank of Uncle Clinton and Saddle, I never got thrown either forward or backwards because I created my own style of riding, which I called "one long, one short." It's a little difficult to try to describe it exactly, but that style made it impossible for horses to throw me, providing a great advantage in races.

One jockey, a guy by the name of Charlie Gibson (we nicknamed him "the Diamond Kid"), began emulating my style and we became rivals -- this kid who copied my style and I were always facing off. Charlie, who was only 12 years old when he started racing, would go on to be the top jockey on the islands for two years in a row -- but not without a fight from me. I remember once that I won three races, came in second in another and was third in yet another race on the same day in an attempt to show Charlie up. My efforts did not escape the notice of the people around the track -- I started getting better mounts, and it wasn't long before it was me, not Charlie, who was the top jockey in the Bahamas.

Unfortunately, being the leading jockey in the Bahamas didn't last long. My body, like that of so many other boys in their teens, was changing. As time went on, I got taller -- and heavier -- and there was nothing I could do to stop those changes, which led to an end to my career as a jockey.

Before I continue with my own story, I'd like to tell you about another young guy who was training to become a jockey. The boy, whose name was Serilatikel, was a big fan of a horse named Anzack. One day, Anzack was in a race and broke his leg, and, of course, they wanted to shoot him to put him out of his misery.

Well, that young boy begged the doctor not to do it -- Serilatikel said he could fix the horse...and he set about to do just that. Somehow, he stole Anzack from the stable and took him to a hideout in the back of a pond. Serilatikel had found a couple of trees that were perfect for what he intended to do, and he had everything else that he needed to save his favorite horse.

Serilatikel hoisted the horse's two front legs into a sling between the trees to avoid putting any weight on the broken leg, and he took care of that horse for months -- he fed Anzack and even slept with the horse in the bush. Within a six-month period, Anzack began to heal, and he was able to put his leg back down and stand on it!

Although Anzack never raced again, that boy saved the horse's life. Anzack lived out his life in a pasture and Serilatikel became the hero of Hobby Horse Hall.

I loved horses, too, and I loved racing them, but it wasn't long (I think I was only about 15 years old) before I got wise to the betting game and the underhanded way that owners and trainers fixed races by instructing jockeys to win or lose. So part of my career involved learning how to win (or lose) crooked races -- and I learned a valuable lesson about unscrupulous owners.

One day, Mr. Knowles, the owner of a legendary Bahamian horse named Shoofly, came up to me and asked me to throw a race for the princely sum of 100 pounds. I was going to be riding another Bahamian thoroughbred with the simple name of Bill (we had already beaten Shoofly in a cup race), and the rest of the field included Cedrick Higgs on Shoofly, Uncle Clinton on Asha Vashey, Charlie Gibson (also known as "The Diamond Kid") on Brave Boy and a jockey nicknamed Rat on Bob. I knew that Bill and I could easily beat all of them, but, stupidly, I agreed to Mr. Knowles' deal to let Shoofly win.

Although I was leading the race from start to finish, I allowed Shoofly to pass Bill and me just a few yards from the finish line. Not only did I lose the race, but Mr. Knowles also refused to pay me! From that time on, you better believe that I got my money upfront -- and I screwed the crooked owners over every chance I got! I won – and lost -- when I wanted to, despite instructions to the contrary.

Bill was my favorite mount, so an introduction to our meeting is in order. Although Bill was reputed to be the fastest horse in the Bahamas, he had not trained before he first came to Nassau from Cat Island, where he had been born, to race against Shoofly, who had a worldwide reputation for streaking out of the gate in front of every other horse (no horse had ever beaten Shoofly out of the gate – until I changed that). And this race was especially important -- it was a high stakes race that would feature nine of the top horses in the Bahamas.

At first, it wasn't even a "given" that Bill would be in the line-up - no one thought he would pass the physical inspection required of each horse before it was qualified to run. So there was a scramble to find a jockey after the handicap doctor declared Bill "fit to race." And, as luck would have it, I was aimlessly walking around the track that day, feeling sorry for myself because I didn't have a mount.

I was surprised to learn that Bill had not been exercised all summer -- and even more surprised to learn that it had been determined that the maximum weight that Bill should carry was 120 pounds; if I rode Bill, I would have to ride him overweight. I decided Bill would not be troubled by ten extra pounds, so I asked Bill's owner, Carlton "Fuzzy" Lightburn,

"Do you want me to win the race?"

"I'm not betting on this race because Bill has not trained much,"

Fuzzy replied. "Whatever you do is okay with me."

Well, I had a strong hunch about Bill as I sat on the horse at the starting gate next to Shoofly, who was straining to run. And, Bill, who had never jumped out of the gate first in all of his racing career, didn't disappoint me. When Bill heard the bell ring and saw the gate swing open, he was off so fast that the announcer didn't even have time to finish his announcement about the horses being off and running. No horse had ever beaten Shoofly out of the starting gate before Bill and me, which led to the term "shoobill" being introduced in our racing circle.

Shoofly was eating dust as Bill and I disappeared down the track, and, in no time at all, we were in the winner's circle! Almost no one -- not even Bill's owner or even my mom -- had bet on Bill (Fuzzy had bet on Shoofly, and my mom had, too, because she was mad as hell at me when I won), but I had put my money on Bill and won quite a few pounds, as the odds were about 20-1.

For the rest of that year, Bill and I were a team -- I rode Bill in every race – no matter how heavy I was. I would take Bill and beat Shoofly, but later I would ride Shoofly and beat Bill, and I also rode Beauty, a horse from Great Exuma, and beat both Bill and Shoofly.

But I had a special place in my heart for Bill -- especially when he was responsible for my finally getting revenge on Uncle Clinton. Uncle was riding Asha Vashey, a very fast horse, against Bill and me in one race, but I beat them out of the gate – and I beat Uncle with my whalebone whip for the entire race, which was a mile and three-quarters. I stayed on Uncle, whipping him all the way, and by the time we were almost at the finish line, he was screaming,

"This boy is about to kill me!"

Uncle was also crying about having a wife and children, but that did not stop me. I remembered what he had done to me, and I wouldn't have stopped beating him except that we crossed the finish line and the steward had me on film then. I didn't care about that – I had gotten my payback – but they took first place away from me.

Wow, was the public mad at me for allowing myself to come in second! They called me all kinds of names, including a crook, but that's the way life goes. I didn't give a damn – I had repaid Uncle for what he had done to me...and I gained his respect. When Uncle saw me from then on, he stayed away from me.

But the public wasn't too far off in calling me a crook -- I was always making my own deals so I would win big. My blatant disregard for the dishonest owners could have gotten me beaten up or even killed, but I knew I didn't have to worry about that. Although I was living at the track during the time I was racing, my mother depended on my winnings to keep food on the table, so she furnished bodyguards for me from among her willing brothers. I never needed to worry about being threatened for throwing a race or winning one the "wrong way" -- I was protected...and I was making a lot of money on the swindles.

I had mixed feelings about participating in fraud, of course, but Henry and I were making great money. By the time I was 16, he and I were able to pitch in (each of us put up half of the money) to build a beautiful stone house for our mothers. At the time, you couldn't separate the two women, and Henry and I were proud to have become the men in our families (even though I wasn't living at home at the time).

During the time I was a jockey, I also found time to pursue other interests. By the time I was 15, I was dancing the limbo in the stable yard. All the young jockeys would do the limbo, and I got pretty good at it. But one night when we were out in the back yard of the stable, something happened. I fell back onto my back on the cold ground, and a chill ran straight through me.

I ended up sick as a dog, and my mother was called. She took me home, which was a good thing, because the ailment that I had almost killed me. The next day, mom took me to Dr. Lorenzo, who told my mom that I had contracted a very bad case of the flu. Before sending us off with some medicine, he also warned me about my practice of depriving my body of food so I would stay small enough to race. He said that if I did not stop starving myself, I would die – and soon.

Well, that flu kept me sick for a month – and I was so severely ill that I don't remember much about what was going on until one day when I woke up to find my mother's black ass on my face. She was crying out to God, begging Him not to take her child.

I guess she had reason for her concern, as I could also hear the kids out in the yard, crying,

"Errisson's dead! Errisson's dead!"

I struggled to push my mother off me, slowly raised myself up, and asked,

"What's all this crying about? Get me some food."

My mother -- who was probably shocked by my sudden revival -- then started praying and praising God for bringing me back. I had suffered greatly during the time I was ill, but, thankfully, I survived that bout of flu.

After I was up and about for a little while, my mom took me back to the doctor for a check-up. I was so small and had lost so much weight (I was just skin and bones) that you would think that a little puff of wind would blow me to the ground.

Despite having been so ill and losing weeks of work, I was right back on the track as soon as I was able because I was determined to be the next Eddie Arcaro or Willie Shoemaker. That dream was put on hold when we skipped a season after there was a fire at the race track. That incident, although it was unfortunate, gave me plenty of time to build my strength up, and I was able to keep busy with my other duties at the track, which included keeping the horses fit and taking them for a sea bath, which they loved. I remember that there was one big, black horse by the name of Mighty Casey who loved the sea so much that he would bolt straight across the road (and into oncoming traffic) if you were not careful. When he got to the ocean, Mighty Casey would dive in head first like a man. I had to keep alert and ready or he would have thrown me off.

Mighty Casey was a fast horse, and I won a few races on him, but by the next season, I had gone from 125 pounds to 140 pounds, and trouble started for me. I wanted to continue my career as a jockey, so I began starving myself even more so I would be able to carry the right weight to be eligible to race. I didn't have to worry about working for a particular owner at this time -- after I became a freelance jockey, all I had to do was walk around the track and I was sure to get a mount.

By the time I was 18, though, I was ready to quit the race game. Even though I was starving myself so I could meet the weight requirements, my body continued to get heavier (I think I weighed about 135 pounds by this time). And, of course, my conscience was pressing me – I was getting tired of the crookedness and fraud.

If I had been smart, I would have ended my career on a high note, but I continued to sign up for races. One time, when I was approached to ride a thoroughbred named Tular, I had to lose 20 pounds overnight in order to qualify. But I was used to dieting and taking emetics (used to flush out my system) – in fact, every jockey who competed on major racetracks the world over knew what was required.

I began the torturous procedure the day before the race. I always kept Epsom salts, bitters and lime juice on hand, so I boiled the salts, dropped in some bitters and added the lime juice to make my laxative drink. After stirring and swallowing the hot mix, I then bolted over beyond the horse stalls, where my trainer was waiting for me by a huge pile of horse dung that the manure truck had not yet hauled away.

As soon as I arrived and greeted Alonzo, I stripped off my clothes, hung them on a hook on the wall and stepped into a large bag that Alonzo was holding open. When empty of the oats that it once contained, the bag had the capacity to hold an average human body, so Alonzo tied the bag at my throat and helped me to hop over to a cavity dug in the pile of horse dung. As soon as I fitted myself into the body-sized hole, Alonzo began shoveling dung around me until the manure was all around my body (only my head was sticking out). Alonzo then walked away, assuring me that he would return in three hours.

He was hardly gone before the Epsom salts began working and my feces ran uncontrollably down my legs. And, since horse manure packed around a human raises the body temperature, sweat was running out of my pores in rivulets (like small rivers). I don't think there has even been a sauna as hot as horse manure.

Before Alonzo returned to dig me out, I remembered the warning of Dr. Lorenzo, who knew all about the dung heap weight reduction process:

"You can't go on like you're doing, King. You'll kill yourself if you do. You're supposed to be a big man – there's nothing you can do about that. If you keep abusing your body, your heart or something else is going to give out and you'll die. Is that what you want?"

Dr. Lorenzo obviously knew what he was talking about. By the time Alonzo and his groom dug me out of the dung heap, I could barely move. I smelled of a high, hot stink that burned the nose, and they had to support me between them until they reached the place where the water hose was located. Holding weakly to a wooden support, I then had to endure the blasts of cold water that buffeted my body until the draining water was clear of brown taint.

Alonzo and the groom then dried me with towels and brought me to my room, where I fell into my bunk to sleep off my exhaustion. I was ragingly thirsty and weak when I awoke, but I sipped only a spoonful of water. I had tried to drink previously after I'd endured the manure pile shrinkage method but had instantly felt puffy. Just one full glass of water in a dehydrated body would put weight back on me.

When I tried to dress myself on the morning of the race, I felt dizzy and light-headed, and I could barely drag myself to the track. When I finally stepped up on the official scale, I still had loose bowels...and I weighed 115½ pounds! After all I had been through, the horse I was to ride could only carry 118 pounds, and there was no saddle light enough for him to be eligible to run with me on his back.

I not only didn't ride that day -- that was the beginning of the end of my career as a jockey. I rode in only a few more races that season before being sidelined by an act of arson -- someone deliberately set fire to Hobby Horse Hall, and the fire and smoke consumed everything, including the spectator stands.

I returned as a jockey after the track reopened in 1959, winning three races and coming in third on opening day, but I knew that my days were numbered. Not only was I too big to be a jockey, but my heart just wasn't in the race game anymore -- I had bigger dreams for myself.

By the time I was running my last races, I was playing music in some small clubs over the hill. I will never forget the big guys (guys older than me) who would come over to the bandstand at the clubs and point at me, making sport of my playing. Despite their ribbing, I was convinced that I would eventually become the greatest drummer in the world. They only had age on me – they didn't have talent – and before those guys died, some of them actually came to me for lessons!

I had resumed my interest in drumming after the track burned for the first time. I knew that I was getting better, but not everyone appreciated my playing -- there were a lot of people who complained about me making too much noise. One occasion that sticks out in my mind had to do with a tenant in a small house that Henry and I had built behind our mothers' stone house.

One of my cousins, who was the wife of Melford Clark, came flying out of that house one day and yelled at me to shut up.

"Why don't you take your fat behind out in the yard and put your head in a hole so you can't hear me playing!" I screamed back.

That was the kind of kid that I was – I didn't take crap from anyone. But everyone got mad at me over that incident. By that time, things weren't going well between mom and Tettie – Tettie and Henry seemed to act as if they owned that house (even though I had put in half of the money for it).

Fortunately, I had two "safe havens" where I could play my drums to my heart's content -- without causing trouble for my mom. The first was on the porch of one of the most wonderful man I have ever known -- and a man that I have always strived to emulate. His name was Justin Roberts, and, in 1955, he had made a promise to his cousin, Terry Roberts, who was dying of cancer. At the time, Terry was married to Zelma Bowe and had three children, Terrance ("L'il Terry"), who was just a baby when his father died, Elizabeth ("Betty"), who had been born in 1953, and Paula, who was born in 1952.

Justin promised Terry that he would look after his wife and children and he did just that, becoming an "unofficial" husband to Zelma and a loving father to Terry, Betty and Paula. Justin and Zelma would also have two boys of their own, Antonius ("Tony") and Bruno.

You can see the kind of man that Justin was from his love for his cousin's family, and he extended that love to me. Justin, Zelma and the kids became my second family; I was as close to them as I was to my own family, and I can't begin to describe how much Justin did for me, encouraging me every step of the way -- both when I was a teenager and into my adult years.

Justin did so much for me, in fact, that I could probably fill a book about him, but there were two gestures in particular that made me that man that I am today. First, Justin not only bought professional bongos for me, but he also let me play on the family's porch whenever I needed a place to practice. In fact, I used to play while I babysat the kids when Zelma, who was very sweet and kind to me, had to go shopping or to some event.

Justin also played a big part in my racing career -- not only did he offer encouragement, but he also bought three racehorses for me to train and ride! I'll never forget the thrill of taking the mail boat to Great Exuma to pick up my first horse from Max Bowe, who was Zelma's grandfather (Max was also the grandfather of the mother of my first son - I'll tell you about them later). Justin named the horse, who was a nine-month-old colt at the time, My Son, and what a runner he was! But he was also the first horse to slap the crap out of me.

I was an experienced jockey by that time, of course, so I knew how to handle any kind of horse -- or at least I thought I could. When we got off the boat and I was walking My Son home to the stables, which were ten miles from the docks, I guess that the walk got too much for him -- My Son just stopped walking. When I walked over and (foolishly) pulled on the rope, My Son started walking on his two hind legs (it was like something you'd see in the movies or something)! And in no time, his front hoof was against the side of my head!

Well, we had one hell of a fight on that road, but I finally got My Son home to Justin's beach house and horse stable at a place called South Beach at the end of the island (that place was much like the resort I would later build on Pestell Beach on Acklins Island).

Unfortunately, the fights between My Son and me didn't end that day. About three months later, I had to break My Son for racing, and, although I was an experienced trainer, it took days for me to get him to the point where someone could ride him. But we did eventually have success with My Son and the other two horses, winning a number of races.

Anyway, to get back to my music, when I wasn't at Justin's I often used to walk over Blue Hill Road into what I thought of as the jungle. There, I would play my drums for the birds and bees; they seemed to understand what I was playing, and they seemed to sing and buzz in response to my beats. Those were some wonderful times.

Despite my playing away from home, things grew steadily worse between my mom and Tettie. My memories of that time are a little fuzzy, but I think that my mom went back to America on contract because the story is that she met up with a childhood friend, Otis Clark, while she was in the States -- and, in September of 1959, the month before my 18th birthday, she gave birth to my half-brother, Gerone Clark, in Miami.

I didn't get to spend a lot of time with Gerone -- it wasn't long before I was away working most of the time. But Gerone and I did have some good times (and a scary episode as well) when I returned to Nassau a few years later.

After the track reopened for the second time and I ran my last races, it took two months for me to recover my strength and be able to eat properly again, but with money I had saved from riding and some cash from my mother, I bought a pair of professional congas. Grateful that I had real instruments to practice on, I knew that the next step should be to seek advice on who could help me connect with people who would recognize my talent and give me a break.

I hadn't gotten a real drum or had any "professional" training until I was about 15 or 16 years old. Before then, my first influence was Hubert Johnson, who played bongo drums. At my request, Hubert made a pair of bongos out of coffee cans for me, but he braced them together and tuned them so I could actually make recognizable music on them.

Fortunately for me, when I was about 15, I was able to get some invaluable instruction from a self-effacing, sharp and kind instructor, an islander named John Chipman. "Chippie" was a hero to the kids of Nassau who wanted to learn music. On any given day, a group of brown children – his "goat-skin trust" – gathered in his front yard and listened raptly to every word he uttered.

John welcomed me, although I was older than most of his students. He taught me both drumming techniques and discipline, and his advice was invaluable. John insisted that I master each new drumming lesson, practice it at home and then return for the next step after I had committed the previous one to memory. He also taught me how to develop stamina for long sessions of drumming.

I owe a huge debt of gratitude to John for helping me along the way and teaching me. John was more than a teacher -- he became a good friend -- and John and I are still good friends. He is over 80 years old now, and I still go to see John when I am in the islands.

A very sad thing happened to John, though. One day, his son,

Phillip, jumped off a dock. It was not unusual for me and my friends to dive off docks – we would wait for the tide to come in and jump in while the waves were at their highest. On that day, though, we tried to talk Phillip, who was about 14, out of diving.

Well, Phillip didn't listen. He missed the tide and had a tragic accident that left him paralyzed. From that day until he died at age 40, Phillip was in a wheelchair and couldn't move anything from the head down. That was a very sad day and a very sad time for John. He had a half a dozen daughters but only one son, and his only son got totally messed up at an early age, never to be a man again.

I wish I could say that I learned from that tragedy, but a month later, I also jumped off a dock into water that was shallower than I thought. I didn't break my neck, thank God, but I struck my head so hard that it seemed that my neck had gone into my shoulders. A couple of the big boys who were around at the time pulled me up and pulled my head up a bit, so I wasn't hurt too badly – but it was a scary moment.

During the time I was working with John, my mother surprised me with a windup Victrola. It was a wonderful gift, and I spent hours playing records performed by artists I admired. I had already discovered the Cuban radio stations, but now I bought albums from the different drummers that I admired. I listened to recordings from such artists as legendary Cuban drummer Ramón "Mongo" Santamaria, bongo and conga drummers Carlos "Patato" Valdez, Armondo Perazo and Candido Camero Guerra, and the jazz stylings of American pianist George Shearing, as well as records produced by Berry Gordy, who blazed to fame as the co-founder of Motown. At the time, I never would have imagined that I would later work closely with and become friends with Berry.

Every night, I went to sleep with Armondo Perazo in my dreams, and soon I could play every lick and sound that Perazo made. My most important discovery, however, was that I was not imitating just one person, but six – I had perfected the sounds of the entire percussion section! I was elated, and I knew I was on my way to becoming a real musician. But I also knew I had a long way to go -- and that I needed help from someone who already enjoyed a successful career as a musician.

As luck would have it, my Uncle Jethro ("Jet"), who thought that I would appreciate observing how an outstanding drummer performed, took me to the Tropicana nightclub in Nassau. I should tell you that my Uncle Jet, who never married, was a very big, strong guy who loved to fight – he was always beating up four or five guys at a time. But his fighting would be the end of him. Before that year was out, my Uncle Jet got drunk one Sunday afternoon and seven guys jumped him and beat him to death. I loved Uncle Jet, and his death hurt me deeply.

On the night we went to the club, Uncle Jet and I had a wonderful time. I was fascinated, almost mesmerized, by the way the little man on the stage handled his drums. That drummer was "Peanuts" Taylor, the world-renowned percussionist who was an iconic figure in the Bahamian music world. Peanuts, who, like me, had begun drumming at the age of four, had been given his nickname by Paul Meeres, who had won international fame as a dancer.

Meeres, who was the son of an Ethiopian mother (she was over six feet tall and black as tar) and a father from Argentina, was 6'2" tall but he moved like a gazelle -- probably because of his ballet training. Meeres had starred at the Cotton Club in Harlem and appeared with Josephine Baker in Paris, but, despite his being an acclaimed star, he always seemed willing to talk to me and encourage me about my music.

Meeres, who owned a club on Market and Deveaux Streets in the 1950s and early 1960s as well as the first black movie house in the Bahamas (the Cinema on East Street), was a close friend of my father. In fact, Meeres and my father had "arranged" an engagement between Paul's daughter, Delores, and me when I was six years old. Although that was a custom practiced in the Bahamas to forecast a marriage between the offspring of close families, it was mostly just talk; the arrangement was not binding.

That arrangement between Meeres and my father, though, was a perfect example of dad's habit of thinking big. He wanted me to have the best, and I couldn't have done much better than Delores Meeres. Delores, who was very light-skinned like her father, was a couple of years older than I was – and a whole lot richer.

Meeres thought that Peanuts would be the perfect person to help me along with my music, but I hadn't approached Peanuts until the night that Uncle Jet and I went to the club. I went up to Peanuts after one of his sets, told him how much I admired his talent and asked him if he would be willing to help me to develop my skills on the drums. Unfortunately, Peanuts, who was only about 5'5" in height, was too busy to help me at the time.

Although I was disappointed, I was also overcome with the conviction that I could play as well as Peanuts -- and maybe even better. So, although he couldn't help me at the time, Peanuts played an important role in my efforts to become the best, and he and I would become rivals before we later became good friends (in fact, I would tune Peanuts' drums on several occasions).

Over the next two years, I investigated every opportunity to learn the techniques of drumming, dancing and singing so I could become a pro. I was fortunate to be helped by several people, including a man named Babaloo, who demonstrated simple beats to me and introduced me to Tojo, the Black Korean. Tojo was helpful with some basic instruction, but after I learned to play like everyone else, I developed my own style of playing. Although I was making progress toward achieving my dreams, I still had a lot to learn -- and not just in the field of music.

Chapter 5

Love, Heartbreak and a Taste of Success

I'm sure that people who know me wonder why I haven't mentioned any women in my life so far. Actually, I didn't have much time for women when I was a kid -- in fact, I was determined not to get married and I didn't think I ever would.

That belief could be traced back to an old Bahamian superstition. When I was growing up, I loved to eat the pot cake – the food that was burned at the bottom of the pot after cooking peas or beans and rice. I couldn't wait to get to the bottom of the pot -- I wanted that pot cake.

When my great-grandmother, "Ma Delphine," saw me eating out of the pot, she would say,

"Boy, you ain't never gonna get married. Any young man that eat out of the pot that much, no woman is ever going to want him."

The more Ma Delphine told me that, the more I ate out of the pot - I believed it would work. But, boy, was my great-grandmother ever wrong! Despite eating out of the pot as many times as I could, I have been married half a dozen times!

I first started noticing girls when I was in my teens. My Uncle Salvanis, who had many children, had a daughter named Sylvia who was drop dead beautiful. She and I were very close, and if she had not been family, Sylvia would have been my first love. Since that was not to be, I found another special girl during my days as a leading jockey.

Ruth was a gorgeous mulatto girl who was 5'7" at age 13. She was the daughter of a white man and a mother who was a 6'2" island woman as black as tar. That woman hated my guts – despite her own color, she didn't want her daughter to be with anyone as dark as I was.

Ignoring her mother's objections, I nurtured Ruth for an entire year. I wanted nothing to do with making love to her or spoiling her – we did French kiss, but that was as far as it went.

For an entire year, it was my habit to walk Ruth to school every morning (I didn't have a car at the time), and I would always be there waiting for her at the end of the day to walk her home. One afternoon, when I went to pick her up at the usual time, some kids approached my three-speed bicycle and started laughing at me.

"You came for Ruth, man, you came for Ruth," they taunted. "The man that take her has gone! The man that take her is gone!"

"What man?" I asked.

"The man in the black car. The little black man in the black car," they answered.

"Sydney," I heard someone else shout.

Well, I didn't know any Sydney -- or any other black man in a black car, for that matter -- so I hopped on my bicycle and rode over to Ruth's house as fast as I could. Sure enough, a black car was parked in front of the door. When I peeked through her window, that little black man was on top of Ruth – who was only 14 years old at this time -- and he was making love to her! Ruth was screaming with delight and having a great time with this little black man – after I had been nurturing her, trying to keep her pure for myself, for our wedding day.

Wow! Ruth was already screwing around and I had no idea. That was my very first bad experience with women, and I was so angry that I picked up three or four of the biggest rocks I could find and I threw them at the windows of Ruth's mother's house, breaking several of them. Then I jumped back on my bicycle and pedaled home.

I was never charged for breaking the windows, and I didn't even bother to apologize to Ruth's mother. Of course, her mother came to my house and raised hell with my mom about the broken windows, but my mom stuck up for me.

"The little slut should not have hurt my son the way she did," she told Ruth's mother.

I found it very ironic that Ruth's mother was more upset about those windows than she was about her daughter having sex at such a young age. Who knows? Maybe Ruth's mother had started having sex while she was a young teenager, too.

Although Ruth's mother didn't seem to think it was a big deal that her daughter was screwing around, I was very angry over Ruth's betrayal -- and I took my anger out on tin water buckets, banging holes in the bottoms of them.

I was already taking drum lessons from John Chipman at this time, so I got a goatskin drum from him and started banging on it. I had never drummed as hard as I did on the day that I caught Ruth cheating on me.

I spanked that drum so hard, in fact, that I tore the skin up – because every time I slapped that drum, I was slapping that woman. I think it was better to slap the drum than Ruth, because I could have gone to jail if I had I hurt her.

In the space of one week, I tore up the heads on five different drums, and my mother finally went out and bought a conga drum with a mule skin head for me. The mule skin head was hard to tear, so every chance I had, I stayed on the porch and I spanked that drum.

During those days when I was so angry, I beat my drum. I didn't play it, because every time I hit it I was hitting that little bitch. I was not a drum player back then; I only learned to actually play the drums after I got over Ruth. Then, I learned to make love to my drums. My drums became my women -- I caressed them and I loved them more than I loved women. To this day, they are me and I am them, so I must give thanks to this girl, wherever she is today, because she actually helped me to achieve my dream of becoming a great drummer.

I never spoke to Ruth after the day that I caught her with that little black man. Sometimes, when I was practicing my drums on the porch, she would walk by and speak to me but I never spoke back. I was that hurt.

One fateful day, I was on the porch as usual, beating my drums, which now included a couple of conga drums that my mother had bought for me. They were cheap drums -- the type that the tourists would buy and try to play -- but it was a great gift nevertheless (my mom believed in me and she didn't deny me anything).

That day, a white tourist who was passing by in a car stopped to listen to me. After about 30 minutes, he got out of his car, walked up to me, held out a business card and asked me to call him. The man owned a nightclub in Boston, and he wanted me to come and perform there because he said I was the best drummer he had ever heard!

I took the card, but I told him that it would be a while before I called.

"You haven't heard great yet," I told him. "Give me a year from now... I'll be the greatest in the world." And I practiced towards that.

Not long after the incident with Ruth, my luck with women began to change. A woman named Lillian, who was a very good friend of both my mother and me, had a sister whose daughter moved from Exuma to Nassau to live with Lillian while she was looking for a house.

The girl's name was Fay, and she was a beautiful Bahamian girl. Her family was well-off – her father used to be the caretaker of an island called Norman's Cay, which later became the dope capital of the Bahamas. Norman's Cay used to belong to Jessica Tandy and Hume Cronyn, who was the first man to own the island privately – before then, it had belonged to the Bahamian government.

Anyway, I suppose that Fay was one of the brightest girls in the Bahamas. She had an I.Q. of about 182, and by the time she was 13 years old, Fay had passed all the required tests to get into college. Since she was so young, Fay wanted to move to Nassau, where she could take more classes at the government high school before entering the College of the Bahamas, which didn't admit students until they were 16 or 17. Her plans (and those of her parents for her) were to finish college before traveling to London to study to become a doctor.

So Fay moved to Nassau, into her auntie's house, to go to school. My mother and I lived just around the corner from Fay's Aunt Lillian, but I didn't meet Fay until she had lived at Lillian's house for several weeks. I was still a jockey at the time, so, needless to say, the charm of King Errisson got to Fay and she fell in love...and the feeling was mutual.

Fay was the spitting image of Ursula Andress, both in face and in figure. She was absolutely beautiful – she looked like a little island princess – and, man, was I in love with Fay. Oh, yeah, I got over Ruth in a hurry.

Fay was so perfect that I can think of only one thing that was wrong with her -- she used to smell like sheep. Her family ate nothing but fresh meat -- they'd go into the pasture every so often to kill sheep or cows or goats or something -- so poor Fay ended up smelling like the sheep that she consumed so regularly. Fortunately, after she moved to Nassau and started being a city girl and using proper perfume, Fay began to smell as beautiful as she looked.

Fay and I not only hooked up shortly after we met, but we also moved in together. Fay had a lot of power over her parents, and she told them that she wanted a house of her own -- and she backed up her request with a threat.

"I'm not living alone. I want Errisson to live with me. I'm not living alone and I won't go to school unless he comes and lives with me."

Now, remember, this girl was still a minor, but her parents went along with her wishes. They came to Nassau and found a nice two-bedroom flat so I could stay with Fay. But they made me promise that I would not get her with child until she finished her schooling. Only then, would they give their blessing to us getting married.

I intended to live up to that promise, but after I moved in with Fay I decided I wasn't petting anybody anymore – it was lovemaking time. I vowed I would never just groom someone for marriage again, and Fay sure went along with that.

During the two years we were together, Fay and I had a lovemaking method. She was an old-fashioned person in some ways – Fay was taught when to make love, I guess, because she never got pregnant. Fay didn't want to get pregnant, of course; she wanted to finish her schooling. I knew she marked the calendar so she always knew the dangerous times, and, although we made love all the time, she called the shots. Fay knew when the time when it was possible to get pregnant, so at those times, she would tell me,

"Get away, I can't be bothered with you."

In my two years of sweet-hearting her, Fay never got pregnant. She would say, "O.K., we can make love tonight," or we could have sex any night until she told me "no." Whenever she told me "no," I knew it was the time that she could get pregnant, so I would not make love to her.

Fay was funny (and she could be a little crazy -- in a good way -- at times) as well as smart, so I loved being with her. She and I had some good times together -- including taking the mail boat to Great Exuma to the regatta (boat races). When we went to Exuma, Fay would stay with her parents, but I could not stay in the same house. I thought that was pretty strange, considering that we lived together in Nassau.

While we were living together, I decided that I had gotten good enough to call the man who owned the nightclub in Boston. I asked if his offer was still open, and I was beyond excited to find out that it was, even though I had waited several months to call him. When I told Fay, I thought she would be happy -- I would have a great job and she could go on to London to continue her studies. But Fay was not happy with the news at all; in fact, she got very upset, even though I promised I would visit her in London every couple of months. Fay was having nothing to do with the idea of us being apart, and she came up with a plan to make sure that I would not leave her.

I'll never forget what happened next. That night, we were making love and I could tell that everything was different about this woman. There was something different about the way her body felt; Fay felt fuller, juicier inside. Sensing trouble, I decided I'd better play it safe and tried to pull away from her before it was too late. Well, I've never been in a death grip like that in my life. Fay threw those long legs and her arms around me and squeezed me with all her might. I have to say that it was one of the best orgasms I ever had in my life, but I could tell immediately that something had just happened. When I looked at Fay and saw the smile on her face, my fears were confirmed -- I knew I had just screwed up…in more ways than one. But that is what Fay wanted.

A week later, Fay came around to my mom's house to visit. The minute she walked in the door, my mother took one look at her and asked,

"Child, what have you done?"

"Nothing, Ma," Fay answered.

"Don't you lie to me. You're pregnant."

"No, Ma, I ain't pregnant," Fay protested.

Now, my mother was a wise woman, and she knew when a young girl was pregnant. And my mother wasn't wrong in this case, either. Some months later, Fay's belly started to show and everybody knew that she was pregnant.

By that time, the gig that I was supposed to have in Boston had fallen through. I had added a second drum after I had met Fay, and I had rehearsed with a guy named Roy Hanna (we called him Duke Hanna) for about three months to go on that gig, but at the very last minute he decided that I wasn't good enough. Instead, Duke took another drummer, a friend of mine by the name of Rudy Pinder, to the three-week gig in Boston.

I was crushed, of course. I had been playing a lot in different clubs in Nassau, and I thought I was ready for my big chance. While I was still nursing my disappointment over losing the Boston gig, a good friend of mine by the name of Solomon Frazier came by the house. Sol was a guitar player, and he and I often played together at the Conch Shell Club in Nassau. That day, Sol came by to tell me about a job he had landed – and he invited me to go with him.

"Hey, man. Let's go to Bimini. I got a job in Bimini at a place called the Famous Door."

Well, I wasn't going to miss out on another job, so I decided to leave Fay to go to Bimini for a few months. Before I left, I took Fay, who was about four months pregnant, on the mail boat to Great Exuma to "face the music." I actually thought that her family would be proud of me for wanting to do the right thing, but Fay's parents were furious at me (as if I was the only one who had anything to do with Fay getting pregnant). In fact, they were so angry that their plans for their oldest daughter were ruined that Fay's father went into the house and returned with his shotgun! I honestly think the man would have blown my head off if Fay and her mother hadn't stood in front of me to protect me.

I politely ran away to get back on the mail boat to return to Nassau, but this time I would be sailing across the water alone; Fay could have come back with me, of course, but she decided to stay in Exuma with her parents. I guess she wanted her mother to look after her while she was pregnant -- especially since I would be away in Bimini and would not be there for her.

When we got to Bimini, I was delighted to find that the man who had booked us into the Famous Door had also provided a wonderful place for Sol and me to live. It was a large, five-bedroom house right on the water in North Bimini, and everyone who performed at the club lived there, including a beautiful voodoo priestess named Rama, who was from Guadeloupe, the southernmost of the Leeward Islands in the eastern Caribbean.

Before I tell you about what happened at the Famous Door, I want to share an incident that nearly scared me shitless. One night, Rama's father's ghost came to visit her, and he stopped in my room to take a look at me. As terrified as I was, I managed to open my eyes and look at the ghost. When I finally could speak, I told him to go to the next room -- and that ghost did just that!

The next morning, I found Rama outside the back of the house (she was doing some voodoo ritual that I can't exactly describe except to say that it involved praying with her hands clasped tightly together and a glass of water in front of her), and I asked her if she had a visitor the previous night.

"Yes, it was my father," she answered.

I told her that I knew that because he had stopped by my room first.

Rama, who was mysterious and exotic, had one of the most fantastic – and dramatic – acts that I have ever seen. She was billed as "Rama the Glass Eater" for a very good reason. Rama would walk up to customers' tables, pick up their glasses of wine or liquor, finish the drinks, and crush the glasses between her teeth – without shedding a drop of blood!

As I drummed, Rama's dancing would become more intense as she resonated to my beat. The faster I played, the more frenzied she got, until Rama was smashing dozens of glasses with her teeth before throwing them on the floor, leaping above them, and landing in the sharp fragments – without even nicking her bare feet.

Rama would roll over the broken glass – scaring patrons when her wild trances turned her into a demon. The customers would flee from her flying arms and legs, but Rama would continue dancing in a fury before leaping into a ring of fire – without getting burned!

It took a lot to stop Rama's otherworldly frenzy. Sometimes, a big, tall, good-looking man from New Jersey would step in. No one knew his name or how he was connected to Rama -- some people thought he was her voodoo partner or just a friend (I thought that he might be Rama's pimp) – but he was usually able to get control over Rama and calm her down.

If that didn't work – if she was so out of control that she would come at me with broken glasses in her hands -- I would sing the voodoo song, "Shango, Shango." That song could either bring a spirit in or take it away, depending on the tone of voice used when singing it and the command I put into it, so I would always sing it in the way that would cause her to stop, listen to me and return to her senses.

If that didn't get her out of her frenzied state, either me – or me and the man from New Jersey together – had to wrestle Rama to the floor! It was really something to see.

Rama's act made a big impression on everyone who witnessed it. I guess the tourists who had seen the show spread the word, because one night I was surprised to see an unexpected visitor to the Famous Door.

That visitor was none other than Sweet Richard, a Bahamian man who had been born Richard Dean. Sweet Richard, who began his career as a street performer in Nassau before moving to clubs, was best known for ushering in a new era in Junkanoo dance choreography. He pioneered the concept of the lead dancer, and Richard gained international fame for introducing the "shuffle" dance.

"The King of Junkanoo" was an iconic figure. Known as the greatest limbo dancer in the world (he once performed for the Duke of Windsor), Sweet Richard was a half-white Bahamian man, the great-grandson of both black slaves and white men -- the kind of person that the people on the islands call a "Conky Joe." A beautiful guy with long black hair that was silky and wavy, he was the wildest man I had ever met – the first real hippie I had ever seen.

Richard always wore a vest and big hat as well as tights or leotards that fit him like a second skin. He never wore shoes, even in mid-winter, but he was never seen without the sword that dangled at his waist – Richard always carried that sword in his belt wherever he went. He looked like Blackbeard the pirate with his huge walrus mustache and that sword.

I have to tell you an amazing story about Sweet Richard. When he was a child, one of his eyes got knocked out. Well, Richard's father, who was a sheep farmer, found that eye and then examined every sheep in his flock to find an eye that matched his son's. He cut off that sheep's head and took the sheep's eye and his son to America, where he had an oculist copy the eye in glass and place it into Richard's empty socket. You know, I knew Richard for years, but I had no idea that eye was false.

Richard was married to a girl named Kitty, a beautiful white girl from South Carolina, who walked like a snake. Kitty was one of the most gorgeous white women I had ever seen; she had long, black hair down to her butt (and what a shapely butt it was) and beautiful dark blue eyes. Richard taught his wife – he always called her Princess Kitty -- how to dance, and they became the greatest dance team in Miami Beach. They starred at the biggest strip club there, Place Pigalle, which was owned by Harry Rich, a big-time gangster who ran Miami Beach at the time.

It wasn't just their dancing that made Sweet Richard and Princess Kitty stars – they were as colorful and flamboyant offstage as they were when they were performing. I wish you could have seen Sweet Richard and Princess Kitty in person – I've already told you that Richard looked like Blackbeard the pirate, but both of them looked like characters out of a Sinbad movie (Richard was never without his big, gold rings, and Kitty wore earrings as big as coffee cups). When the couple walked down Biscayne Boulevard in Miami, the cops used to pick them up and put them in jail because Sweet Richard and Princess Kitty stopped traffic!

I had first met Sweet Richard three years earlier. I was just 16 years old when I began joining him on stage, playing the tub bass (a one-string instrument that had a washtub for a base) at a place called the Pirate's Den. Richard had then left the islands to become a big star in the United States, and by the time our paths crossed again in Bimini, Richard was such a celebrity that the Goodyear blimp had brought him from Miami Beach to Bimini to see Rama's show.

Richard had no idea that I was also playing at the Famous Door, but he recognized me immediately, and I was happy to see him again. After the show, he called me over to his table and exclaimed,

"Crazy, man! You are the greatest -- and I want you to come play for me! You are the best! Crazy, man, crazy!"

Richard told me that he had six drummers on stage with him and I played better than all six of them put together! Wow, that was a great compliment, but the best was yet to come. I was elated when Richard told me that he wanted me to join him and Princess Kitty in their act -- especially when Richard told me he would pay me any amount of money and provide a car and a place for me to live. Of course, it was an opportunity that I couldn't pass up, so I gave my two-week notice to the owners of the Famous Door so they could find someone to replace me.

I was a little sorry to leave Bimini and Sol and Rama. I had a great time playing at the Famous Door, and I had met some wonderful friends on the island, including Adam Clayton Powell. Although I wouldn't see Rama for about 20 years, I did return to Bimini to see Sol and some other friends a few years later. But I would soon be making more friends -- and great (and not so great) new memories in America.

When I returned to Nassau after the Bimini gig to get things in order to join Sweet Richard and Princess Kitty in Miami Beach, I did not have time to see Fay or my first-born son, Anton Avon Johnson. I had received the news about Anton's birth when I was in Bimini, and I had sent money to Fay to help with his needs.

I had looked forward to seeing Fay again -- and even thought about marrying her someday -- but while I was on Bimini I had gotten a phone call from my mother that changed everything.

"Errisson, I went to see Fay this morning and I saw a man jumping out of her window! It was that tall fellow by the name of Bowe. When I asked her if she had seen him before, she told me she had."

Boy, was my heart broken…for the second time. And it was then that I began to wonder if the child was even mine! That's when I decided to put my heart on the shelf -- and I decided I would become the meanest (and greatest) lover of all times. I didn't have anyone to go back to in Nassau, and I didn't have to worry about what I would do or say if I saw Fay when I returned home. Shortly after Anton was born, she had left baby Anton with her mother to return to Nassau to gather her things and give up the flat that she and I had shared. Fay then returned to Great Exuma, and I would not see her or our son for several years.

I hadn't wanted to leave Fay pregnant to have a bastard child, of course -- I wasn't brought up that way -- but I will always give thanks to her father for chasing me away. That was the greatest thing that happened to me – I could have ended up a farmer, raising pigs and chickens, instead of becoming a successful musician.

I've been running from women with babies ever since. As a matter of fact, since Fay, every time I met a girl I'd tell her straight and plain,

"If you get pregnant, you're on your own because I am not going to be a farmer. I will not stay in the Bahamas and raise pigs and chickens."

I would not be trapped – I always left. In fact, I left three women pregnant in the Bahamas – I had three different sons, by three different women, including Fay's cousin, Alice, the mother of my son, Kenny. I'm not proud of that, but I was upfront with those women; they knew how I felt about them getting pregnant.

I refused to be stuck in the Bahamas, and you cannot imagine the pride I felt when I traveled to Miami Beach to appear with Sweet Richard. From the time I was a kid, I had dreamed of getting off the islands and making something of myself. The only time that anyone in my family had been out of the Bahamas had been to work on contract -- but I had no intention of working on contract.

I had been listening to music for my entire life -- music from the movies, music on the radio and music on the records that I had bought -- and I knew that I could play as well as the professional musicians I had heard. And now my dreams were finally starting to come true – I was going to America as a performer.

Chapter 6

On Tour as a Limbo Dancer

Sweet Richard, Princess Kitty and I, along with Babaloo, the drummer, were a huge nightclub act in Miami Beach, where we played at the Place Pigalle on Collins Avenue. Sometimes, Richard would let me dance the limbo when he was offstage, but mostly I drummed for him while he danced. Richard was a wild man when he was on stage -- as was his wife, Kitty; they were exciting performers, and the audiences (all white folks) loved us.

As I mentioned before, the owner of the club, Harry Rich, was a Jewish gangster who pretty much ran Miami Beach at the time, so he was able to stop the prejudicial treatment that Sweet Richard faced at the hands of the cops. But, although he was a very nice man, Harry was a bit racist himself. He was fine with blacks as long as they stayed in the back and didn't mix with the whites. In fact, the only time blacks could be seen up front was when we were coming to work or leaving -- or if someone in the audience asked to meet one of us (sometimes someone would send a note backstage for me after the show, and Harry would allow me to go out and meet with the patron).

And, boy, was Harry adamant about his beautiful white strippers not mingling with us -- although I didn't pay much attention to that rule. Every time that Harry would find out about my goings on -- or even suspect something -- he would fine the stripper. And, once, he took more serious action.

There was one stripper there who was from France. She was absolutely beautiful -- maybe even prettier than Princess Kitty. She was taller than Kitty, and more curvaceous -- and what a great stripper she was.

It didn't matter how talented she was; Harry chased her out of the place when he caught us kissing in my dressing room. I never saw her again, although she did call me for a little while. Then, she just disappeared and I never heard from her again. I was sorry that our relationship had resulted in her losing her job, but that's just the way things were with Harry -- he had to keep us niggers in our place.

I saw a lot of things in those days in Miami and when I later traveled with Sweet Richard (incidents that would continue to rear their ugly heads when I later toured with another limbo group). For instance, I went to places where they had faucets that were marked for coloreds and for whites. You know, you never saw things like that in the Bahamas.

Of course, we had racism in the Bahamas, too. The "Conchy Joes" were boys who were just barely mixed with white people, but they thought they were better than everybody else. We had theaters in the Bahamas that I wasn't allowed to go into, but the racism wasn't nearly as pronounced in the Bahamas as it was in the States.

In America, you had those signs in the South telling you that you weren't wanted, which was better than the North, as far as I'm concerned – you were treated like crap when you walked into places in the North. There weren't any signs in the North; all the "signs" were in people's minds. At least the South had these big signs – "For Colored Only" or "Drinking for Whites" and "Drinking for Coloreds" – so you pretty much knew where you stood.

Well, I refused to think of myself as a second-class citizen because of the color of my skin; I was determined to be treated fairly. One day, as I was walking down the street in Miami Beach with a couple of my friends, I got hungry and decided I would order some lunch. Much to the amazement of my friends, I walked into one of the small restaurants that lined the street and placed my order for a burger and a Coke.

The man behind the counter glared at me and snarled,
"We don't serve niggers here."
"Well," I politely replied. "I didn't order niggers. I ordered a burger and a Coca Cola."

The guy was so taken aback that he gave me that burger and Coke to me - although he said I couldn't eat it in the restaurant. That was fine with me - all I wanted was some food and something to drink. When I walked outside, burger and Coke in hand, my friends were standing there with their mouths open. They couldn't believe that I had the nerve to walk into that place -- and they were beyond amazed that I had actually been served.

Despite the racism that I encountered, I enjoyed living in Miami. I was staying at the Carver Hotel on Ninth Street and Second Avenue. Although I saw a few black tourists there, it was mostly a residential hotel as it was located in the black section of Miami. But you would not believe who else was a resident there!

On January 17, 1962, I was walking through the lobby on my way to my room. I had a conga drum under my arm as I wanted to practice a bit, and it attracted the attention of a young, powerfully built man whom I instantly recognized.

The handsome, mulatto-looking man walked up to me, spanked

my drum, and asked,

"Where you going with that drum? You know who I am?"

I had a very heavy Bahamian accent in those days, and I replied,

"Yes, mon. Everybody knows Cassius Clay – the next heavyweight champion of the world."

Clay flashed a big grin and said,

"I like you, brother! It's my birthday, and I'm having a shindig in my room tonight. I need you to play "Happy Birthday" for me. Would you come up and play some drums for me?"

"I'd be happy to," I replied.

Clay's room happened to be on the floor where I was staying; in fact, we lived only two doors apart! I went to my room and waited until about 7:00 p.m. before going to his room, where I found the door half open as Clay's friends were making their way to the party.

"Hey, little brother, you made it!"

After I told him that I couldn't let the champ down, Clay emphasized that he was the greatest fighter in the world – the whole, wide world! Now Clay had only begun his professional career on October 29, 1960 – and he was still a couple of years away from becoming the heavyweight champion – but he was one impressive fighter. Even at his young age -- that party was to celebrate his 20th birthday!

Some of his buddies and I began to play and sing for him, and I met some great people that night. One boy, who called himself Cornbread, played the maracas and a couple of other hand-held percussion instruments, a guy named Sammy played the timbales, and another of Clay's friends, Beaudine, was on bass (Beaudine was so fond of Clay that he always cried whenever Clay got hit in the ring). We were having such a great time jamming that even Clay got into the act, trying to play my drum!

Amazingly, everyone was having fun without drinking any alcohol – only soft drinks, juices, and water were served at this party. And there was a big birthday cake that was brought up by the hotel staff.

The reason for the absence of alcohol was that most of Clay's friends were members of the Nation of Islam (Clay wasn't at this time, as the group wouldn't accept him as a member because of his boxing career; but he mentioned his beliefs several times during his birthday party, and he was attending meetings regularly). I had never heard of Muslims before that night, but I thought so highly of everyone in that room that I was ready to go to a Nation of Islam meeting with Clay the next day. I would go to many meetings with him during the time we knew each other in Miami, and at one of those meetings I met Clay's mentor and spiritual advisor, Malcolm X (everyone called him "Red" because of the red tint in his hair).

My fondest memories, however, are of the days that Clay would go running in the streets of Liberty City (the poor black section) in Miami. I would sit in the back seat of his 1962 gold Cadillac while Clay and a few of his friends would run behind it. After the run, we would go to breakfast at a place called the Famous Chef Café, where Clay would eat an entire chicken, along with potatoes and whatever else came with it, in one sitting (I saw him do this many times).

I don't remember how many months I spent in the company of the future champ, but the time came when Sweet Richard's act got so popular that Richard decided to go on tour (it would be the first time I ever toured -- previously, I had just played gigs in one place). Our first booking was at the Club 500 on Bourbon Street in New Orleans. A Miami booking agent, Sammy Clark, a little Jewish man (he was only about four feet tall) who was the booking agent for Sweet Richard and Princess Kitty, got the gig for us, and we were all excited about playing in New Orleans. But had we known what would happen to us there, we might have just stayed in Miami.

Although we were as popular in New Orleans as we had been in Miami, Harry Rich wasn't there to protect us from the ugly reality of discrimination. One night, for example, I walked into a bar to buy a bottle of wine. I hadn't seen any signs, but when I walked in the door, there were two white men sitting at the bar, arguing. One of them, a redneck, white-trash type of person, said to the other,

"You know what, Jimmy? You may be white, but you're a nigger just the same."

I don't know if that guy realized how profound his statement was. You don't have to be black to be a nigger. In fact, I think that there may be more white niggers than black niggers. This man didn't even understand the truth of what he was saying.

Anyway, when I went into that bar, I had a hundred dollar bill, which I handed to the bartender for my bottle of wine. He looked at it and looked at me and said,

"Hold on. I'll be right back."

Well, that man went to the back and called the cops. Before you know it, the cops were there to get me.

"Where did you get a hundred dollar bill?" one of them asked.

"Are you familiar with Sweet Richard or are you familiar with limbo dancing? Are you familiar with King Snake?" I asked (in those days, I went by the stage name of Lord King Snake).

The cop then turned to the bartender,

"Why did you call us about this man? Didn't you think he could have a hundred dollars?"

"Well, I just wanted to know," the bartender responded. "A nigger shouldn't have a hundred dollars like that."

That's the way people were in the South in those days. And it was quite funny that an incident like that happened in a place like New Orleans. Even today, most of the people there have mixed blood. Yet I was treated badly by a bartender who didn't think that I – a man who came from a long line of whites – should have a hundred dollar bill!

But that act of discrimination against me was nothing compared to what happened to Sweet Richard while we were in New Orleans. Although he was a big star, Richard was of mixed races - and that resulted in him facing life-threatening discrimination.

Right after our first week at the Club 500, Richard got sick from taking sleeping medication. The next night, he overdosed and was rushed to the hospital.

The rest of our group, knowing nothing about Richard being in the hospital, were backstage in the dressing room of the club, waiting for him to show up. The club was packed with people by that time, so the owner or manager or whoever the guy was who was in charge, came into the dressing room to report the news.

Well, stupid me, with my smart-ass attitude, said,

"Well, I guess there's no show tonight."

"Not so fast," the guy growled. "Those people out there don't care which one of you is Richard. They just want to see a show tonight."

"But nobody here can come close to Richard," I protested.

"Well, one of you is gonna dance tonight or you don't leave New Orleans -- not alive, anyway!" he threatened in reply.

By this time, Princess Kitty, who had accompanied Richard to the hospital, had made her way to the dressing room.

"Let's go, guys," she said. "King, you dance with me tonight."

Well, that night was a big boost for me. Our act went over well, and I was still feeling the flush of excitement when we went to the hospital the next day to see Richard.

It didn't take long for my "high" to be deflated. When we blacks walked into that hospital, we were followed to Richard's room, where Princess Kitty was sitting on the bed next to her husband. We all greeted him enthusiastically, of course, but it couldn't have been more than a couple of minutes later that the hospital's head person -- a big, fat white pig of a woman -- walked in and demanded,

"All you niggers get out of here." And she didn't stop there.

"I thought you were a nigger," she snarled to Richard. "Get out of this hospital. This bed is for white people."

Believe it or not, they pushed Richard out of that hospital -- with the tubes still in him! And, when we got to the black hospital, where we immediately took Richard, they didn't want to take him, either! Those southern blacks were just as foolish as the whites -- they thought that Richard looked too white to be admitted to the black hospital!

I knew I had to do something -- and fast -- so, I stepped up and said to the nurses,

"This is a black man -- he only has fair skin. We are Bahamians, and Bahamians come in many colors."

I guess my explanation counted for something, because they kept him, but Richard's troubles were not over. When he got out of the hospital, he went back to his hotel -- only to be told that he could not stay there anymore because he was black! So Richard and Princess Kitty came over to the black side of town, where the rest of us were staying at a place called the New Patterson Hotel.

The hotel was indeed owned by a man named Patterson, but, despite its name, there was nothing new about the place -- it was falling apart! At first, Mr. Patterson refused to let Richard and Miss Kitty stay at the hotel because they were not black. What a crock that was -- Patterson himself was of mixed races, although he was not as fair-skinned as Richard.

I was finally able to convince Mr. Patterson, that Richard was, indeed, a black Bahamian. I didn't bother to tell him that Richard was half white, but I did explain that Richard was from Long Island, where the people were fair-skinned. Mr. Patterson finally said that Richard could stay -- but Miss Kitty could not! I managed to talk Mr. Patterson into keeping both of them for that night at least. After all, Richard had just gotten out of the hospital and kicked out of one hotel already.

Boy, that was some crap we went through in New Orleans, and we had enough of it. That night, Kitty and we blacks went to the club to do our show. After we finished, we snuck all our equipment out -- limbo sticks, limbo bars, everything -- and the next morning we packed our van and left New Orleans, never to return.

Our having to leave wasn't Richard's fault. Harry Rich, who was a much bigger gangster than those Bourbon Street boys, whoever they were, had found out what happened and told Richard to leave town before it got ugly.

Sammy Clark got very upset over Richard leaving the gig in New Orleans, but it wasn't like we were out of work or anything -- Harry Rich was more than happy to have us return to the Place Pigalle. But things were a little different for me this time. One night, Sammy walked up to me, held out his business card, told me he wanted to be my agent!

Sammy knew that I liked working with Richard, so he asked me to do a gig in Daytona Beach as a favor to avoid any problems between Richard and me. To tell the truth, I was ready to move on -- I thought I was good enough to do my own show, so I jumped at the chance. I was anxious to go out on my own and see another part of Florida, so I gave Richard a two-week notice. My decision to leave -- even though I explained I was doing it as a favor to Sammy -- did not sit too well with Richard, who had given me my big break. I truly appreciated all he had done for me, but I really felt that I was ready to do something on my own.

Sammy had booked me into a small Daytona Beach tourist club called The Tropics for two weeks, so I had to come up with an act pretty fast. I brought along a beautiful black lady named Tina, whom I had met at the Sir John Hotel on 9th Street (the hotel was famous for its nightclub and pool scene). Tina was a very good dancer, so we opened the show with me playing my drums while she danced. After she would go under the limbo bar, I would jump up into the air like a mad man! Tina would then step aside to the congas to play a little riff. I waited for the last three bars (which was sometimes too much for Tina because she wasn't that good on the congas), before making my entrance and going under the limbo bar myself. Then I'd go back to my drums while Tina danced again -- and that was the way it went until I went under the lowest bar, which was about the height of a Coca Cola bottle (needless to say, I was very thin and limber in those days). I admit that it wasn't much of an act, but the people seemed to love us.

One of my fondest memories of our gig in Daytona Beach began one evening when a man and his family came to see my show. After Tina and I finished our act, he introduced himself and his party, and it turned out that he was the grandson (or maybe the great-grandson) of Mary McLeod Bethune, the influential black educator and civil rights leader who had started a school for black girls in Daytona way back in 1903!

In 1923, Mary's growing school merged with the Cookman Institute, a school for black men, and the school later became a junior college before becoming Bethune-Cookman College in 1941 (the year I was born). I was honored when this man, who had such personal ties to the school, invited me to visit.

During my tour of Bethune-Cookman, I got my first lessons in American black history. I learned about Sojourner Truth and other blacks who were involved with helping their people up from slavery through such endeavors as the Underground Railroad, and I also learned about other blacks, such as the great scientist, botanist, educator and inventor, George Washington Carver, who had overcome their ties to slavery to make important contributions to the American way of life.

I returned to the school several times to soak up what I could about my people and their struggles. In fact, those visits started me on a quest to learn as much as I could about why things were the way they were in America -- and I started to understand that, for the most part, white people didn't really hate me…they were just afraid of me because of the way they treated my people. I could only imagine that when we black people smiled and said, "Good morning," that we were probably scared to death. The thought that they mistrusted me -- never knowing when I would "snap" -- was very funny to me.

After our gig was over, Tina and I took a train back to Miami. And what a train ride that turned out to be -- the train was running late, so the engineer "put the pedal to the metal" to make up time…and ended up hitting a semi full of oranges!

The truck driver said he thought he could beat the train, but when he realized the train was moving toward him so fast, he had no choice but to jump out of the cab, leaving his rig on the tracks. Well, our train took that truck about 400 feet before stopping. The engineer was killed instantly, and a second engineer died some time later in a Miami hospital. The sad part was that the engineer's wife was driving to meet him in Miami, so I guess it was his impatience to see his wife that killed him (and could have killed us, too).

When the police and medical personnel boarded that train, I was surprised to find that people all around me were pretending to be hurt in order to get money! I had never seen anything like that in the Bahamas -- sure, Mr. Carey had gotten money from PanAm, but that was because there was real damage to his house (my Uncle Cecil would never have thought of suing PanAm simply because he had a close call). Anyway, as the police and doctors walked through the train, those old white people were complaining about their aches and pains.

When they asked Tina and me if we were hurt, we (truthfully) answered that we were not. I guess we were the stupid ones – I knew nothing about making false claims, so we lost out (we didn't know the games that people played in life). And, to add insult to injury, we had no train, of course; we had to stay on that train for 12 hours before we were able to get moving again.

When I got back to Miami, Sammy had yet another offer waiting for me -- and what a great gig it turned out to be! Sammy wanted me to meet another young limbo dancer from Nassau by the name of Percy "The Deacon" Whylly. The Deacon was probably the second greatest limbo dancer in the world – second only to Sweet Richard himself.

At this time, The Deacon was about to start a gig in Hawaii, but his drummer, Leroy Epps, was being drafted into the army, and they needed someone to take his place right away as they not only had the gig in Hawaii, but The Deacon and his group would also tour Japan for six months after that. Ironically, Leroy's brother, Preston Epps, co-wrote "Bongo Rock," which would be recorded by the Incredible Bongo Band, in which I was a featured member (that would come much later in my career).

When I met with The Deacon in Honolulu, he was due to begin his month-long gig in Hawaii two nights later. Fortunately, he was impressed with my performing skills in both drumming and dancing, and he wanted to hire me for the princely sum of $750 a week. Wow, more of my dreams coming true – I was going to be making "big bucks" to perform in Hawaii and then tour Japan! Before this, my only exposure to that exotic country had been watching the movie, *Thirty Seconds Over Tokyo*.

Before I tell you about my days with the Deacon, I'd like to say that I will always have wonderful memories of Sweet Richard and Princess Kitty. They were such colorful characters, and they taught me so much about being a performer as well as a musician. I learned the importance of charisma – of putting my personality into every performance -- and developing rapport with my audiences. Those traits would play an important part in the next phase of my career, when I broadened my horizons and ventured beyond America.

Sadly, both Sweet Richard and Princess Kitty met tragic ends. They were so inseparable that after Richard died in 1964, reportedly choking on a piece of steak just months before his 34th birthday, Princess Kitty killed herself. I didn't hear about that until much later -- after I had finished touring with The Deacon and returned home to Nassau.

My gig with The Deacon and his limbo dancers couldn't have started on a higher note. We opened at the Hanabasha Club (the man who brought us to Hawaii to work was a partner in the club in Honolulu and in a club of the same name in Tokyo, where we would perform next), and the experience would prove to be a magical one. You won't believe what happened on the very first night I performed at the Hanabasha Club

-- I met my first big movie star!

Rita Hayworth, who was a friend of the man who owned the club, was there! She was pretty drunk (but she was a sweet drunk), and when she saw me, she said,

"C'mon, let's dance."

The club owner didn't try to stop me, so I danced one number with Rita. She was older than me, of course, but she was still very beautiful and very sexy and I had a ball dancing with her. It was an amazing experience to be dancing with one of my favorite stars, and I also got the chance to tell Rita how much I had enjoyed her film, *Fire Down Below*, which had been released in 1957.

After the gig in Hawaii, our group went on to Japan, where we were supposed to work for six months (that six months turned into a year and probably could have gone on longer if we hadn't been booked back in the States). Before I tell you about Japan, I have to tell you about one of the dancers in The Deacon's troupe. Her name was Regina, and she would not only become a muse to me -- she also became my first wife.

Although Regina means "queen" in Spanish (and Regina was, indeed, a queen), Regina was not Spanish -- she had been born on an Indian reservation in Alabama. Regina, who had skin the color of copper, was about 14 years older than me -- but, although she was already in her 30s, she looked like a 16- or 18-year-old girl. Regina was in great shape and she was so beautiful that people would stop her to ask for autographs, thinking that she was Diahann Carroll or Dorothy Dandridge.

Regina's father was a tall, red, full-blooded American Indian whose last name was Penn, and her mother was a big, red Indian woman, although I think she had some black blood mixed in -- I would later meet Regina's brothers, and some of them were almost as dark as I was! Regina had half a dozen brothers, but she was daddy's pet since she was the only girl in the family. Mr. Penn would take Regina everywhere with him – he was a drunken man, I heard, so he'd take her to different bars with him and she would get up and dance (Regina said she danced on bar tops for nickels and dimes to help buy her dad's rum). She became a tough girl because of her early experiences, but her great sense of rhythm would really pay off for her.

Although I mostly performed as a limbo dancer during my time with The Deacon, I also played lots of congas because there were only three of us in the act. Regina encouraged me to develop my talent on the congas. She would teach me beats and how to keep a rhythm going so she could keep shaking her booty to it. She taught me how to hold a rhythm long enough to make it infectious, and she let me know when it was time to change the beat. We'd practice and practice, and she could dance to just about anything I'd play.

Regina was one of the best dancers I had ever seen, and she especially loved to dance like Josephine Baker. As a matter of fact, Regina had costumes much like those that Josephine Baker used to wear – like those banana outfits. Regina also had an unusual accessory – she always walked around with a seven- or eight-foot python around her neck. That python used to scare the crap out of me – I wasn't too afraid of snakes, but I just didn't like anything that big hanging around. Later, after Regina and I got together, that snake used to sleep on the couch – and he would move me away whenever he felt like it. Whenever that snake came up on the couch, I got up and left it to him.

When I met her, Regina was married to a man named George Washington, who lived in Dallas, Texas, and she had already been married once before that -- when she was about 15 or 16 years old, her family had married her off to an old man in Memphis, Tennessee. Although she had been born in Alabama, Regina had grown up in Memphis (according to her, she grew up next door to Elvis Presley, whose great-grandmother was a black woman who raised him). Her first husband was an undertaker -- and very rich -- but Regina left him after a year or two.

I think that Regina's dislike for men began during that first marriage – she wanted to be the boss, so she resented what men represented. In any case, Regina ran away and became a great dancer – almost a second Josephine Baker – performing in New York and Miami and other places. During that time, her husband died, leaving her hundreds of thousands of dollars. Amazingly, Regina never went back to claim that money – she was too busy dancing. By the time I met up with her, she was enjoying great success with The Deacon (she had joined his troupe after she met him in Miami).

Although Regina was so beautiful (and was in fantastic shape), I wasn't interested in her romantically (at first). Part of that had to do with her being married, but an even bigger reason was that I enjoyed being footloose and fancy-free. I was like a kid in a candy store -- I wanted to explore the world and all the delights it had to offer. And there was no shortage of delights in Honolulu -- I had a great time playing around there.

Regina didn't seem to mind that I was playing around so much. In fact, she encouraged me to go out with other women while we were in Hawaii (as if I needed any encouragement). If she had any jealousy, she didn't show it -- in fact, she wanted to know all about my escapades (she couldn't wait to hear my reports when I got home). Our relationship sure changed before we left Hawaii, though.

Maybe Regina wasn't worried that her husband would suddenly appear -- after all, we were in Honolulu, not Cleveland, so it wasn't likely that George Washington would just hop on a plane to travel to Hawaii (although if I had a woman like Regina, I sure wouldn't let her out of my sight). No matter what the reason, one night Regina not only asked me to tell her what I did, but she also wanted me to show her.

On that particular night, I had played around with three sisters -- one right after another (they had actually lined up to wait for their turn, and I think that their brother -- who was right there -- probably wanted in on the action, too, although I wasn't interested in that). No one wanted me to leave, and I didn't want to go, either, but I knew that Regina would be waiting for my report so I politely excused myself and went back to my hotel.

Although I was quite puffed up about my exploits that evening, I guess that Regina wasn't as impressed. She mentioned something about me "not getting the body," and when I didn't understand what she meant, she said,

"Here, let me show you."

The next thing I knew, Regina had taken off her clothes and was standing naked in front of me. I was stunned, of course -- I hadn't expected that, but I can't say that I was going to complain…Regina was a beautiful woman with an incredible body.

"I've been meaning to teach you," she said.

And teach me she did. I'm not going to get graphic here, but, suffice it to say, Regina made love to me like that was the only thing on earth that she wanted to do (it was as if she had been looking forward to the day that we would finally get together). And, amazingly, it would always be the same every time we made love -- it was always wild, exciting and just like the first time (even during our marriage and after our divorce). When Regina was finished teaching me how to love a woman, both she and I were convinced that no woman would want to be without me. Regina not only taught me how to please a woman, but she turned me into a tiger. And by the time we got back to the States, where she would finally see her husband again, Regina was Queen Johnson, not Queen Washington!

Looking back, I think that maybe our love-making was so intense because any time we had sex could have been our last time. Regina knew that her husband loved her, and, although it was unlikely that he would show up while we were in Hawaii or Japan, that would change when we returned to the States a year later.

Chapter 7

Fame in the Land of the Rising Sun

When we got to Japan, we toured all over the country. Although we were based in Tokyo, we never stayed longer than two weeks in any one place. And, we were so popular that we worked day and night -- sometimes our shows would start as early as 9:00 or 10:00 in the morning, and we would play matinees in addition to our evening shows.

If I thought that Hawaii had been a paradise, my experiences there were nothing compared to what happened in Japan -- I had a slew of Japanese girls just swarming over me all the time. Although I was getting closer to Regina (we were lovers the entire time we were in Japan) and she certainly had deep feelings for me, she would say,

"I love you, but I want to see you have fun. Go out with these Japanese girls and have some fun. And let me know what you did."

Even though Regina was a beautiful and very special woman, I was not in love with her at the time. I couldn't resist all those beautiful Japanese girls. I was young (about 21 or 22 years old), so having two or three Japanese girls a night was much more fun than having just one girl.

Regina had a heart of gold, and she always looked out for me -- and I sure paid when I didn't listen to her. One night after a show, a beautiful young Japanese girl walked up to me and asked if she could keep me company, despite the fact that I was with Regina. When I asked Regina about that, she gave her O.K. -- along with a warning not to have sex with the girl.

Well, after an hour or so of drinking at the bar, I invited the girl up to my room. Our booking agent had gotten separate rooms for all of us in the troupe, so it was no problem for me to keep Regina from knowing that I had ignored her advice.

Although the girl kept saying "no" when I wanted to have sex with her, I got all macho and wouldn't take "no" for an answer. I didn't understand much Japanese at the time (although I certainly understood "no"), but I'm sure that this girl was trying to explain to me that she was sick, because about an hour after she had gotten up and ran out of my room, my penis was burning like a sewing needle was being pushed up into it. I was in so much pain, in fact, that I had to call Regina, who immediately took me to the hospital.

The doctor took one look at me and asked who the girl was that I had been with that night. I had foolishly not asked the girl what her name was, but the doctor told me that there were some nasty girls running around town and passing along some very serious diseases (I had no idea that a person could catch a disease so easily -- and so quickly).

I don't know exactly what it was that I had, but it was bad enough that the doctor said that I might have died if I hadn't gotten to the hospital when I did. As it was, I had to get four shots in the cheek of my behind that night (all with needles that looked like horse needles), and I had to return to see the doctor three more times!

When Regina took me home, she certainly could have been angry and said, "I told you so" -- after all, she had warned me not to have sex with the woman (I guess that Regina, as wise to the ways of the world as she was, had already sized the girl up and realized that she was a whore). Instead, Regina took care of me for the two weeks I was sick (I even moved into her room for a week because I couldn't stand the smell that girl had left behind in my room).

Yes, Regina was always there for me -- and she never steered me wrong. As she began falling more in love with me, though, Regina must have thought I was fooling around too much -- so she tried to put a cap on me. But, amazingly, she was all for it when I introduced her to a couple of young Japanese girls who were more than one-night stands to me. The fact that Regina approved made me feel better -- because I certainly didn't want to hurt her.

One of those girls was named Fumiko, and we had a great time together for a little while. The other girl, whose name was Kawaguchie, made even more of an impression on me -- I even considered making her my first wife! And I wasn't the only one who was smitten -- Regina thought so much of Kawaguchie that she said she would go after her herself if she was a man.

Kawaguchie was the tallest Japanese girl that I had met (she was about 5'8" or maybe even 5'9"). She was also very slim and had beautiful straight black hair that floated gracefully down her back. Another thing that impressed me about Kawaguchie was the way she dressed -- she always looked like a movie star.

I especially remember Kawaguchie's silk lingerie -- everything had to be silk (her bra, her panties, her stockings). Her thigh-high silk stockings were held up with a garter belt, and I used to love to take my time with that -- unhooking each strap as she removed each piece of her jewelry. Those were some incredible nights!

Since Kawaguchie was so beautiful, I'll never forget the day that she was wearing a black eye patch when she came to see me. I asked her what was the matter, but she said that nothing was wrong -- she had undergone surgery to change the shape of her eye!

Well, there was nothing wrong with the shape of that girl's eyes -- they were beautiful -- and I loved the way Kawaguchie looked naturally. But, despite my telling her that if I wanted someone with eyes like a white woman I would go out with a white woman, Kawaguchie wanted to look like Lauren Bacall, so she had the other eye done about two weeks later. And, as if that wasn't enough, she also had her nose done.

I guess I can't blame Kawaguchie too much -- she was simply following the fad of the day. The Japanese sure had funny ideas at the time -- everyone wanted to look western. The women wanted to look like their favorite movie stars, while the young men were having their faces fixed to look like those of Hollywood leading men (I remember that the Robert Mitchum chin was "the thing"). I had never seen such bull in my life -- people wanting to look like somebody else. There were a lot of Japanese (both men and women) who were very attractive just the way they were, so why would they want to change their looks?

I was away from Kawaguchie a lot because of our touring schedule, but I certainly wasn't lonely because Regina was always there. Our relationship really got complicated though -- one day Regina came to me with some unexpected news,

"I'm two months pregnant with your baby."

I had started studying karate as well as drama while I was in Japan, and I would often show off my karate kicks to Regina. On the night that she told me she was pregnant, I was fooling around, practicing my kicks as usual, and I accidentally kicked Regina in the stomach. Regina had a miscarriage right then, and she swore that I kicked her on purpose, but I would never have done a thing like that.

I guess I was muscular enough to look like a fighter at the time, because one night when I was walking through the lobby of our hotel, I was stopped by a giant of a man. That man, who was 6'4" and weighed about 300 pounds, was a wrestler from Phoenix, Arizona, by the name of Ricky Waldo. Waldo, who had been a contender for the heavyweight wrestling championship, knew I was too small to be a heavyweight, but he thought that perhaps I was a lightweight boxer or wrestler.

Our conversation that night was the start of a wonderful friendship with both Ricky Waldo and his promoter, Rikidozan. Rikidozan was actually born Kim Sin-Nak in North Korea, but, knowing the prejudice of the Japanese against the Koreans, he had adopted the Japanese name of Mitsuhiro Momota and said he was from Nagasaki (I don't know if Ricky Waldo knew the truth, which wasn't revealed publicly until years after Rikidozan's death).

Adopting the name Rikidozan, which means "rugged mountain road," he became a legend in Japan. Known as the "Father of Puroresu" (Japanese wrestling), Rikidozan had boosted the spirits of the Japanese after World War II by popularizing wrestling. Not only did he thrill crowds with his own wrestling (he won several championships during his career), Rikidozan also booked wrestlers for Japanese matches. He mostly booked rude white boys (the Japanese loved seeing those crackers being beaten to a pulp), but Ricky Waldo was a black man. Although the two were rivals (Ricky Waldo and his partner, Luther Lindsay, defeated Rikidozan and his partner, Toyonobori, for the All Asia Tag Team Title in 1962), they had a mutual respect for one another and were great friends. And I was very happy when both of those popular wrestlers took a liking to me.

Whenever I wasn't working, I would spend time with Waldo and Rikidozan. Most of the time, we went to wrestling matches (sometimes, one or both of my friends were participants and I was just a spectator). A couple of times, I tried to bring Kawaguchie along, but she didn't like the fights too much.

I guess that was because those fights could get pretty violent at times. I thought that the wrestlers were usually just joking around with each other, but there were times when they would get serious and beat each other up real good. I remember one night in particular that someone hit Ricky Waldo on the head with an iron chair and he went straight to the ground. Immediately, Rikidozan came out with a steel pipe and beat the offender on his knees so bad that the guy had to crawl off the mat. That was one mess.

Besides being a wrestler and promoter of both wrestling and boxing matches, Rikidozan was also a successful businessman. He owned hotels, night clubs, golf courses and a lot of real estate, so the three of us also spent time in some of Tokyo's hottest night spots.

One of our most memorable outings, however, was my first visit to a Japanese bathhouse. Everyone -- men, women, sumo wrestlers, you name it -- would bathe naked together in the 120 degree water. A person could get cooked pretty good in that water.

The first time that I went with Ricky Waldo, I did not want to take my clothes off in front of all those people. I had gone swimming naked lots of times when I was a kid in the Bahamas, but this was totally different. Here I was in a room full of strangers -- and their attention seemed to be directed at Ricky Waldo and me.

"Get them clothes off," Ricky ordered. "Are you a girl?"

"Hell, no," I shot back, and stripped down.

Well, you could have heard a pin drop in that room. Everyone started pointing at me and making comments about my manhood. I guess that I had even Ricky Waldo and the 400- to 600-pound sumo wrestlers beat, because there were several gasps and I heard a couple of comments about my "tail."

Of course, I didn't always have a lot of time to spend with these friends. Our group was so popular in Japan that our tour was extended for another six months. At that time, we were only allowed to stay in Japan for six months at a time -- although we could leave for as little as one day to qualify for another six months when we returned. We opted to travel to Okinawa, where we worked for a week or two before returning to our home base in Tokyo.

The people in Japan were very happy to have us back -- in fact, our fame was almost scary. By the time our second six months was coming to an end, we were all doing movies -- especially me. I was tall compared to most of the Japanese people, and I was very good looking (if I do say so myself), so I had no trouble not only getting roles, but attracting the attention of one of the country's biggest movie producers.

That movie producer offered me a five-year contract to stay in Japan and make movies for him, but I was a little uneasy about the deal. I had picked up quite a bit of Japanese during my stay, and when the movie people talked to me, they would do it in the regular dialect. But, there are hundreds of dialects in Japan, and when the movie people spoke to each other, they would speak in some dialect that I didn't understand. I didn't care one bit for that crap, so that was one reason I decided to continue on with The Deacon on his tour of America, which would start with a booking in Las Vegas.

Believe me, I was very tempted to stay in Japan -- I was in love with Kawaguchie and I didn't want to leave her. And I was even more reluctant to leave after what happened when my beautiful Kawaguchie accompanied me to the airport to say good-bye.

She had tears running down her cheeks as she hugged me -- and delivered some incredible news: she was pregnant with my baby!

Needless to say, I was shocked -- and I was determined to cancel my trip to the States. Regina, though, convinced me that it would be hard for me to stay behind in a strange country where I only had a few friends -- and, besides, both Regina and The Deacon needed me to carry on with their act. She also reminded me of the good money I would make -- money that I could use to help Kawaguchie and pay for a return trip to Japan. I was still reluctant when I agreed to go with The Deacon and Regina -- and I didn't leave Japan without promising Kawaguchie that I would come back to her.

After six months, though, I lost touch with Kawaguchie. I wrote faithfully, but her letters stopped coming. Looking back on it, I think that maybe Regina was intercepting and destroying those letters (Regina was certainly possessive of me at that time -- and maybe she realized how close she had come to losing me forever).

Anyway, after a year, I gave up hope of ever finding Kawaguchie again. Even if I went back to Japan to look for her, I would not begin to know where to start. Not only might she have moved during that time, but I also didn't know anyone who might be able to put me in contact with her.

I don't know if Kawaguchie was a loner -- or if she had another boyfriend (or even a husband) -- but she never introduced me to any of her friends while we were dating. She would come directly to me from work and we would have dinner in the restaurant of the hotel where I stayed. She would always leave right after dinner and then come back (sometimes, she would stay the night; other times, we would just make love and she would leave).

It was a shock to realize how little I actually knew about Kawaguchie. And I often wondered about the little half-black Japanese kid I had left behind. Of course, that child would be a middle-aged adult by now -- maybe with children of his or her own. Unfortunately, I don't have any answers to this puzzle…I have no way of knowing if Kawaguchie shared our little secret with her child.

Unfortunately, I wasn't able to ask Ricky Waldo for help in finding Kawaguchie or learning what had happened to her -- he didn't stay in Japan much longer than I did. Ricky went to Calgary, Alberta, Canada, where he won the Stampede International Tag Team title in April of 1963, and he also invested in an airplane company in Canada.

While that was good news, I also got some bad news from Ricky - he told me that Fumiko, the other Japanese girl that I had dated, had killed herself by jumping from a train (apparently, she thought that no Japanese man would want her after she had been with me). That saddened me greatly, but, unfortunately, it was not the first time that a woman had tried to kill herself over me (although I think that she was the only one who actually succeeded).

More bad news came at the end of 1963, when Ricky Waldo told me that Rikidozan had been murdered. Rikidozan's success had put him on the radar of Japanese gangsters, and one night in December, he had gotten into an argument over "territory" with one of them at a Tokyo hotspot. The gangster stabbed Rikidozan in the chest, and he had to be rushed to the hospital. Although he was told that the wound was not life-threatening and he was patched up and sent home, Rikidozan was dead from an infection from the wound a week later at the age of 39. Thousands of mourners turned out for his funeral, and his death was a terrible blow to both Ricky Waldo and me.

Ricky and I remained good friends for many years. If I needed something, Ricky was always there for me, but, unfortunately, we lost touch after he left Canada and returned to Arizona. When I finally started making a little money (even though I hadn't made it big at that time), I wanted to repay some of the generosity he had shown to me -- but when I made contact with his family they told me that they believed he was dead. That was another big blow to me -- as well as the end of any connection I had to Japan.

After we left Japan, Regina and I toured all over America with The Deacon. We were booked as a "novelty act" in a lot of hotels as well as Jim Crow redneck bars and saloons all over the country. We performed in "Deep South" states, including stops in Georgia, Alabama and Louisiana (we made a return visit to New Orleans, but, fortunately, it was much less dramatic than when I performed there with Sweet Richard). And we also performed in Texas, Kentucky, Ohio and Missouri -- and as far west as Colorado and Nevada (ironically, our first and last gigs together were in Las Vegas, where I would make my home several years later).

We were never booked into black clubs -- just white joints where blacks were only welcome on stage or in the kitchen (you never saw a black face in the audience). I guess that no club for blacks wanted to hire some niggers dancing around doing the limbo -- maybe it reminded them too much of slavery.

The limbo was very popular at the time because of Chubby Checker's limbo dance (he was nearly as famous for his limbo dance as he was for the Twist). I played some drums in those days, so Regina, The Deacon and I sometimes grooved to my African rhythms. More often, though, we just danced to chanting by the three of us.

Before our first gig in Las Vegas, Regina wanted to see her husband, George Washington, in Dallas, and she asked The Deacon and me to go with her. While we were in Dallas, Regina stayed with her husband and The Deacon and I stayed in a small, run-down hotel that was "For Coloreds Only" (being for coloreds only, it was a dump, of course). Despite the accommodations being less than appealing, The Deacon and I would stay there whenever we returned to Dallas during our touring days (since we toured on a circuit, we often played several different gigs in one city).

While we were in Dallas for that week, we stopped by Regina's home, and I finally got to meet her husband. George Washington, who was a big black man, also must have had some Mexican or Indian blood in him because he was not as dark as I was and his mother looked like an American Indian. I thought that George was a great guy -- very nice and friendly -- so I could see how Regina could have fallen in love with him before she met me. And, I could see why she could still love him in some way.

I also found out the reason that George didn't follow Regina around -- he was his mother's only child and somewhat of a "momma's boy." I don't blame him for wanting to take care of his mother, though -- she was a very nice woman.

George's mother was a teacher and also a fantastic pianist, so during the week I spent in Dallas, I took my first piano lessons from her. I really began to like playing the piano -- and learning more about music.

George was also a talented man -- one of the things that he did to bring in money for himself and his mother was to make items out of leather, including belts with heavy conchos on them (the conchos, which were round or square disks, were most often made out of silver or turquoise). I loved the belts that George made, so I asked him to teach me how to make them, too. George was happy to oblige -- he even brought me down to the store where he bought his supplies and asked me to pick out what I would want on a belt. Man, I had a ball -- I not only picked out some far out conchos, but also some great leather and other things that were needed to put the belt together.

When we got home from the store that day, Regina was waiting for George. Apparently, they had some family event to attend, so they dropped me off at my dumpy hotel on the way. When George said he would come to get me the next day, Regina said he didn't need to bother - that she would pick me up -- and it was left at that (George never seemed suspicious or showed any jealousy about Regina and I being together).

Since The Deacon and I were on our own that night, we decided that we would go out to a black club. The Deacon was a bi-sexual, and on this particular night he decided to be a man when he saw a beautiful mulatto girl at the bar. That girl was a stunner -- a King Errisson kind of girl -- but I guess she took a liking to The Deacon, because the girl, whose name was Geneva, and The Deacon started to play around.

That didn't sit too well with the three men she came with, especially since one of the guys was her husband (it didn't seem to matter to Geneva that she was married). Anyway, as we were leaving that night, the three guys jumped on The Deacon and started to beat him. Of course, I tried to pull the guys off him, but then one of them pulled out a knife and held it to The Deacon's throat. Wow, did that set me off -- I had just left a woman pregnant in Japan and was going to perform in Vegas in two days, so the last thing I wanted was to lose my partner. So, stupidly, I pulled out the gun that Regina had given to me to take with us (even though I didn't know anything about guns at the time, Regina said that was O.K. -- all I had to do was just pull it out if anyone messed with me).

Well, it was a damned good thing that I didn't know how to use that gun. When I aimed it at the guys who had jumped on The Deacon and tried to shoot them, I didn't know that the safety was on (in fact, I don't think I even knew what a safety was)! The guys started running away when they saw the gun, but I did manage to hit one of them upside the head with it -- and ran down the street after them (still trying to shoot them, but, of course, nothing happened).

That was one close call -- and I know that God loves me because He kept me stupid during my early years. Can you imagine what would have happened to me if I had actually shot one of those guys? Since they were black, I probably would have spent my life in a prison cell (if I had shot a white person, I would have gotten the electric chair)!

I was a little sad to leave Dallas, as I had a great time with George and his mother, and I would have loved to spend more time with them, learning how to make those beautiful belts (I left with a special "going away" gift -- the beautiful concho belt that George had shown me how to make) and furthering my piano training (I would continue to get piano lessons from George's mother every time we were in Dallas). It was clear that both George and his mother loved Regina, and I felt a little guilty for taking Regina away from them, although, technically, I didn't take her away -- she volunteered.

Before I tell you about some of our gigs, I'd like to mention something else that happened during our touring days in America that would greatly influence my career and play a large part in my success -- Regina introduced me to jam sessions. She took me to my first jam session in Atlanta, Georgia, and I have to give her a lot of credit for doing that -- I learned a lot in those jam sessions.

Anybody could get up on stage at the jam sessions as long as they could play something, and it was a great learning experience to go on stage with musicians that I didn't know, and playing -- especially with the jazz musicians -- helped my playing, too. I have to admit that I was a little shy at the beginning, but once I began to play and cut loose, I was always a winner. Once I started clipping, I knew what I was doing -- and

I had a good, good time.

The beauty of those jam sessions was that everyone who played wanted everyone else to look good. Once, in fact, when I was playing with a group, the horn player said to me,

"Man, you've got to tighten those drums; they're not tight enough. We need to hear some sounds out of them."

That was a lesson I needed to learn. After I tightened my drums, the horn player said in approval,

"Yeah, now that sounds good."

If there was any jealousy during those jam sessions, I didn't see it. I learned a lot from those pros, and I had a lot of opportunities to learn; after that first jam session in Atlanta, Regina took me to jam sessions every Sunday evening. No matter where we were performing, she would search for a jazz club that was having a jam session and I would go there to play. I loved playing in those jam sessions all over America.

Before I move on, I want to mention one more thing about Atlanta. We had gone there to play in one of those tropical garden-type calypso clubs, and, as fate would have it, I ran into a young man who was playing at the club next door. That man was Dennis St. John, a very talented white drummer. Dennis was as great a person as he was a musician, and I'll be forever in his debt -- he would be the one who would start me on the most exciting phase of my career some years later.

Chapter 8

Adventures in America

As I said, our first U.S. gig was in Las Vegas, where we opened at Diamond Jim's Nevada Club. The club, which was located on the same spot where the Four Queens Hotel & Casino is today, was owned by a couple of gangsters, but they were real gentlemen to us. It was a pleasure to work there, although Las Vegas at that time was as racist as some of the cities we had toured in the South. Headliners such as Sammy Davis, Jr., Nat King Cole, Dinah Washington and many others could not stay at the hotels where they played – even though they drew large crowds into the showrooms. Black performers either lived in grungy motels off the Strip (on streets such as Koval Lane and Paradise Road) or stayed at overpriced boarding houses in the black area of town.

We lived in a motel around the corner from the Moulin Rouge, which was the first desegregated hotel casino in the country. The Moulin Rouge, which was located on Bonanza Road, on the border of the black section of Las Vegas, had been home to some of the most popular black entertainers of the day -- Sammy Davis, Jr., Nat King Cole, Pearl Bailey and Louis Armstrong, to name just a few -- when it opened in May of 1955, and white performers, including Frank Sinatra, Jack Benny and George Burns, would often go there to gamble and perform after entertaining audiences at their shows on the Strip. Unfortunately, the Moulin Rouge closed in November of 1955 and declared bankruptcy a month later, so by the time we got to Vegas, the place was shuttered and getting as rundown as the rest of the black neighborhood.

During our first gig in Vegas, I met Sammy Davis, Jr. Despite his talent, Sammy had endured a lot during his career, but he managed to rise above the abuse and disrespect. He was a wonderful man who later became a good friend after we had the opportunity to play together professionally a few years later.

While I was in Vegas, I also met a couple of other people who were inspirations to me. First, I met a drummer named Francisco "Chino" Pozo (he is not to be confused with the Cuban percussionist, singer, dancer and composer, Chano Ponzo. I never met Chano, who was best known for his Latin jazz stylings for Dizzy Gillespie, as he was killed in a bar fight in Harlem in 1948 at the age of 33). Chino, who claimed to be Chano's cousin, was also from Cuba, and he specialized on the bongos, congas and drums. Best known for his Afro-Cuban jazz,

Chino had also played for Dizzy Gillespie as well as for a number of other prominent performers, including Charlie Parker, Peggy Lee, Stan Kenton, Herbie Mann and Xavier Cugat, before coming to Vegas, so I enjoyed listening to -- and learning from -- him.

Not long after I met Chino, Preston Epps, the brother of Leroy Epps (the guy I had replaced in the Deacon's troupe), came into Diamond Jim's. Preston was a tall guy who looked a lot like Harry Belafonte, and, man could he play the bongos -- he had to be the greatest bongo player of all time.

Preston, who released a number of bongo-themed singles and albums during his career, including songs that were featured on my later recordings with the Incredible Bongo Band, also had great success as a sessions musician. He was a wonderful guy who shared some profound advice with me -- he told me to go with what I knew and to stick with it. Maybe that's why I never found out how good Preston was on the congas (or on other percussion) -- he knew he was amazing on those bongos and he stuck with them.

Hearing guys like that play made me all the more anxious to get some real training in music. I had learned a bit about the technical aspects of music from George's mother when I was taking piano lessons, but I was determined to get a real music education. Fortunately, I got the chance to really study the mechanics of music while we were in Vegas. I met a drummer by the name of Owen "Mo" Mahoney, who had played with the Dukes of Dixieland (the group made two albums with Louis Armstrong) before coming to Vegas in the 1950s. Mo had been appalled that there were no real music stores in the city (there were just a few piano shops), so he opened Mahoney's Pro Music and Drum Shop on Maryland Parkway.

In addition to selling music and instruments, Mo also gave lessons at his shop, and I became an avid pupil. I soon learned how music was written and what signatures meant, and I learned about the timing, scoring, arranging and other techniques that came so easy to players who had been actually educated in music (Regina was one of those people -- she had been a music major, so she knew exactly what was going on when musicians played).

I was thrilled to finally have some sort of music education, and I thought that what I learned would enhance my playing. It wasn't long, however, before an old white musician who had been coming to see me at the club since we opened, approached me one night and said,

"You're taking music lessons, aren't you?"

When I told him that I was, he said,

"I could tell -- you are not as natural as you used to be."

"Is that good or bad?" I asked.

"That depends on what type of musician you want to be. When you first came here, you had soul, but now it seems that you are losing it. You don't want to sound white, do you? If you don't want to be like us, forget about that technical crap and be yourself."

That really opened my eyes -- before I knew about bars and four counts and eight beats, I just played naturally; now, I found myself counting every beat I played. I was technically correct, but my playing lacked my natural free-ranging and adaptive style and energy. I was grateful for the advice of that old white musician, and I resumed playing in my natural style.

That doesn't mean that I forgot my technical education. When another musician asked what I was playing, I was finally able to answer - without having to resort to bullshit because I didn't have a clue. My training would also play a very large part in my later successful career as a sessions musician, arranger and songwriter, but that was a few years in the future.

After we left Vegas, we toured on a circuit. Whenever we went to Dallas, which was a frequent stop on that circuit, Regina would stay with her husband – for a while, anyway. After our shows, she'd sneak out to spend several hours with me before going home again.

During one of our trips to Dallas, I had the great fortune to meet Abe Weinstein, who owned the Colony Club on Commerce Street. Abe was a very nice man, and it was a wonderful experience to work in his club (the experience meant even more after I learned that Abe handpicked the acts who performed in his club -- he once turned down Johnny Mathis, although he did book a young singer by the name of Elvis Presley).

Abe, his brother, Barney Weinstein, and Jack Ruby were Dallas gangster-types. Jack's place, The Carousel Club, was two doors down from Abe's club, while Barney owned another club, The Theater Lounge, just around the corner. They were rivals for the same customers (the clubs were all strip joints), and they also shared a connection with a famous woman stripper.

Back in the 1950s, Barney had hired a young lady as a cigarette girl at his club, and Abe had been so taken with her beauty that he took her under his wing (and into his bed) and transformed her into a featured stripper at the Colony Club. He had this girl bleach her hair, and he gave her the stage name of Candy Barr (supposedly because she had a fondness for Snickers candy bars). Candy became acquainted with Jack during the time she was Abe's sweetheart, and she renewed her acquaintance with him in early 1963 (just months before JFK was assassinated in Dallas), but, supposedly, they were never more than friends.

Because of Abe's involvement with Ruby (who killed JFK's alleged assassin, Lee Harvey Oswald -- on national television, no less), he would be interviewed three times by the Warren Commission. The Warren Commission also interviewed Candy, but both swore that they knew nothing about the plot to kill JFK -- or Jack's intention to shoot Oswald.

I never had the opportunity to meet Candy -- at the time we played at Abe's club, Candy was in prison (that's another story), but I sure heard about her. I can only imagine how beautiful she was and how great a stripper she must have been if Abe was so taken with her.

Abe's club was famous for its strippers -- white girls who were all so beautiful that they once literally stopped traffic (or a parade, anyway). The story was that the strippers came out (in various stages of undress) to watch a parade, causing the marchers to stop in their tracks to gawk at them. The police finally ordered all the girls to go inside so the parade could resume!

Anyway, one of the girls at Abe's place (I believe she was his office girl) was a beautiful white girl who was just as gorgeous as his strippers. She was a little on the heavy-set side but very nice, and I, being a dumb-ass Bahamian, had no idea that I was taking my life into my hands when I accepted her invitation to lunch one day. We walked to lunch together on Elm Street, the street where President John F. Kennedy would get shot just a short time in the future, and after we ate she asked where I lived.

Well, foolishly, I took her to my hotel, which was called the Jackson Hotel (it was another one of those dumpy hotels for coloreds only). When dumb ass me took her there, the hotel attendant saw me walking this white woman up to my room.

"Where the hell are you going with that white woman?" he shouted.

When I answered in my Bahamian lingo – my very heavy accent – they knew right then that I was stupid, and they allowed me to take her to my room. We spent a couple of hours upstairs before coming down to begin the walk back to Abe's club.

When we got to the main street, we ran into half a dozen white boys who were also walking on that street. They looked at us and I heard them saying to each other,

"That white man sure got a dark tan. 'Cause he can't be a nigger being with a white woman."

I finally realized that I was in deep trouble, but, thankfully, those white boys didn't go any further than their taunts. By the time we got back to the club, though, Abe was standing outside the door, and when he saw us walking down the street together, he screamed at my companion,

"What are you trying to do? Get him killed? You know better than that!"

She was young, and I guess that she was stupid, too; at least stupid to the fact that I -- or even both of us -- could have been killed by the racists that populated the city. At any rate, Abe fired her on the spot. He was a nice guy, but he did fire that girl.

"You no longer work here," he told her. "You're trying to get this man killed – and we need him to work."

Maybe the only reason that Abe really gave a damn was that I was working for him. But, unfortunately, I didn't learn my lesson after that episode (it would not be the last time I would get in trouble because of a white girl).

Amazingly, those big-time gangster-types weren't very racist themselves; as long as you were a decent person, it was O.K. to sit down and have a drink with them. In fact, I used to sit at Ruby's bar and have drinks with him. Ruby was a friend for the few weeks that I spent in Dallas -- I could go by his bar and sit down and have a drink with him anytime. It amazed me that I never had to worry about gangsters -- they were all decent guys to us.

Unfortunately, there were people who weren't as decent, and we experienced more than one racially-motivated incident while we were on the road in America. One time, The Deacon and Regina and I were walking down Elm Street in Dallas, and an old white woman walked up to us and screamed,

"Niggers! Niggers! Niggers! Where are you going, niggers?"

Well, I just looked at that woman and said in a very gentlemanly way,

"Good evening."

At that the woman replied,

"Crazy niggers!"

I had a big laugh over that, but Regina wanted to kill the woman. And things weren't any different another time, when the three of us were in Kansas City working at the state fair. As we were getting ready to go onstage, an old white man started singing,

"Shine or Shine."

The Deacon and I didn't pay any mind to that kind of nonsense. Because we grew up different than American blacks, I thought that all the bullshit was funny -- and I knew that it hurt the racists more than it hurt me. But there were a couple of times when the racism got really ugly -- and potentially dangerous.

One time, when we were in Denver, Colorado, The Deacon, Regina and I were working at a place called the Tropical Gardens. After the show, four white girls followed us back to the motel where we were staying, and The Deacon brought them to his room.

I sure wanted to help The Deacon out with those white girls, but I couldn't take them to my room because Regina was there. Although our booking agent had gotten us separate rooms while we were in Japan, we weren't making much money on the circuit we were working (despite our popularity), so we had to share rooms on our U.S. tour. I was supposed to share a room with The Deacon, I guess, but why would I do that when I could share one with Regina?

At any rate, Regina was right there when The Deacon called me over to his room. I should have known better, but I foolishly went over there to play around with the little white girls, not knowing that Regina followed me and peeked in the window of The Deacon's room to see what was going on.

We hadn't gotten around to anything except sitting down and talking when Regina kicked in The Deacon's door and came flying at me – with her favorite frying pan in her hand. When she slapped me upside the head with that frying pan, I thought I was seeing stars! I certainly wasn't seeing any white girls -- they had fled the room in terror.

Regina was a no-nonsense kind of woman, and she gave me the first bitch-blow I ever got in my life -- and I faced more of her wrath when we got home. I hadn't wanted to start a fight with her in front of The Deacon, but when we got back to our room, you'd better believe that there were fireworks. She beat on me and I hit her back -- but after that the love-making began.

Regina had some very funny ideas about our relationship -- it had gotten to where she didn't believe that I loved her unless I would beat her and then make love to her. You know, it makes me laugh now when I look back on those days and think about how tough she was. I should have expected that, though -- she did, after all, grow up on the streets with her father.

But that wasn't all that happened in Denver. Not long after the incident with the white girls, The Deacon left our little motel for his daily walk. On this day, unfortunately, he attracted the attention of a bunch of rednecks in a pickup truck. Those guys pulled over and one of them started beating The Deacon like he had done something. The Deacon hadn't done anything; his only "crime" was that he was black. Of course, this was in the early 1960s, and the country was very, very bad at the time (there is still racism now, but it was much worse back then).

The Deacon was bleeding and crying when he got back to our motel, and I was determined to do something to right the injustice that he had suffered. I was a pretty good fighter back in those days -- especially since I had taken those karate lessons in Japan -- so I was more than ready to take matters into my own fists.

I asked The Deacon if he knew where the guys who had beaten him up had gone, and when he said that he had, I replied,

"Well, just take me there and let me see."

The Deacon, Regina and I then headed off to the little redneck bar where The Deacon had seen his tormentors go. And, as luck would have it, the pickup truck that belonged to them was still in the parking lot.

The bar had the usual sign, "No Coloreds Allowed," so when I walked in the door, one of the crackers stood up and sneered,

"Can't you niggers read?"

I didn't bother to answer him. Instead, I demanded,

"Which one of you bastards beat up my brother?"

There was a big guy -- he had to be about 6'2" tall -- sitting at the bar, and he jumped up and replied,

"I did, and what are you going to do about it?"

Everyone in the bar started laughing -- I guess it was because I was much smaller than the guy who had beaten up The Deacon. Besides, all the crackers thought the big guy was one bad dude. Well, it wasn't him, but me, who got the last laugh.

Although this was a bar for whites only, the bartender was a little black man, and he was so scared that he started shaking and waving his hands for us to leave the place. But I had no intention of leaving until justice was served.

I was wearing the heavy cowboy belt that George Washington had made for me in Dallas, and -- as if the conchos that adorned it wouldn't do enough damage -- I had also put a nine-millimeter pistol inside my back pocket. When I had swung the door open and walked into that bar, I felt like John Wayne or Lash Larue or one of them.

At any rate, before the guy who had jumped up and sneered at me had a chance to sit back down, I slapped him upside his head with my concho belt. Blood immediately spurted from his nose, but I continued to beat him.

I think the unexpected beating frightened the others, because after I kicked the first guy's butt, I continued beating those crackers -- one man at a time. In the meantime, Regina took off her shoe -- in those days she wore pumps that had four-inch spiked heels made of iron -- and she jumped into the fray, swinging the heel of that shoe with a vengeance. I've never seen a woman fight so much (and so effectively, I might add); fortunately, she used only her shoe that night -- she didn't pull out the pistol that she had brought in her bag. Regina and I cleaned up that bar, putting at least half a dozen white cracker boys -- as well as a female patron who had thought she could take on Regina -- out of commission.

Just as we were finishing up, we heard a siren -- the police were coming down the road! We didn't stick around to greet them -- we ran through the back door of the bar and back to our little motel. The guys we had beaten up were in no shape to follow us, but, evidently, someone knew who we were and where we were staying, because the police came to our motel and told us we had to get out of town if we wanted to live.

After we told the guy we were working for what had happened, he tried to smooth things over. He was another big shot gangster, I guess, because he told the angry white folks to leave us the hell alone -- and he also saw that we had taxis to take us back and forth to his club. Sometimes, when we were riding in those cabs, we would see the white cracker boys that we had beaten up -- they were cruising the streets looking for us.

It didn't take us long to decide that we had enough of that nonsense -- and the club owner agreed. He told us to cut the engagement short and get out of town. All of us knew that those crackers would not stop until they had found -- and killed -- us.

So, just two weeks into our month-long gig, we played our last show. We packed our bags in the middle of the night and were at the bus station at six o'clock the next morning to catch a bus to Louisville, Kentucky. In those days, I played seven drums, so it was a hassle to move so fast, but we did manage to pack all our stuff into a cab and make it to the bus station to get the hell out of Denver (never to return again).

Since we had cut our gig short, we had two weeks to kill before our next booking in Louisville. Although she could have gone back to Dallas to see her husband, Regina decided that she wanted to spend time with her family in Memphis instead -- and she invited me to go along with her.

Regina had grown up in Memphis and considered the city her "home," and she and I had a wonderful time when we were there for those couple of weeks, although I was surprised to see that Regina's family still had an outdoor toilet. I had been shocked to see outdoor toilets when I first got to America -- I didn't think that outdoor toilets existed in the States (especially in the 1960s).

I really enjoyed meeting Regina's family and learning more about her Indian background. Her father was dead by that time, but I did meet Regina's mother and brothers. Regina's mother was a beautiful woman with very nice ways, and she took to me right away. She treated me like family -- and she certainly fed me well. In fact, Regina's mother was the one who introduced me to chitlins, the pig's belly (she cooked the best and sweetest chitlins I have ever tasted). It was this southern delicacy that gave its name to the "chitlin circuit" where The Deacon, Regina and I played.

Regina's mother also presented me with a wonderful gift -- a special treasure that I have been wearing for over half a century! In my early days, I always wore chain vests as well as big chains around my neck. One of the most beautiful of those neckpieces did not come from my great-grandfather (as I have told people just to make a long story short); it had belonged to Regina's great-great-grandfather -- and it was a gift to me from Regina's mother.

Regina's family had a trunk (one of those big, old-fashioned trunks) that was full of Indian jewelry. One day, her mother opened that trunk and told me to take whatever I wanted. The piece that I picked up was breath-taking -- it was a heavy gold chain that had large bead-like charms that represented the sun and the planets.

Regina's mother was in awe when I picked out that piece. She told me that it had been her great-grandfather's piece and that he had used it as a rosary. Even though I didn't use it as a rosary, that piece is more than jewelry to me (and it remains my favorite piece of jewelry to this day). That piece has given me power throughout my life -- and I got so accustomed to using that piece as my strength that I never go onstage without it. In fact, I can't even play onstage if I don't have that piece on - I don't have the strength to play. It is a powerful piece, and it's only been out of my sight once since the day I got it.

Besides spending time with her family, Regina and I went out a lot when we were in Memphis. One night, Regina, her brothers and I went out to a nightclub on Beale Street, the famous Memphis Street that is called "the birthplace of the blues." Regina was a star in her adopted hometown, so she got a big welcome from the MC, who seemed to know her.

Someone else who was getting attention that night was the girl who was singing at the club -- a young Aretha Franklin. That was the first time I met Aretha, and I also met a young girl by the name of Carla Thomas and her father, Rufus Thomas, that night. It was a thrill to be getting to know some of the "big people" in the music business -- and many of them were coming to know me because of my playing in jam sessions (of course, I didn't miss the opportunity to play in a jam session in Memphis).

We were having a wonderful time at the club -- until I made a comment about the drummer in the band. He was older than I was, but he played very good drums. I noticed that the guy seemed to have a bad leg, though, and I said something about it to Regina.

Regina quickly jumped to the drummer's defense. I don't know if he was just a friend or if she had slept with him in the past, but she retorted,

"Don't worry -- he knows how to work everything just fine."

I guess I took her comment the wrong way -- and I slapped the hell out of her. She asked me if I was crazy -- slapping her like that in front of her brothers -- but I told her I didn't give a damn. Fortunately, I didn't have to worry about my fate at the hands of her brothers. Her brother, Jimmy, had taken Regina's comment the same way I did, and he told her,

"Leave us out of that crap. I would have slapped you myself."

Fortunately, the incident blew over quickly. By the time we left the club that night and got into the car, Regina and I were making out like we were young lovers.

Our time in Memphis came to a close all too quickly, and it was time to "get back to business." We went on to Louisville to work our gig, and it was there that I played the bossa nova for the first time. Even though the bossa nova was hot at the time and everyone was playing it, I didn't know what the hell the bossa nova was. But when Regina took me to a jam session in Louisville, I heard the other guys -- the drummer kicked it off -- and I knew exactly what to do.

I had a great time on the road. I was a buck in my earlier days, and I showed off my broad shoulders, muscular arms and big chest by working shirtless. Sometimes, I could hear the women in the audience gasping for breath and muttering among themselves about my body, so I took advantage of that. I could get any white woman I wanted, but one night Regina educated me on the folly of my actions.

We were working in Missouri, and a beautiful blonde, blue-eyed, 22-year-old girl walked up to me after the show. She put her hands on my shoulders, sucked the sweat off one hand, and said,

"You have such beautiful, broad shoulders."

Well, Regina would have none of that -- she pushed the girl away and screamed,

"Keep away from him, bitch! He's mine!"

The girl walked away in a hurry, but not before saying,

"I'm sorry."

"You should be sorry, bitch!" Regina shot back. "Do you want to cause his death, you white bitch?"

Regina then turned to me and commanded,

"Get your ass in that dressing room before you get lynched!"

I was appalled that Regina was so mean to that young girl -- and told her that she had to be better to people. But Regina argued,

"No, you belong to me, and I don't want those white bitches coming to you. Stay away from white women because they always lie. The next thing you know, they'll say you raped them and you'll be lynched."

Regina could tell countless stories about how white women had screwed around with black men -- only to cry "rape" if a white man caught them together. She had actually seen black men hung on trees because white women had lied about them, and Regina was determined that wouldn't happen to me.

As we traveled around the country, I'd see why Regina was sometimes so adamant about white people. They could really have some screwed up notions and ways. But she really went off about them when we were dating. If a white woman approached me, Regina was right there -- at least most of the time.

Chapter 9

Becoming "That *Thunderball* Drummer"

On our last trip to Texas, we were working at a place called the Stork Club in Houston. The girls who worked in Abe's club in Dallas had been goddesses -- tall, gorgeous white girls -- but the girls at the Stork Club were absolutely breath-taking as well, and I was in heaven when one of them took a liking to me (I sure took a liking to her, too).

By this time, Regina had gotten very possessive of me. She didn't want me to look at other women -- especially white women -- but that didn't stop me from seeing that stripper on a regular basis. Sometimes, I would tell Regina that I was going to the store or to the gym -- I sure couldn't tell her that I was going to the stripper's apartment.

One night, the stripper got very bold -- just before we went out on stage, she came into the dressing room that I shared with The Deacon to wish me luck. Unfortunately, Regina had heard her, so she came to the dressing room, too – and found that girl rubbing my shoulders!

Wow, did all hell break loose! Regina was furious – and ready to fight. She stormed into my dressing room and started beating on this white girl as if the girl had stolen something from her. And every time Regina hit that girl, she would shout,

"Keep your hands off my man! He's my man!"

Both The Deacon and I tried to stop Regina from beating the girl, of course, but as we tried to pull Regina off the stripper, Regina slapped the hell of out both of us as well. As I ran out of the dressing room to get help, I could hear the stripper screaming, louder and louder,

"Get these niggers off me! Get these niggers off me! These niggers are killing me!"

Well, there were no niggers beating this woman up -- there was only one person, and that was Regina. Finally, the club manager, who was a big guy from Oklahoma, was able to pull Regina off the stripper (the guy was so strong that he was able to simply lift Regina off the girl). That poor girl hadn't done anything that night, but she sure got a cut ass for paying some attention to me (I can only imagine what would have happened if Regina found out that we had been playing around).

I paid for what happened, too -- when I got home that night, there was certainly no love-making. In fact, Regina was so angry that I had let that white girl anywhere near me that she hit me upside the head -- not with her frying pan this time, but with a pot!

I guess that you can see by now that Regina did not like anyone who was white. When we worked in those little country-looking resorts and hotels, white women would sometimes come up to me to shake my hand or tell me how beautiful I was and how broad my shoulders were. Regina would have none of that.

"Stay away from him! He's my man, you white bitch. Leave him alone," she'd yell.

Unfortunately, our problems did not only involve white girls. One night while we were working in Houston, there was another incident that would change the course of the future of our group. The Deacon was caught fooling around with a young white boy in the park, and you can only imagine what happened next. Of course, The Deacon went to jail; in fact, he spent two weeks in jail while we were trying to get papers to get him out. Once we were finally able to get him released, we left Texas in a hurry and went on to Las Vegas.

Our gig at Diamond's Jim was supposed to last for six months, so Regina and I got an apartment on Eastern and Charleston, which wasn't too far from Fremont Street, where we worked. Regina, who had grown up in the south, was very resourceful in making that place cool and comfortable -- we had no air conditioning in those days, so Regina would buy a block of ice, cover it with a blanket and set up a fan in front of the ice to send the cooled air into the apartment.

And, since we were somewhat settled in one place and had more space than we would have had in a motel room, Regina presented me with a wonderful gift. She knew that I had loved to watch "Lassie" on TV, and one day she found out about a place (not far from where we lived) where some of Lassie's offspring were for sale. It was a great surprise and thrill when Regina brought home the most beautiful collie puppy I had ever seen. That dog, whose name was Lobo, was as smart as he was beautiful, and within a few weeks Lobo was bringing in the newspaper. But that dog would play a part in a very close call I had with Regina not long after.

Since she had grown up around bars with her father, Regina knew more about the street and guns than anyone I had ever met. She was a tomboy -- but what a beautiful tomboy she was -- and she always carried a gun.

One day, she handed her .45-caliber pistol to me so I could learn how to operate it. She had taken the clip out, but forgot that there was still one bullet left in the chamber. While I was playing around with the pistol, I stupidly pointed the gun at Lobo before moving it away from him and aiming it at Regina's head.

It was then that the most frightening thing in my life happened – the gun went off and the bullet just grazed Regina's head! I almost crapped – it was the loudest thing I had ever heard and I was suddenly aware that had I not put that gun on the side of Regina's head, I could have blown her head off. Here we were, just lying in bed fooling around with that gun, but our day could have had a very tragic end. Regina was so shaken that it took me all day to stop her from crying -- and she said that her ears rang for weeks.

Regina forgave me, of course -- and she taught me how to properly handle a gun. I was thankful for that -- I'm sure that if I had killed her there would have been no way to convince the police that it had been an accident…and I probably would have gotten the electric chair!

There was also another incident that happened in Vegas that could have put an end to my career. One day, when Regina and I walked into a supermarket to buy groceries, a little white boy (he was probably about five or six years old) pinched Regina on the ass. Well, not only was that a "no-no," but, at the time the kid pinched her, he was also chanting,

"Nigger, nigger, nigger."

Well, even though that boy had been holding on to his mother's hand, Regina kicked him -- sending him about 20 feet down the aisle. Of course, the boy's mother began screaming,

"You kicked my son, you kicked my son!"

Regina immediately responded in that very high pitched Indian voice she had, "You need to put that boy on a leash and keep that little cracker bitch away from me! Calling me a nigger! Don't you know how to teach your kid manners?"

"He don't need manners," the mother responded.

Regina looked at her and said,

"Lady, if you don't shut up, I'll kick your white ass across the floor as well."

That's the way Regina was. She really didn't care – she would jump on you in a minute, especially if you were white and were trying to mistreat her. Regina didn't buy into that game.

I asked Regina if she realized that her actions could have landed us in big trouble; it was very possible that she could have ended up in jail. But Regina didn't seem to care about that -- she was not going to let anyone, not even a young white boy, assault her either physically or verbally. Thankfully, the boy's mother never pressed charges -- maybe she realized that she had been wrong.

After being in Vegas for six months, it was time to renew our papers to stay in America (back in those days, The Deacon and I had to go to immigration to get new visas every six months). When The Deacon applied for his new papers, however, he couldn't get them because of his arrest in Texas. Even though he had married Geneva so that he could stay in the U.S. (I was the best man at their wedding), The Deacon was deported for fooling around with that white boy.

The Deacon returned to Nassau, and Geneva went along, but she left him after a few months and returned to the States. The Deacon kept in touch with both Regina and me for several years (in fact, he was the one who kept me posted on what Regina was doing after Regina and I separated and were divorced). The Deacon later died of AIDS, which was expected, I guess, because of the type of life he led.

After The Deacon was deported, leaving Regina and me behind, we tried to carry on by ourselves -- I played the congas and Regina danced. We did get some help with our act from a big black lady named Charlene, who was a wonderful organ player. At the time, Charlene lived in a beautiful, four-bedroom house on Cheyenne Avenue, which was so far from town that you could shoot a cannon down the street and not hit anyone (in fact, in those days you could shoot a cannon from Sahara to Lake Mead and probably only hit a couple of prairie dogs). Charlene's home had only cost around $20,000 or so, but that was the way Vegas was in those days…you could get a lot of property for very little money.

Although my playing attracted a good crowd in Vegas, Regina and I finally decided that it was too much for us to continue to perform by ourselves (even with the help of Charlene). We decided that we would pack up our Chrysler and head for Miami to try to find a gig there. As we were making our preparations to leave Vegas, I got a telegram from Fay's mother. I couldn't believe the message -- she was begging me to come home and marry Fay!

Fay's mother thought it was about time that we got married because one of Fay's sisters was getting married and the family wanted me to come home so we could have a double wedding. And, to make the proposition more attractive to me, Fay's family would give five acres of land to me and build whatever house I wanted if I agreed to come home and marry Fay. That sure seemed strange to me – after all, when I had first asked for hand in marriage, Fay's father had pointed a shotgun at me! Now, here he is offering five acres of land and a home if I marry her.

Well, it didn't take long for me to figure out what was going on. I looked at Regina and said,

"You know what's happening right now? Fay is pregnant by somebody else and they want to pull the shame away from the family -- they don't want her to have another bastard."

My guess was that Fay's father wanted to keep his family's good name – and use me to do so. Well, I couldn't go for that -- I was making good money in America and stars were in my eyes – I knew that the best was yet to come.

Anyway, I wrote back to them, saying that I would not come back and marry Fay because I believed she was pregnant. It wasn't long before I got another telegram telling me that I was wrong.

By this time, Regina and I were ready to begin our drive to Miami, so Regina suggested,

"Why don't you just fly to Nassau to see if your intuition is right?"

So I did. Right after we got to Miami, I flew to Nassau. When I got there, I learned that Fay, her mother, her sister and her sister's husband were already there from Exuma. I went by Fay's auntie's house on East Bay Street to see them, and when I got there, Fay's mother started crying.

"Why are you crying?" I asked.

"I'm sorry I brought you back from the States," she replied tearfully, "I didn't know it, but Fay is pregnant by somebody else."

"Well, I figured that," I responded.

"How did you know?"

"I had the feeling that she was pregnant and that you all were trying to trap me."

"Oh no," she cried, "I'd never try to trap you. I didn't know and I'm truly sorry."

That very day, in front of her mother, I held Fay in my arms and wished her good luck. I was happy to see my son, Anton, for the first time while I was home, but I wouldn't see Fay again for many years.

While I was in Nassau, I also spent some time with my family, which now included another half-brother, Henry Shivers, who had been born in June of 1962 (Henry was the son of mom's friend, David Shivers). Henry would be a great blessing to mom, especially in her later years -- he and his wife, Stephanie, moved into mom's home and took care of her for nearly a year when she was suffering from the Alzheimer's disease that would take her life.

That was many years in the future, of course, but I did feel a sense of loss during the time I was home. While I was in Japan, I had received word that Paul Meeres had been killed. Like my dad, his dreams had been shattered, causing him to become a drunk in his later years. On September 13, 1962, Paul had staggered into the path of a Customs Department bus that was driven by Dyanza Burrows (Dyanza and I had gone to school together, and he was a good friend). Paul was severely injured, and -- despite efforts to save him -- he died several hours later at Princess Margaret Hospital.

Of course, I had immediately sent a card expressing my condolences to Paul's daughter, Delores, hoping that it would be special to her because it came from me. I didn't have any delusions about our having a future together, though -- she married a guy who owned a chicken shack restaurant (every time I saw him, I would joke that he had stolen my "wife"). It was good to see Delores again, but I greatly missed my old friend -- Paul had been such an inspiration and encouragement to me.

I was happy to get back to Miami to Regina. We weren't there for very long before Regina came up with a plan -- she wanted to leave her husband and marry me! That would mean that I could qualify for U.S. citizenship, and, because I wanted to be an American citizen, I didn't mind Regina twisting my arm. So Regina and I got married by a Justice of the Peace in Miami -- even though she was not yet divorced from George Washington!

I wish I could tell you that our careers were going as well as our relationship. Although Regina and I did a couple of gigs in Miami, we were not finding the success that I had dreamed about -- we could never find another dancer as good as The Deacon to keep our show hot. I couldn't help but wonder what people we would have met and what breaks we would have gotten if The Deacon hadn't gotten caught with that white boy. So I blamed The Deacon for what Regina and I did next - about two months after we got married, we decided to go back to the Bahamas.

Before we left Miami, however, I was able to reunite with Cassius Clay. On the day before he left for London for a fight with an English heavyweight boxer, Henry Cooper, Clay said "good-bye," held up six fingers and said,

"Little brother, watch me. I am on my way to England. Watch me knock this white boy out in six."

Well, that fight didn't even last six rounds; it was stopped in the fifth round due to Clay opening a deep cut under Cooper's eye – but not before Cooper had stunned Clay with his famous left hook, "Enry's Ammer," in the fourth round. Fortunately for Clay, he went into the ropes and avoided being knocked down to the mat, but what followed led to considerable controversy: Clay was administered smelling salts in violation of British rules that limited stimulants to water. But Clay's prediction of six rounds was pretty close.

I didn't go to any more Nation of Islam meetings with Clay after that fight. In fact, he was becoming such a celebrity that it was difficult to get close to him. That became even more impossible after Clay knocked out the reigning heavyweight champ, Sonny "The Bear" Liston, in Miami Beach on February 25, 1964.

I was not in Miami at the time of that fight – or when the Nation of Islam finally accepted Clay, who changed his "slave name" of Cassius Clay to Muhammad Ali, after he won the heavyweight championship. In fact, I would not see Ali again until 1971, just before another epic fight (I'll tell you about that later).

Regina and I were back in Nassau at the time Clay won his title. She and I were enjoying a wonderful life together in the Bahamas -- but that only lasted for about ten months...and I take the blame.

When we first arrived, Regina was welcomed like the queen that she was -- my mother fell in love with Regina and treated her like she was her own daughter – and I became very successful. Following my father's example, I was always looking for ways to make money, so I opened a place called King Errisson's Chicken Shack. But my restaurant was my secondary job.

Regina and my baby sister, Maddie, ran the place for me so I could concentrate on my music. They did a great job, too -- Regina was so beautiful that she sold a lot of chicken…and kept the place packed. Men would flock there to eat chicken and play pool with my stunning wife.

During the time that Regina and Maddie (with occasional assistance from my mother) were taking care of business for me, I was hired to work at the Conch Shell Club -- the very place for which I had cooked barbecue as a young boy. I should mention that I would own ten percent of the club, along with its president and founder, Roy Bowe, who had hired me to play there. And I did more than just play -- I ran the band with a guy by the name of Lord Swain. When Lord Swain left for Freeport about a year later, I took over the band, which was playing to large crowds of locals and tourists alike.

Although I was the star of the show, my backing band included some great and talented guys. First, there was my friend, Herbie Edwards (we called him "Ninny"), who was a 6'3" giant of a man; he sang and played maracas, but, since he towered over me, we had to keep him in the back. The rest of the band included Bill Anderson, Brother Shallow and

Little Foxie (Little Foxie later met a tragic end when he got drunk one night and dove into an empty swimming pool).

One evening when we were performing, a large party walked into the club. It wasn't unusual for us to have groups of people in the audience -- tourists often came together from the tour boats that stopped in Nassau -- but this party was different. I couldn't believe it when I saw a face familiar to millions -- it was none other than British actor Sean Connery!

And Connery was accompanied by nearly the entire cast and crew from the future blockbuster film, *Thunderball*! The party included the two female leads (Claudine Auger, who starred as Domino, and Luciana Paluzzi, who played the Fiona -- the girl who gets shot in the famous nightclub scene), the director, Terence Young (*Thunderball* would be his last James Bond film), and Ken Adam, the production designer, among others.

I was thrilled to be performing before an audience like that, and I was determined to rock their socks off that night (apparently, I did just that). I was singing the song, "The Wings of a Dove," when they walked in, and I never would have imagined that Sean Connery would fall in love with the song -- and the way that I sang it -- and would want my version of the song featured in the film.

Exhausted but exuberant after my set, I walked over to the bar, where Roy Bowe was sitting with Connery, Kevin McClory, who was one of the screenwriters on the film, and Kevin's first wife, Frederica Ann "Bobo" Sigrist, who was the daughter of millionaire aviation pioneer Fred Sigrist. Bobo was one of the most beautiful women I had ever seen -- she looked like a princess then, and she would eventually marry a prince (her second husband was Prince Azamat Guirey; the two would be prominent in Dublin society before retiring to the Bahamas in the 1990s). Bobo was a very special woman, and even when she returned to the islands as Princess Guirey, the locals affectionately continued to call her "Bobo."

McClory, a tall, good-looking and talented man who had been born in Dublin, had met Ian Fleming, the creator of the popular James Bond books, on a trip to the Bahamas in 1959. The two agreed that Bond was a "natural" for spectacular films that would gross big at the box office. Unfortunately, there were some legal problems that delayed the production of *Thunderball*, but by the time I met McClory, filming was finally about to begin -- and Nassau was the base for the movie.

Everyone in Nassau was excited about the film being made there -- especially since the film people were going to recreate Junkanoo, the national Bahamian festival that is similar to Mardi Gras in New Orleans and Carnival in Rio. Bahamian Junkanoo celebrations, which include bands, dancers and colorful costumes, are held on a number of islands (the biggest celebration is in Nassau) during the early hours of December 26 (Boxing Day) and New Year's Day. The making of *Thunderball* gave people another chance to celebrate in March (during what is usually called Spring Break in the U.S.).

Roy Bowe had told McClory and Connery about me, so they had come to the Conch Shell Club to see if I was as astonishing on the congas as Roy had claimed. I guess that I was, because Connery praised my magic hands – and asked if I would audition for a part in the new film.

That role would take place in the Kiss Kiss Club and would feature Connery dancing with Luciana as the beautiful but evil Fiona. A conga drummer would frantically beat on his drums to warn James Bond of impending danger as Fiona's henchmen moved in to kill him. Of course, Bond was smarter than any evil henchmen -- especially being alerted by the music in time to see a gun emerge from the curtain behind the bandstand. He would spin Fiona around just in time so that she would end up being the one killed -- and Bond would carefully lower her into a chair because she was "just dead."

Of course, I would have loved to have that part, and I thanked the international star for his compliments on my playing. But I also said to him,

"Mr. Connery, you just saw me audition. It doesn't get any better than that unless you want it more intense or a solo."

"You're right," Connery replied with a smile. "Let me buy you a drink. I'd like to know how you learned to overwhelm an audience with your drums."

I knew, of course, that there were other great drummers who could have performed in the film. Some of them, including "Mongo" Santamaria, "Patato" and Candido, had been major influences on my own playing. Another was "Peanuts" Taylor. In fact, Peanuts and his people had already approached the movie company about hiring Peanuts, although the final selection had not been made at the time that I met the star and his producer.

Over the next week, McClory and Connery returned to the Conch Shell Club nearly every night to have drinks and observe me. When they came back at the end of the week, I heard McClory and Connery talking about me, and it was only then that I thought that I actually had a chance at getting the part. My hopes were confirmed during my break -- when I sat down with them, Connery enthusiastically announced,

"You got it, King!"

We toasted the happy occasion with drinks (in those days, I drank Pernod and milk -- I always had my drinks with milk). But that special evening got even better when I danced with Lucianna Paluzzi! She was much safer dancing with me than she would be dancing with James Bond in the film, of course, so we had a wonderful time dancing.

My band and I had a great a time filming that scene at the Kiss Kiss Club -- despite an incident that could have left me in relative obscurity. The original bandstand banner, which stretched across the entire stage and featured my full name, was created at a cost of hundreds of dollars. The banner must have been placed too close to the lights, though, because it caught on fire after the first night of shooting. When I got to the set the next day, the movie people told me that rather than hold up the shooting – it would take too long and be too expensive for the artist to create another banner – they would just do without it. Well, I was having none of that – I wanted my name to be up there for all to see, so I took a razor, cut up what was left of that banner and taped it back together. While I couldn't salvage my entire name, I got enough of it up so people would know who I was.

While that episode had a somewhat happy ending, there were a couple of other incidents that happened during the filming of *Thunderball* that didn't turn out so well for me. First, I have already told you that Sean Connery loved my rendition of "The Wings of a Dove," and he wanted to include it at the end of the film. The director, Terence Young, bought the song from a man, Carlos Malcolm, who claimed he had written it, but the real author of the song sued the producers for millions of dollars, so the song was pulled. Therefore, instead of hearing me at the end of the blockbuster, filmgoers heard Tom Jones' rendition of the title song, "Thunderball," which became a huge hit for him -- and I am sure "The Wings of a Dove" would have been just as big a hit for me.

Another disappointment was my compensation -- I received only $5,000 for my role in *Thunderball*. If the film had been produced in the U.S., I would have gotten a higher salary and been entitled to residuals.

As if that wasn't enough, Peanuts' people made sure that he was promoted instead of me – even though he had not appeared in the film. Peanuts' manager, Sir Stafford Sands, was a white economist who was considered to be the driving force in the Bahamas' tourism industry, so it was no problem for him to arrange to have the poster that featured me replaced with a poster of Peanuts displayed at every theater at which the film was shown!

You can't imagine my surprise when I first saw that life-size poster of Peanuts when I attended the premiere of *Thunderball* in Nassau (in fact, Peanuts' poster was so large that it almost seemed as if he was the star instead of Connery). And, since that poster was displayed at every movie theater (not just the ones in Nassau), I came across it again when I later toured Canada!

People were always asking me why my picture was not displayed, since it was me, not Peanuts, who had played the congas in that famous nightclub scene. Can you imagine how well known I would have become (and how much sooner) if my picture and band's name had been promoted? I learned a valuable lesson from that experience – you must have a manager in my business to get the right exposure (today, it would cost a fortune to get that kind of exposure).

But appearing in *Thunderball* was the biggest break of my career. Not only did I now have a movie under my belt, the recognition that I got from my brief appearance opened doors for me not only on the islands but also in Canada and America. And, my popularity was largely responsible for my success in the romance department as well.

Chapter 10

Success and Forbidden Love

Although *Thunderball* wasn't released until December of 1965 due to legal battles, the filming had caused a lot of excitement in Nassau, and I became a "hot ticket." The Conch Shell was filled every night with people who came to hear me play and sing. Besides the tourists, more locals than ever before came to the club (some of them were the guys who had harassed me about my playing when I was a jockey), and they always requested the drum song that I had played in *Thunderball*.

By this time, I was considered one of the top three drummers in the islands (along with Peanuts and John Chipman), so Peanuts' manager, Sir Stafford Sands, sponsored a drum duel for us at the Lyford Quay Club. Before I tell you about the duel -- and how unfairly I was treated -- I'd like to share an interesting story about Lyford Quay.

Lyford Quay had been developed as a sanctuary for old, sick white folks -- blacks were only welcomed as hired help. Today, however, the place is full of blacks who think they have "made it." Unfortunately, people (including my beautiful sister, Maddie, who built her dream home there with her husband, Dennis, in the 1980s) don't get well on Lyford Quay -- they get sick. The truth about that exclusive little piece of land is that Lyford Quay was a leper colony about a 100 years ago and the ground is still contaminated.

At any rate, I was delighted to be invited to participate in the drum duel -- I couldn't wait to show everyone up. Since my band started at about 8:00 p.m. at the Conch Shell Club, I asked for the duel to begin at 10:00 to give me time to get there.

I should have taken a couple of hours off and let Ninny start the night off at the Conch Shell, but I didn't want to disappoint our audience. I knew that some of the tourists had to get back to their cruise ships, and I always wanted to give them a show -- something to talk about on the way back to their boats. So, I stayed at the club and played until about 9:30 p.m.

Was that a mistake! By the time I got to Lyford Quay at about 10:10, both Peanuts and John were receiving their awards as the best drummers on the islands! I wasn't expecting that outcome – even though the duel was sponsored by Peanuts' manager, who was still bitter over me being chosen over Peanuts for the role in *Thunderball*. Of course, I congratulated Peanuts and John and shook their hands as we departed that night, but I was disappointed that I hadn't kicked their asses in a big way.

My disappointment over that duel would not last long. One night in March of 1965, I was on stage, singing "More" ("Theme from *Mondo Cane*"). Little did I know that the song would be prophetic -- that night, which had started off so normally, would be the start of a magical love affair.

As I was performing, the most gorgeous white woman I'd ever seen walked into the Conch Shell Club. One of the first things that I saw was her smile as she walked in the door -- from fifty feet away I could see that woman's smile, it was so big and beautiful. The gorgeous blonde looked as if she was happy to see me -- as if she knew me, although she had never seen me before. And I felt the same about the woman I would come to call "my JMC."

Joan Marie wasn't a skinny girl, but she wasn't fat, either. She was like a Kim Novak type. In fact, she looked very much like Sophia Loren – absolutely breath-taking. JMC was wearing a dress with stripes; a dress that matched the color of her skin. It was sort of a rust-tan dress with beige stripes, and the dark part of it blended right in with the suntan she had gotten during the week she had already spent in the Bahamas.

Although she walked in with two guys and her friend, Xavia, who had come to the islands with her from New York City, JMC walked straight up to the bandstand, looked at me and smiled that incredible smile. She then reached her hand out to me and I reached mine out in return.

I turned to Ninny and said,

"You take over, I'm going dancing."

The stage was about three feet off the ground, so I stepped down - right into this woman's arms -- not knowing that I was about to dance with a self-avowed racist! JMC later told me that she had never even touched a black person before. In fact, when she was a teenager in East Orange, New Jersey, a black family had moved in next door to her family and JMC had asked her mother to move away. JMC and her family packed up and left because she didn't want to live next door to a black family! And now here she is dancing with a black man!

JMC told me that she didn't know what came over her, but she felt as if she had known me all her life and she wanted to be a part of me. And, boy, did I fall for that, because I wanted to be a part of her, too. It was love at first sight for both of us.

I can't explain why I had such an attraction to -- and even a connection with -- JMC. Of course, she was beautiful -- before she was 19, JMC had already been the "face" of one of those hair-coloring companies (Clairol, I think) -- but I'd seen (and had sex with) beautiful white women in Japan and all over America, and I had never felt this way about any of them.

I never thought I could love, much less marry, a white woman. Sure, I had plenty of one-night stands with white women who wanted to "live dangerously" with a handsome black performer, but I never had feelings for any of them -- I just had my fun and went on my way. I would screw every white woman I could get my hands on to avenge my brothers of yesteryear who had suffered for having anything to do with a white woman. But revenge was the last thing on my mind when I met this beautiful, young white girl.

The first night that I met JMC, she and I danced until the Conch Shell closed and then I took her to my favorite beach, where we stayed until the wee hours of the morning. I went home, not thinking anything of it, only to find Regina sitting up on the porch, waiting for me. This was the first night since I'd brought her back to Nassau that I had stayed out so late.

Before I could get to the porch, Regina demanded,

"Who's that white woman you've been f**king?"

I knew I was in hot water, so I tried playing innocent,

"What are you talking about?"

"I can smell the perfume a mile away. When you entered the gate I could tell you've been with some white woman."

I had forgotten about the sharpness of the nose of an Indian, but I did reek. I didn't know how much I reeked until I took my clothes off and the smell of the JMC's perfume filled the house.

Regina went crazy. She ran outside, picked up a stone, came back into the house and hit me upside the head with it. I didn't like that, of course, but there was not much I could do about it. The side of my head was bleeding – this was the first time anyone had hit me hard enough to draw blood, even though Regina had hit me pretty hard with her frying pan and a pot in the past. Despite being hurt so badly, I did not fight back -- I knew I had wronged Regina.

Later that day, I got up and drove out to the British Colonial Hotel, where JMC was staying. I had made a date with her the night before, so I drove out to meet her for lunch. I knew that I was falling in love with this woman. I wanted her to stay in Nassau and she wanted to stay – even though I had told her that I was married, that I had a woman at home, and that I never had any intentions of meeting anyone else. But I never thought I would meet a woman of JMC's caliber – a beautiful white girl who wanted me.

I had been so intrigued by JMC that I had done something that I had never done before – I'd left home and gone out to have lunch with another woman. By the time I got back home, Regina and Maddie were in my restaurant, and I tried to patch things up – I tried to be nice and pretend that nothing was wrong, but my uncharacteristic behavior made Regina suspicious that I'd been with the white woman again.

I went to work that night as usual, but JMC wasn't at the club. When she returned to the Conch Shell a couple of nights later, we went out again -- she was really getting to me. We stayed on the beach all night and I didn't get home until 6 or 7 o'clock the next morning, so Regina knew something was definitely wrong.

As I walked toward the house, she was sitting on the porch, crying.

"What are you crying about?" I asked.

"Where've you been?"

She knew there were times when the boys from the band and I would go to a place called Hutch Chicken Shack or Father Alan's and just shoot pool until early in the morning. But this time Regina could tell that something was wrong. She said I was totally different.

Regina allowed me to sleep until about noon. She didn't bother me (she didn't fuss or anything); she just lay down beside me, crying.

When Regina woke me up, she said,

"I want you to take me for a ride."

Now, Regina's been on the island all these months and she knew her way around, but she was insistent,

"I need you to take me down to the Grove to see your sister."

"But you know how to drive and you know where my sister Aries lives."

"No," she replied, "I want you to take me."

So I said, "O.K." and got up and got into the tub (in those days we still had a tin tub for bathing). After taking my bath, I got dressed and we got in the car and headed off, supposedly to see my sister.

As we approached an abandoned street, Regina said to me,

"We can go over this way. You can reach Aries' house down this road."

I was wondering why Regina wanted to take this roundabout way to get to my sister's house, but I went along with her. As we got farther into the bushes, she pulled out her .45 caliber pistol and put it to my head! Regina had already crossed the bullet and split it so that my brains would splatter over the car when she shot me.

As Regina was pulling the trigger, I knocked the gun out of her hand and the bullet blew a hole in the roof of the car. I grabbed Regina, threw her out of the car and started beating her. A man who was passing by in a truck stopped when he saw me.

"What are you doing?" he asked, although it was pretty obvious what I was doing.

"This woman just tried to kill me," I shouted. "Look at the car!"

"Well, that's no way to handle it. Don't beat her anymore. Just go to the cops or something. But you have to stop this."

That guy saved Regina's life – and probably mine -- because I was so angry. All I could do was think about how this woman had almost killed me – and just when I had found a new love. It was selfish of me to feel the way I did, but, to put it bluntly, I was scared. I knew that if Regina tried to kill me with my eyes wide open, while I was sitting next to her, I was a dead man if I ever went to sleep again.

It was about 1:00 in the afternoon when I got Regina back in the car. She was crying as she said,

"See, there are only two bullets in the gun – one for you and one for me. I was going to kill myself after I killed you because I don't want to live without you."

"Well, I don't want to live without you either, and I don't know why we can't work this thing out. But I believe that if you tried to shoot me when my eyes were wide open, I am a dead man if I ever shut my eyes around you again. You have to get on a plane tonight and go. If you don't go, you're going to kill me or I'm going to kill you. I'm sorry for what I've done to you, but you have to get on the plane tonight."

We drove back home, where I had Regina (who was crying the entire time) pack her bags, and then we drove to my restaurant to tell my mother what Regina had tried to do to me. Both Regina and I were crying as I related what had just happened. Now, my mother loved Regina as if she had birthed her from her own body, but when she found out that Regina tried to kill her son, my mother agreed with me.

"If you tried to shoot him while he was awake, he'll be a dead man when he goes to sleep. I can't trust you – that you won't kill my son. So I agree with him – you need to go home. Go back to America."

My mother had loved to tell me stories about American women and how they loved to kill men -- shoot them and chop them up or cut them up with knives and stuff like that. But Regina...oh, man, what a letdown. I don't think I would have gotten so tied up with JMC if I had been able to hold on to Regina. We possibly could have worked it out. After all, what had happened with us was not a unique situation in the islands.

We used to call the white girls who came to the Bahamas "yellow birds." They come into your life for a time and then they fly away. It was not unusual for Bahamian guys to screw the white girls who came in for a weekend or a week or two, so Bahamian women were pretty much used to that. A lot of Bahamian boys were selling themselves, technically speaking, but I didn't put myself into that category -- I thought I was in love with JMC.

My mom and I were able to get Regina to the airport and on a plane, much against her will. Regina had cried all the way to the airport, and she continued to cry all the way to the plane. As I walked her to the plane, she continued to cry and beg,

"Please don't send me away. I wouldn't try it anymore. I wouldn't kill you -- I love you too much."

But I was too afraid. I just couldn't take that chance.

Now that I was free, JMC stayed on. She had come to Nassau for a two week vacation; she stayed for six months after that, refusing to go back home. We had a wonderful time together -- JMC was so much fun to be with…you could laugh with her, run with her, play with her.

To show you what a great sport JMC was -- even though she had leased an apartment on Bay Street, the main street in the Bahamas, a beautiful apartment with everything going for her, she wanted to be a part of me so much that she used to come down to our little clapboard house in the back of the Grove (I found out later that the Grove would be called a ghetto in America, but we didn't call them ghettos when I was growing up -- we just lived over the hill).

Anyway, Joan Marie would come down to the Grove with me and she would help me fill the big washing tub full of water and put it on the fire to boil. We'd jump in it and she'd bathe with me in this tub in the middle of the living room floor.

Sometimes we'd have big brown cockroaches flying overhead, buzzing around her head. JMC couldn't stand that, so she'd get up and rinse herself off, put her clothes on and go sit in the car until I came out. But that was the life we had in the Bahamas – cockroaches, big black ground spiders, centipedes and scorpions were frequent around the house, especially during rainy times.

JMC and I were a beautiful couple. I would always dress in white or black – whatever it was, it was always the same color, straight out -- and she was always in a tan dress or something that matched her beautiful blonde hair and suntanned body (JMC loved the sun; she lived in the sun).

When we'd walk down Bay Street, tourists were always walking up to us and saying how beautiful she was and what a good-looking couple we were. And these were white folks. It was so wonderful to live in the Bahamas. Tourists who would never speak to me in America would walk up to me and say,

"Oh, what a beautiful wife you have. What a nice looking couple. We heard about you all the way in Pennsylvania."

We got so much praise that it seemed like we were living a fairy tale -- you just didn't see a handsome black man and the most gorgeous white woman in the world walking down a main street in America. People would look at her, and sometimes I could see the envy on the white men's faces, as if they were thinking,

"How the hell did he get her?"

JMC and I had only one troubling incident – and that was quickly put to rest. One night, we went dancing at a place called Dirty Dick's on Bay Street, and I guess this white man just couldn't take the way we were dancing and hugging and kissing on the floor. He came over and pushed JMC.

He was a big guy, but that didn't make any difference to me. When he pushed her, I grabbed him by the collar and demanded,

"You apologize to my wife."

"What did I do?"

"You pushed her. Now apologize or I will wipe the floor with your ass."

The guy was stunned – if I had tried something like that in America I'd have been arrested...or maybe even shot. But I was home now. And, boy, did that guy apologize.

"I'm so sorry. It won't happen again."

"Don't you let it happen again. You're not in cracker town, you know. You're in the Bahamas now."

It didn't take much time before the word got out that King didn't take any crap, especially when it came to this woman. She was his pride and joy.

Joan Marie was such a unique person. We'd be driving down the street on the way to a movie and she'd say,

"Honey, there's a dark alley there. Let's go make love."

I'd have to pull the car through the alley and make love to her and then we'd go on to the movies. One of the things that she used to love to do was make love and then go out. She was the second woman I had who wanted to do that.

JMC was also a daredevil. Sometimes, in the middle of the night after work, she'd borrow a car from one of my friends and I'd use my car

-- or she'd use my car and I'd borrow somebody's car -- and we would race down a street on the outskirts of town. We were young – she was 20 or so and I was 23 – and we would race like two kids. We had the most wonderful time, and I think I was beginning to know what love was all about with Joan Marie. She was everything that anyone could want in a woman.

JMC and I did more than have fun together – she became my muse. When I did drum solos at night and didn't capture the audience, she would sit there and look at me with a disenchanted smile. When the night was over, she'd say,

"Well, you didn't do well at all. We're taking the drums with us tonight and we're going to the beach the first thing in the morning and you're going to practice and I'm going to listen. I'll tell you what you should do and when you should do it."

Yes, my JMC was a pusher. She always told me,

"You have to work. If you want to be the best you have to practice."

She'd have me up – and I mean up – by nine o'clock the next morning and we'd be at the beach by ten, practicing. That practice would go on from ten until two or three o'clock in the afternoon. I had just enough time to get back to the apartment, get a shower and grab a nap before having to head back down to the Conch Shell. Thank God, the Conch Shell gig didn't start until 8:00 or later (sometimes 8:30 or 9:00), so I had a little bit of time to rest.

JMC used to watch the way the people danced when I played, and she said certain beats I played made people dance even more -- it was more infectious if I kept the same thing going for a longer time so I could get the people into the mood. I started listening to her and started obeying my "instructor," and it worked out. It worked out just fine.

On the nights when I'd worked real hard and Joan Marie was completely, totally pleased with my performance, she couldn't wait to get home to the apartment and fix a special treat for me -- warm milk and butter with a tiny bit of sugar. After making love, we'd sleep like two babies until the middle of the next day.

Joan Marie would also go with me to different clubs in the evening before I went to the Conch Shell to play. I'd go to these clubs and sit in on people's drums and I'd show everybody up – I used to love to do that. And she liked that, too.

She'd say, "Let's go show Peanuts up."

Peanuts, who was supposedly the number one drummer in the country at this time, owned a number of clubs, including the Drumbeat

Club, which he opened in 1964, the year before I met JMC. Suffice it to say, we'd jam and I'd out jam everyone else. That was always my intention – to show JMC that I was better than anyone else in the world. That was the thing about JMC – you had to be the best if you were going to be a part of her life. I liked that about her (although I liked everything about her).

Joan Marie always used to say that she wanted to be married to the best. Although we were not married, JMC and I called each other "husband" and "wife" for the six months that we lived together. That was our thing -- our Bahamian way. We were husband and wife as far as she was concerned. But little did we know that our happy life together would be shattered…and soon.

Chapter 11

Loss and New Beginnings

Unfortunately, our love was doomed from the start. There was something that I didn't know about JMC -- she "belonged" to one of the biggest gangsters in New York City – and a Jewish gangster at that (I don't think there's anything worse than a Jewish gangster). The guy's name was Alan, and he was married with a couple of kids, but Alan took care of Joan Marie; she was his moll and he did everything for her. By the time she was 19, JMC owned two beauty salons in Manhattan (gifts from Alan), and she was moving up the ladder of success. JMC had it all -- until she came to Nassau and started playing around with a black boy.

We later found out that Xavia, the friend who had come to Nassau with Joan Marie, had gone back and told Alan that JMC was sleeping with a black man in the Bahamas. To make matters worse, JMC's mother also found out about our relationship, and she and Joan Marie's father were deathly against it. Being of Italian descent, they didn't want to hear that their daughter was involved with a black man. Not only did they forbid JMC to continue seeing me (there was a letter from her mother waiting when we got home from the beach one day), but they also told Alan that they wanted him to bring her back (Alan must have been like a breadwinner for that family).

In the beginning, we faced minor annoyances -- Alan began sending people down to Nassau to check out JMC's black boyfriend. Then, more and more of Joan Marie's girlfriends were coming from New York. They would come and try to have one-night stands with me. I say try, because Joan Marie kept everyone away.

It seemed that Joan Marie had Alan by the balls because, even though he knew about me, he kept sending money to her. I used to love to play the horses, so JMC and I would go to the races whenever the horses ran. Because I used to be a jockey, I thought I knew what was going on – but I didn't know crap. Sometimes, we'd win, but most of the time we'd lose. We'd get tips that weren't right – and I should have known better because I used to make all kinds of deals and I didn't always do what I was supposed to do, either. Anyway, we were gambling a lot and I'd lose a lot of money.

When I lost money on the horses – no matter how many hundreds or thousands of dollars we'd lose -- Joan Marie would call New York and money from Alan would be in the bank the next day. We were never broke, but I guess Alan got tired of JMC spending his money on her black boyfriend – and things turned deadly.

Alan decided that he wanted me out of the way -- and permanently. So I was marked for death by a Jewish gangster in New York. Although he was hundreds of miles away, Alan had a target on my back, and he was determined to put an end to me and my relationship with his girl.

The first attempt on my life came one day when I was practicing my drums on the beach. I used to consider that part of the island mine for some reason. It wasn't mine, of course – the land and the castle-like home that was built on it had once belonged to white folks who had abandoned the place after black people started coming into power. I guess those white folks "got out of Dodge" because they thought they would be overthrown. That had happened in Africa years before, but there was none of that in the Bahamas.

Because the place was abandoned, Joan Marie and I took over the property, technically speaking. We used to say it was our house, and we even kept the gate locked; when we'd go in, we'd lock the gate. The beach was "ours," too – and I'll always have the picture in my mind of JMC (so gorgeous in a red bathing suit) sitting on that beach. She had her arms stretched out to her feet and she was so in love -- it was a picture to behold.

There was never anyone around but us when we went to that beach – until one particular day, which had already started out with a heart-pounding incident. Joan Marie had insisted that we stop by my mother's house to pick up my half-brother, Gerone, who was about six years old at the time, and take him to the beach that day. JMC was lying on a blanket, my congas at her side, and Gerone was playing in the sand while I swam about 200 yards out into the ocean – quite a good distance away from the beach. As I was cruising along, Joan Marie suddenly got up, screaming – in fact, she and Gerone were both screaming –

"Shark! Shark!"

I looked around and, sure enough, there was this big shark behind me – I could see its fin hanging out of the water. I'd been around sharks before, so I wasn't too afraid and didn't get panicky. I took my time paddling back toward shore because had I rushed back the shark would have come after me faster than he did. But, since I was swimming slowly, the shark took his time, too. Occasionally, I turned around to look at the shark to see how fast it was moving; he wasn't moving that fast so I knew that I was in no danger. I kept slowly paddling on until I got about ten feet from the beach -- where I could get up and run out of the water.

I was not afraid because when I was growing up on the island of Exuma as a young boy, I learned that if you didn't get panicky the sharks didn't come after you. But I did stay the hell of the water for the rest of the day.

JMC and Gerone, on the other hand, had panicked. Gerone was screaming, "Brother, didn't you see that?"
Joan Marie had quite a fright, too, and she clung to me, hugging me close to her on the blanket, after the scare. Little did we know that the most frightening event of the day would come about 20 minutes later, when we were confronted by a scene that could have come straight from a James Bond film.

All of a sudden, a frogman with a spear gun in his hand came up from the ocean. And from the way he was looking at JMC and me, you could see that he was not there to be friendly and make small talk. I walked over to the frogman and asked him what he was doing there and why was he coming out of the water on this end of the island. The way the island was shaped, nobody should be coming from that end of the beach -- in order to get into the water in a wet suit, he would have had to go to the eastern end of the rock and jump over on the eastern end and swim around to the point where we were. Therefore, he must have been there for some time, watching our movements – likely wanting to see how far I would be away from Joan Marie before he shot me.

As I turned around, I saw two men up on the ridge overlooking the beach. Both were wearing gray suits and felt hats – certainly not attire for a day at the beach – and they had driven to the spot above us in a rented Volkswagen. I suppose that they were hit men – either there to do the killing themselves or at least see that it was done.

Joan Marie, sensing danger, grabbed up Gerone and pulled me close to her. She wouldn't let go of either one of us. Not wanting to harm JMC – and possibly not wanting to kill me in front of a young boy -- the men in the gray suits waved the frogman off. The frogman wished us a good day and jumped back into the ocean and the guys in the suits got back into their car and drove away. But Alan wasn't finished with me yet.

By the time we got back to our apartment on Bay Street – the apartment that Joan Marie had rented -- there was a telegram lying on the floor just inside the door. JMC's hands and voice were trembling as she read,

"Your boyfriend almost died today, and if you're not home by the end of this night, he <u>will</u> die tomorrow."

Joan Marie went immediately to the telephone and made a call. I could hear her screaming,

"Alan, if you harm him, I will go to the authorities and let them know what a bastard you are."

The way this woman was screaming, you would swear I was already dead. And, that evening, when I went to work at the Conch Shell, JMC went on stage with me. She stood beside me while I was playing, never once leaving my side that entire evening. For a week, she stood beside me as I was playing.

"Nobody's going to shoot you in front of me because they don't want to hurt me," she said. "They've been paid to kill you, not me."

JMC stayed with me for an extra two weeks, regardless of the threats that had been made against me, and she would argue with Alan every day. She would always tell him,

"If you hurt King, I'm going to tell people who you are because I know what you are and what you have done and what you are all about."

To further protect myself, my friends (and band members), Ninny and Brother Shallow, and I became – well, we were already our own little gangsters. Nobody could just come to the islands and kill somebody – especially me. They could dream about that, but it was far-fetched the way we lived in Nassau as a unit. We weren't too worried, but, because of the way the club was set up, we had to walk outside for quite a distance to get to my car. I was always between Ninny and Brother Shallow – you would think I was the Godfather or something the way everybody protected me after the word had gotten out that there was a hit on me.

For three weeks, the gangsters tried to find an opportunity to shoot me down in the street. Fortunately, my group and I were able to avoid them, but things were far from over. The last time I heard Joan Marie crying on the phone, Alan had told her that he didn't give a shit or something to that effect. She dropped the phone, screaming, after he told her that he no longer had any jurisdiction over the matter. He had already paid for the hit, and when you pay somebody in Miami to do a hit, you can't take it back.

"You'd better take it back. I don't care how it's done, but don't hurt him. I'll get on the plane in the morning."

JMC then began started crying. She leaned over on me, and it wasn't too long until she was sobbing.

Well, we went to work that night, and, as usual, she stood on stage with me, close by me while I was singing and playing. She was my guardian angel.

The next morning, however, JMC was packed. As I drove her to Nassau airport, the hit men followed in a car behind us. In fact, they followed us all the way to the airport.

At the time, JMC was wearing a diamond ring that was shaped like a hibiscus flower. That ring cost around $20,000 – and this is back in the 1960s -- but she took that ring off and flung it into Lake Killarney as we were passing by. She just took that beautiful ring off her finger and flung it and said,

"Screw Alan and screw everything he can do for me. I love you and you're all the man I want in my life. You're everything that I want and need."

I was amazed when JMC threw that ring into the lake. I had always admired that ring and I wished that I could have given something like that to her.

"Wow, why did you do that?"

"I don't need it. It's just a thing and it means nothing to me," she replied.

When I stopped the car at the airport, I went to open the car door for JMC as I usually did. Almost before I knew what happened, the two hit men who had been following us walked up to the car, grabbed JMC and escorted her to the plane. And they boarded the plane with her. What a scene that was -- like something in a gangster movie.

The next time I heard from Joan Marie was five days later; she called me through the phone at the Conch Shell Club. When Roy Bowe got the call, he came over and got me while I was on stage. He knew how much I loved JMC and how important the call would be to me since I was so heartbroken. I think it was the first time I really got my heart torn apart -- JMC hadn't left me, she had been taken away from me.

When I picked up the phone, JMC said,

"I'm sneaking this phone call because I love you. But I can't move, I can't do anything. I'm locked up in a room. I'm being fed in a room like a prisoner and I can't do anything about it. But the first chance I get, I am coming to you. The first chance, the very first chance, I am coming to you, my darling."

About a week later, I got another phone call from her and I couldn't believe what she said,

"I'll see you later."

"What do you mean later?" I asked.

"I will see you later," was her only response.

It turned out that Joan Marie was able to get away from her prison. She told Alan that she needed to go shopping, and he allowed her to do so -- but only in the company of two gangsters. But JMC was able to get away from them. She ditched them in New York City and took a plane to Chicago. From Chicago, she flew to Pennsylvania before heading down to Miami. JMC landed in three different states trying to dump those gangsters before she ended up in Nassau at a place called the Royal Victoria Hotel.

JMC hadn't told me that was where she was when she called me. She had simply said,

"I'll see you later."

An hour later, she walked through the door of the Conch Shell Club, just like she had done the very first time I saw her. My heart jumped into my mouth. I was so happy – I was like a little boy in a field of candy. I jumped off the stage, ran to JMC and hugged and kissed her.

When I got through working that night, we drove out to the beach and made love. We had the most wonderful time making love on our favorite beach. But by the time we got back to her hotel room, early that morning -- around 5:00 or 6:00 or so -- the two gangsters were waiting for her again.

They snatched JMC out of my car, escorted her to her room and picked up her luggage. She was already packed – these people had already been in her room and packed her clothes. They checked her out, put her in their car and drove to the airport. Those guys snatched my woman and there was nothing I could do about it.

Now that I think about it, if I had more sense back then, I could have called someone. I had so many friends -- policemen who could have done something about JMC being taken against her will. That was just wrong.

After Joan Marie had been taken away and the gangsters couldn't get to me the way they wanted to, they started sending different women to try to trap me. One night in particular, a beautiful -- a very beautiful -- blonde girl was sitting in the very same seat where Joan Marie always sat. When I took my 20-minute break outside on the patio, she walked up to me and said,

"So you're the mighty King Errisson."

"I don't know about the mighty, but I am King Errisson," I replied.

"Well, I've been hearing about you from Miami to New York – everywhere. Everybody knows King Errisson."

"How did you know me?"

Instead of answering my question, she asked, "Well, where's your wife? The beautiful blonde girl?"

"My wife is back in New York. Haven't you heard? If you know who she was, you've heard she's been taken away from me."

"Oh, I heard about that. That's why I've been sent down here – to take a good look at you."

When the night ended, she asked me to take her for a ride.

"Can we go to the beach?"

"Sure."

I believed that something was up – maybe she was sent to kill me -- so I had my boys follow me. The guys from the band followed me out to South Beach, where I usually take all my girls. It's a beautiful beach -- and a great place to make love.

When we got to the beach, this girl – before I could say, "what's that?" – had stripped off her clothes and jumped into the water. Of course, I followed – and the rest is history. We made love like two mad dogs – I didn't have Joan Marie anymore, so I had nothing to worry about.

After cavorting around on the beach for a few hours, we jumped into the car, headed back to the hotel where she was staying and spent the rest of the morning making love in her room. When I finally got up, I said,

"I'll see you later."

"Yes, you will," she smiled.

But I never saw that woman again. She didn't come to the Conch Shell that night as she had promised she would, and she probably left the islands, because I never saw her again.

That woman did to me what I used to do to women. I would find them, screw them and forget them. But this girl was such a beauty -- and such a good lay -- that I was hoping to see her again (I never did).

About a month later, JMC was able to tell me about my little romantic escapade. She called and asked me if a certain girl had come into the club and did I see a woman come into the club and on and on.

I knew right then that this had been a set-up, maybe by Alan, because Joan Marie knew that the woman had been with me. I had thought at first that the woman might have been sent to kill me and then just couldn't go through with it, but maybe she was just sent there so JMC would find out that I had been cheating on "my wife."

At any rate, I didn't hear from JMC again -- but that doesn't mean I forgot about her. I loved Joan Marie so much, needed her so much and missed her so much that I would go to New York to look for her – like in the movie, *Dr. Zhivago*. I never knew her address, so I'd just go to New York and hope to see a beautiful blonde girl walking down the street. But I could never find her – and neither could Roy Bowe. Sometimes, when Roy would go on business trips to New York, he would look for her, too. But neither one of us ever saw JMC.

Despite our lack of success in New York, I never gave up my search for JMC. When I was walking down the streets of Miami or wherever I went in the world, if I saw a beautiful blonde girl, I would walk faster to look at her face to see if it was JMC. If a blonde girl had a nice shape, if she had shiny blonde hair (JMC had the prettiest, shiniest blonde hair you'd ever want to see) – every time I'd see a girl like that I would run to see if it was my Joan Marie.

I was so hurt that I promised myself never to marry or have anything to do with anyone until I saw JMC again. There was something so special about Joan Marie. She was so beautiful, but she wasn't just pretty -- she was a nice person, just a lovely woman. So when she was taken away from me again, it couldn't have hurt more than if she had gotten killed.

About a year after I saw JMC for the last time, I was still performing at the Conch Shell Club, and you'll never guess who walked in the door -- it was Regina! I was very surprised, but also very glad to see her. Regina had gained a little weight, so that beautiful dancer's body was gone, but she was still beautiful

Since I had already lost JMC to the gangsters, I ended up taking Regina to South Beach. As we sat on a blanket, Regina began telling me what she had been through since she left the islands. She never mentioned whether or not she had gone back to her other husband, George Washington, after she left me, but she did tell me that she had ended up in an asylum for six months. The people at the asylum had said that the only way they could cure her was to find the scent of the perfume that JMC was wearing. Since Regina could describe the scent so well to them, the asylum people found it -- and once Regina smelled it again, she sort of got over the hurt.

Regina said she had forgiven me for what I had done to her, and she asked me if I still found her beautiful, and, of course, I told her that I did. I really wanted to make love to Regina, but I was still afraid that she might try to kill me again. Before we did make love, I made sure that Regina was completely naked and that her hair was down so she couldn't hide anything in it.

My fears proved to be unfounded. We had a wonderful time together that night -- and over her three day visit -- so when she left for Miami, I thought she might come back again -- even though I was still afraid of what she might do to me. After all, Regina had begged me to let her stay with me when I sent her packing after the shooting incident and there were still sparks between us.

Before she left Nassau, however, Regina told me that she had just come to see me to make sure she was over me -- and her hurt over my fooling around with a white woman during our marriage. So, when we said good-bye, I would not hear from Regina or see her again until the early 1970s.

I heard that Regina ended up getting married to some guy in Miami, whose last name, ironically, was Johnson, like mine. They would have half a dozen kids (I didn't think she could have that many since she was so much older than I was) and many grandkids.

Seeing Regina had brought back a lot of painful memories, so, although I was enjoying great success at the Conch Shell Club, I was determined to leave the gig -- and the islands -- partly to ease my hurt over losing JMC. My antidote was accepting a gig a long way from home -- at a place called the Caravan Club in Toronto, Canada.

Before I left for Canada, I decided to make my first album, which was called *Drums of Nassau*. Before the actual recording began, I practiced for three weeks with my backing band, Lou Adams and his Orchestra. Lou was a talented trumpet player -- one of the best I had ever heard -- and his orchestra was composed of several other wonderful musicians (Clarence Bain on guitar, Eric Cash on bass, Bruce Coakley on the sax, Maurice Harvey on the piano and Maurice Flowers on the trap drums).

We flew to Miami to record, but I must admit that I was a little worried about the timing -- my flight to Canada left that evening! Well, Lou and his group didn't let me down -- they were such professionals (and I was so confident with them) that we had that entire album finished in plenty of time for me to catch my plane!

I had a great time in Canada -- I was able to study drama while I was headlining at the Caravan Club, which was on Queens Street, for almost a year. The man who owned the Caravan Club was a Czech whose name I could never pronounce, so I called him Gus. Gus had booked me because of my drumming scene in *Thunderball*, and I guess that the audiences were as impressed as he was -- we had some great crowds at the club.

One night when I was playing, two men walked in. One of them was Wes Thompson, an old friend from Nassau. He was with Martin "Marty" Hearst, a 29-year-old man of German descent who was rich as hell. Marty had taken over his father's roofing company, which was called Mule Town, and turned it into a multi-million-dollar business within 18 months. Part of the reason that Marty made so much money was that he hired a lot of rednecks and blacks, giving them an incentive to work by awarding his top salesmen with gifts and cash prizes.

It turned out that Wes was now working for Marty, but not in his roofing business. Marty also owned a lot of real estate, and Wes was his rent collector -- and Marty's right-hand man. It turned out that Marty had seen me at the Conch Shell Club when he was on vacation in the Bahamas, so when the two men heard that I was playing in Canada, they came to see me from Buffalo, New York, where Marty lived and had his roofing business.

Marty told me that he was having a big party (a couple hundred people or so were invited), so he wanted me to come and play for him on my day off. I didn't have a manager or agent at the time, so I agreed to work for free. The next week, I drove to Buffalo, passing through immigration on my way.

When the immigration officers asked me where I was going, I told them -- stupid ass that I was. I did not know that Marty had not gotten work papers for me or the other people who were performing at his party (although it was a private party, it was still against the law to work in America without the proper work papers).

I should have been able to work in the U.S. by this time. After all, I had married Regina so that I would be eligible for citizenship. Regina had filed my papers before I put her on the plane for America, but I hadn't made any further arrangements to get a green card.

At any rate, there were a number of performers booked for that party, including a singer, a fire dancer and a limbo dancer. I was the star of the show, so I was going to be the last performer that night. Well, I never got to finish my act – in the middle of my performance, the police stormed into the room and arrested all of us, saying that we were breaking the law.

We were all taken to the downtown jail and locked up because we didn't have papers to work in America. I couldn't help but blame myself for that. But, as if being arrested wasn't enough, I was so dumb that I got into an argument with one of the officers. When he told me that I was taking the bread out of an American mouth, I told him that I was doing a favor for a friend and that there was no money involved.

That didn't seem to matter to the officer. He told me that someone else could have done the job and gotten paid. Well, I had to disagree with that.

"Man, there's nobody that can play like me. That's why my friend asked me to do the favor for him," I retorted.

So, talented or not, we all spent the evening in jail before being deported the next day. I went back to Canada with a deportation mark on my passport. That mark wasn't visible to me, but it was to immigration officers, so I was unable to perform in the States, where several gigs had been lined up for me.

I really wanted to play in the U.S. again, so I decided to return to Nassau to get my green card situation straightened out. As fate would have it, my plane had a short layover in New York City. When we touched down, I was one of the first ones off, and I dashed into the terminal. I had left my things to be shipped back to Nassau by air freight after I had settled down, so I didn't have to worry about any belongings -- the only thing on my mind was getting into that terminal to call the friend who had arranged my American gigs. I was desperate to see if there was anything he could do for me.

Chapter 12

Leader of the Band

I had met that friend, Tommy Murray, when I was performing at the Conch Shell Club in Nassau. Tommy, who was then a police detective in New Jersey, had approached me one night and said,

"Your playing is like magic. I can make you the best-known drummer in the world and book you in places you've never even dreamed about. I can get some guys around you in a band that'll be welcome in night spots all over the U.S."

Tommy said that he loved jazz, and, although he had never booked a single music artist into any club, he had major connections. That Tommy was a super salesman -- he was so positive that I said I'd think about his offer. And, before I knew it, I agreed to head up a band that he would build around me.

At that time, however, I had already accepted the Canadian gig, but Tommy was there for me when I called him from the airport in New York. After I explained my problem, Tommy, who had a lot of pull, said,

"Just stay where you are. I'll pick you up at Kennedy Airport and I'll get you straightened out."

It was great to see Tommy again, and I filled him in on all the details -- that Regina and I had been married and that she had already filed papers for me to legally be in the U.S. Once Tommy knew the whole story, he made some calls and found out that all I had to do was to go to the immigration office to fill out some additional papers, since the original paperwork had already been filed.

Of course, I wanted to do everything the legal way, so I stayed with Tommy in New Jersey for a few weeks while things were being straightened out, and then I went back to Nassau to finalize the process. It was great to be home and see my family and friends again, of course, but I couldn't wait to get back to the U.S. -- and my gigs. A month after I arrived in Nassau, the King, now a resident with a green card, returned to New Jersey, where my career took off.

True to his word, Tommy had hooked me up with a band – and not just any band. My band would include some of the best jazz players in America – men who were heroes in my eyes when I was growing up. These men helped me break into my jazz life – they were my ticket to acceptance in jazz clubs.

For starters, there was Specks Williams, one of the greatest organists of all time (Specks got his nickname because of the thick glasses that he wore). Another member of the band, Jimmy McLinton, a big man with red skin, also wore thick glasses, but his bad eyesight didn't stop him from being one of the best guitar players in the business (Jimmy played as well as the great American jazz guitarist Wes Montgomery). And, Tommy also found two extraordinary drummers for me.

The first was Bill Elliott. I met Bill, who was an excellent drummer and singer, and Dionne Warwick for the first time in a club in Newark where Bill was playing (by the way, Bill and Dionne had an on-again, off-again relationship for many years, and I met them just before they got married). That night, Tommy had talked so extravagantly to Bill about my magic with percussion instruments that Bill got to his feet and said,

"If he's so damn good, send him up here!"

Well, I tore the house down with my playing, and I impressed Bill and Dionne so much that Bill joined my band. He played with us for three months, and, after his departure, Rashied Ali, one of the greatest drummers of all time, replaced him. Rashied was probably one of the best known drummers in the world then – he was right up there with Max Roach and Louie Belson.

What a thrill it was to headline my own show with that band! That first year, I was the youngest player to lead his own band, and we played at all the big jazz clubs in America. Most of those clubs were on the "chitlin' circuit," like my gigs with The Deacon had been, but Tommy also got us into some very famous places. We were a hit at the Village Vanguard in New York City, where we also played at Basie's Lounge, and we were booked into Memory Lane in Los Angeles – places where you had to be "somebody" to perform.

We also played gigs in jazz clubs all over Canada, from Montreal to Calgary. The biggest club we played there was the Esquire Showroom in Montreal. That club held about 200 people, so, while it held half as many people as The Conch Shell Club in Nassau, it was twice as big as most of the other jazz clubs where we played.

My first gig with my new band was at the Key Club in Newark. I believe that was the first time since the club opened that so many white people were in the audience. There was barely enough room for the regulars because I was known to whites who had visited Nassau and to fans of *Thunderball*. In fact, I was billed as "That *Thunderball* Drummer" for all my bookings, and you should have seen the people lined up to see me on opening night at the Key Club -- and at clubs where we later played.

The Key Club held only about 100 people, and I kept that place packed from opening to closing time. The bandstand was in the middle of the bar, and there was just enough room to squeeze three or four players in. But that was what most of the clubs on the "chitlin' circuit" were like at the time.

We spent a month in Newark before performing at the Fantasy Lounge in Trenton, New Jersey, for another month. After that, it was on to a club in New Bedford, Massachusetts, for two weeks and then to Harrisburg, Pennsylvania, where we played at the Famous Door for another three weeks.

For our first couple of gigs, I had bought an old green hearse to take us around. Sometimes I would lie down in the back, and when we pulled up to a stoplight, I would raise up very slowly – frightening the people next to us, who thought a dead person had suddenly came back to life.

Not long after we started out, we got a one-week booking in Rochester, New York, at a place called the Playmate Club. Marty Hearst heard about it, so he came down to see me. When he saw my hearse, Marty said,

"No, man. You are a King. You have to do better."

Well, I was doing my best, but I was only just starting, and I had no big-time manager or even a real agent (Tommy booked our gigs, but he didn't know a lot about the music business). During his visit, Marty asked me to perform at another big party he was throwing in Buffalo. I had a couple of days off coming up, so I agreed -- but, although I had played free for Marty the first time, I made sure that I gave him a price for this gig.

Marty was not only willing to pay that fee, but you wouldn't believe the "bonus" that he threw in. I was shocked when I got to his place in Buffalo and Marty presented me with a beautiful white Chevy van! On the side of that van was painted in bold, red letters: "That *Thunderball* Drummer/King Errisson." That van was a beauty, and now our band had two vehicles to get ourselves and our equipment around -- we were really moving up!

While we were at the Playmate Club, I met a young girl who had just finished her nursing studies at a college in New York City. At age 21, she was already a head nurse at Rochester State Hospital, where her mother was the administrator. This girl, although she was not as beautiful as some of the girls I had known, reminded me very much of actress Karen Black (in fact, she was named Karen, too). Although Karen was not gorgeous (she certainly wasn't ugly, either), she had a great body -- and I would also find out that she was a fun person with a wonderful personality.

Anyway, while I was playing, Karen came up to me and said,
"I'm taking you home tonight."
"We'll see about that," I answered.

I was hoping that a fine-looking mulatto girl that I had met on our opening night would show up, but when she didn't, Karen got her way. I took her to my room and we made love all night. She just couldn't get enough – and I had a great time.

The next day, I realized that I had left my stage clothes in my dressing room at the Playmate Club, so I called the mulatto girl to ask her to bring them to me. Well, that woman had other things to do, so I called Karen to see if she could do that favor for me. Although Karen was at work at the time, she jumped at the chance to help me. She must have moved like Wonder Woman, because within 90 minutes she was walking through the door with my things.

I kissed Karen and thanked her and then asked if she wanted to go to my show and have dinner afterwards. Of course, Karen said, so after we got back to the club I found a table for her and she met Marty and Mrs. Hearst. I performed for about an hour and then, leaving the packing to the band, took Karen out to have something to eat. We ended up driving up to Buffalo and staying at one of Marty's rental properties that night – Marty had a lot of rental properties in those days, as well as his home in Buffalo, which was a 6,500 square foot beauty right on Lake Erie, overlooking Niagara Falls and Ontario, Canada.

While Karen and I were in Buffalo, we decided to check out some clubs. Since Karen was from Rochester, she wasn't too familiar with the streets in Buffalo. When she accidentally turned the wrong way down a one-way street, we were pulled over by the police!

The officer was extremely rude to us at first. When he saw that I was black, he ordered me to get out of the car.

"No," I replied (in my thickest Bahamian accent). "For what reason?"

The cop couldn't understand me, of course, so Karen took over.
"What is the problem, Officer?" she asked. "I'm the one who is driving. What did he do wrong?"

Well, when Karen spoke up, that officer recognized her.
"Sorry, Miss Karen. You are going the wrong way on a one-way street," the officer responded (in a much more courteous tone).

"I'm sorry, Officer," Karen replied sweetly. "I'm not too familiar with the streets in Buffalo. And, even if this is a one-way street, it is 2:30

129

a.m. and we are the only car on the road."

The officer then asked about her father – it turned out that Karen's father was a well-respected justice of the peace (that was the first time I had heard about her father and learned what he did for a living)! And, to top it off, that cop had worked for Karen's father before moving to Buffalo.

Things were starting to look better, so I should have left well enough alone, but I didn't.

"Do you still want me to get out of the car?" I asked. "And are you going to give us a ticket? If you aren't, please let us go -- it's very late."

Of course, the officer chose to let us go without writing a ticket, and Karen thanked him.

"No problem. Be sure to say hello to your father for me," replied the officer, who then got back into his cruiser and drove away.

The next day, Karen and I drove back to Rochester so I could finish the band's engagement at the Playmate Club. The club's management wanted to extend the band's gig, but I had my eye on another club, the Johnny Ellicott Grille, in downtown Buffalo. I asked Marty if he had any pull with the club, and, sure enough, Marty secured a booking for us there before the week was out.

In the meantime, a number of black entertainers, including South African-born singer Miriam Makeba, who had a huge hit, "Pata Pata," at the time, Nancy Wilson, Herbie Mann, George Kirby, Slappy White and some other top black entertainers were in Buffalo for a convention at the Shrine Auditorium. Boy, I wasn't going to miss an opportunity like that; that was one gig I was willing to play for free because I wanted to let people know that I would be at the Grille.

Since I wasn't going to get paid for performing for the conventioneers, I wasn't able to pay my band members, and only one of them – Jimmy McLinton – understood what I was doing. Although the rest of the band declined to work for nothing, Jimmy was supportive and encouraging,

"Come on, Kid," he said. "You and I can do this."

When it was my time to perform and I was being called up on stage, Jimmy helped me carry my drums – a large rack of six drums -- to the center of the stage. I hadn't wanted to drag those drums across the stage, so I greatly appreciated Jimmy's help, but I told him,

"Thanks. I can handle the rest by myself. I need to show these people something."

So there I was, all alone on the stage -- just me and my drums -- in front of a sea of people who were probably wondering what they were about to hear. I started with "John Henry," the "steel-driving man" song, and then went into "Who's Gonna Be Your Man?" and then performed "Betty and Dupree," which was a big hit for Harry Belafonte. After that, I treated the crowd to several drum solos.

I got seven standing ovations that night, and people did not want me to leave the stage. Of course, I told them that if they wanted more they could come see me at the Johnny Ellicott Grille. My performance that night made the newspapers the next day; "The Buffalo News" raved about "That *Thunderball* Drummer" doing a solo performance at the Shrine Auditorium and bringing the house down!

As great as that was, I was even more elated that I finally gained the respect of my band members. They realized that I could do it all on my own -- and that I loved playing my congas and singing by myself. Now a cohesive group with a mutual respect for one another, we packed the Johnny Ellicott Grille every night for the next three weeks.

One night when we were playing there, a big black guy and his party came into the club and sat down at the table nearest to the bandstand. Well, the first thing out of the guy's mouth was,

"Play 'Misty.'"

"Sorry, man, I don't know that song," I replied.

Well, the guy would have none of that. He stood up and shouted, "You heard what I said. I said 'Play Misty,' Mother F**ker!"

Now, I am sure the band knew the song – it's just that it's one we never rehearsed. As for me, I knew of the song, but never thought I could sing it until that night. You better believe that I learned "Misty" on the spot -- you should have seen how fast the band and I got into that song!

The guy had obviously had a few drinks before he got to the Grille, so he was satisfied with our hasty (and probably very "off") rendition of the song. Later, when we didn't feel we were in danger of losing life or limb because we hadn't known "Misty," we had a good laugh over the incident.

Since we played in so many places -- and some of them more than once -- it is difficult to remember everything about our travels on the road. But some of my experiences definitely stand out.

One of the places that we played several times was Bertie's Hurricane Club, which was on top of a hill in Pittsburgh. On our first opening night there, I met two of the players for the Pittsburgh Pirates -- Maury Wills and Andre Rogers, the first Bahamian baseball star (Andre had started with the Giants and also played for the Cubs before playing for the Pirates from 1965-1967). In fact, most of Pittsburgh's baseball players and basketball stars met at "Bertie's on the Hill."

It was during one of my gigs there that I got my first offer for a major recording contract, but that came later, so first I'll tell you about my rather unsettling experience at Bertie's. I had been given a dressing room in the basement -- although some of my band members came dressed for the gig, I was a different kind of star…I had to have some place to change my clothes because I would change shirts after every set. I would always come back to the stage in a different shirt and sometimes even change my belt -- my pants didn't matter too much because my rack of drums hid them; besides, my congas were all black, so I always wore black pants so I didn't need to change them.

Well, that may sound like a cushy deal, but I wasn't totally alone in my dressing room -- I shared it with the biggest black rats you have ever seen! Sometimes they would scare the crap out of me. Not only were they big suckers (some of them looked like they could wear my shirts), but they also weren't afraid of anything. They would stand up on the beams, sharpening their teeth as they watched me getting ready. It gave me the feeling that they were getting their knives and forks ready for a King Errisson snack!

After my first gig at Bertie's, it was back to the Key Club in Newark and then on to the Famous Door in Harrisburg, Pennsylvania. On my opening night at the Famous Door, I met a true African for the first time. The man, who was about 102 years old, was visiting his family in Pennsylvania, and he had read about my gig in the papers.

He was from the Zulu land, and was about 6'6" or 7" (he towered over his 47-year-old grandson, who had brought him down to see me at the African's request). The African man had seen me in *Thunderball*, and he said he thought I was the best drummer that he had ever heard.

"It would take many drummers to play the way that you play alone," he said.

I thanked him, of course, and then played "John Henry" for him. The man and his grandson stayed for two sets. That was unusual, because while a few people stayed for two sets, most of our audience would see one set and then leave. Actually, we liked it that way because there was always another crowd waiting to come in.

Since the clubs we played in were not that big, we knew we were cooking if we could fill them three or more times a night. I was able to do that more than any other artist that many of the clubs booked, which is why the club owners or managers would book us three or four times a year.

While I was in Harrisburg, I almost became a pimp! I met a

beautiful, half-Caucasian woman named Patsy, who told me that she wanted to take care of me – she said that she would come home to me every night and that the money she would make each night would be for me.

Of course, I had to ask the woman why she would want to do something like that, and she replied that she had fallen in love with me from the first time she saw me. I told her that I would have to think about her offer because I had to travel a lot, but she didn't seem to care about that -- she even said she would travel with me!

After my show that night, Patsy took me to her apartment, which was in the same hotel where the band and I had rooms. When I walked in, she pulled me into her bedroom and started ripping off my clothes! I didn't try to stop her, so after she got me naked she ripped off her dress and dropped to her knees.

I don't think that I have to tell you what happened next, but that woman got me so hot that I pushed her to the floor and began making love to her. Man, I had that woman screaming, and I ended up spending the entire night with her.

Call me naïve, but, even though Patsy had said she would bring her money to me when she came home at the end of the night, I still didn't really know what she did for a living! I couldn't believe it when she told me that she was a hooker!

"Why?" I asked. "Why would anyone as beautiful as you do that?"

Patsy had a very long story to tell about that. Her mother had been a poor black woman with half a dozen kids. Patsy was the oldest, and when she was 16, her mother sold her to the insurance salesman, who was a white man. Patsy had to go to live with him, but, although she said that he treated her kindly, she was with him against her will.

Patsy eventually had a couple of kids, but when they got older, she left them with the maid -- never to return. That is when she turned to hustling. It was a sad story, but it got worse when Patsy told me about what she did on her job.

She told me that she didn't really like men, especially her customers, who were always white men, so she never let them screw her…or even kiss her. Instead, she would give them oral sex or just a hand job. And some of those white men would have an orgasm so fast that she would get semen in her mouth. When that happened, she would get up and go to the bathroom to rinse her mouth out and then go on to the next trick.

That is another reason that she didn't want to have sex with these guys -- she said it was nasty and it would take her too long to clean up afterwards. By setting the boundaries she had set, all Patsy had to do was brush her teeth and rinse with Listerine before moving on to another guy. Because she had more time to do more tricks, Patsy told me that she could make as much as one or even two thousand dollars in one night.

Patsy also told me that I was the first man that she had made love to in many years, and, even though she said she wanted me to pull her out of that lifestyle, she said she would take care of me until I had made it. And, she promised she would do anything for me during the three weeks I played at the Famous Door.

Because I was beginning to like Patsy, our relationship wasn't always easy for me. I remember one night, while I was on stage, that a group of guys approached her and Patsy got up to go with them, waving good-bye to me as she left. Boy, she looked so beautiful that I found myself getting jealous.

I guess that Patsy only had to go a short distance, because she was back by the time I finished playing that night and we went for a walk. I felt like eating some soul food, and Patsy knew just the place -- we went to a little joint where we had fried chicken and chitlins and then headed back to my place.

The moment we walked into the room, Patsy emptied her purse on the bed -- and I couldn't believe my eyes. There had to be at least $1,500 in that pile of money!

"It's all yours, honey," she said.

"Why?" I asked, my mouth still hanging open from surprise. That woman had made more money in a single night than our band made in an entire week!

"Because I work for you. Everything I make is yours."

"But what did you make for yourself?"

Patsy replied that she had lots more money, so that money was mine; she must give me whatever I wanted. Wow, was that a turn-on. I took the money and made love to her like a mad dog.

Afterwards, Patsy asked me to come to her apartment, so I got up and walked over there with her. When she brought me into her bedroom, there were two long black leather coats, pants, shirts, shoes -- all the kinds of clothes that a well-dressed pimp would wear -- waiting for me. And, as if that wasn't enough, she also pulled a bundle of cash out of a bureau drawer!

My mouth dropped open again as Patsy said,

"Here, this is for you. And whatever else you need, you just let your momma know."

I took the coats and some shirts, but I didn't take any more money, even though Patsy insisted. I am willing to bet that Patsy had already given me more money than I had made for myself during my entire gig in Harrisburg.

I was sure tempted to have Patsy take care of me, and maybe I would have gone along with it -- but Jimmy McLinton talked me out of it. Jimmy was concerned about my falling for both Patsy and her lifestyle. I wasn't falling in love with Patsy, although I was becoming quite fond of her; my heart belonged to JMC, and after all these years (no matter where I was), I always dreamt that I would meet up with her again.

But Jimmy argued that Patsy was older than I was (even though she looked young) -- and he knew that I would be a superstar one day. Jimmy was afraid that when that happened, I would no longer want Patsy -- but she would show up without warning and embarrass me. It took Jimmy almost a week to convince me to give back the clothes, but I wasn't about to give back the money. That money helped me to pay the band all that I had made for our engagement at the Famous Door and still have something left for myself (I always paid most of the money that we made to the band -- and I don't think we ever made more than $2,000 a week during the entire time we played together).

Once I had made up my mind to leave Patsy behind, though, I found myself praying for our three weeks at the Famous Door to be over - and I hoped that they wouldn't ask us to extend our engagement. Fortunately, that didn't happen, and I waited until the day after we closed to talk to Patsy about our future together.

On the morning we left, I told her to keep the jackets for me until we returned. Of course, that sounded like a reasonable request because we did play the same place a couple or three times a year, so it was very likely that we would come back to Harrisburg. But then Patsy asked where we were playing our next gig. I didn't answer her directly -- I simply answered that we were going to be touring for a long time (and I didn't mention anything about her coming along with us). Patsy didn't ask to come along, but I didn't forget her -- I kept in touch with her for a long time, and I sometimes wonder what direction my career might have taken if I had accepted Patsy's offer and became a pimp.

Chapter 13

Becoming "Mr. Bermuda" -- and Losing My Shirt

After we left Harrisburg and got to the club in downtown Newark, New Jersey, where we were supposed to play, they were not ready for us. But this job (as well as my other jobs) was through the Musicians' Union, which was the second most powerful union in the U.S. at that time. When you worked through the union, you got paid through them as long as you just showed up -- or the union would put a lock on the club's door.

Although the owners of the club, which was called Mr. Wonderful, hustled to get the club open, it wasn't ready by the time we were due to play our next gig. It's too bad that we didn't get to play in that beautiful club (I sure would have loved to), but all my gigs were booked in advance, so I had to stick to our schedule.

Our next booking was at a club in Rochester, New York. I had taken this job on a moment's notice, so I didn't realize that the gig was in a Spanish club -- and that the management there thought that I spoke Spanish and that my band was a Latin group. I knew that I was in trouble when I pulled up in front of the club (where we were supposed to play for three weeks) and saw the marquee. It said, in big, bold letters:

"KING ERRICANO"

My fears were realized on the first night -- when only six people came in. And those six people wanted me to sing Spanish songs! When they realized that I couldn't, they left...and the same thing happened the next night.

On the third night, the club owner fired me -- saying that he did not know what kind of singer I was. He was expecting a Latin group, of course.

I told him that I did not care -- he was the one who was supposed to check that out before he booked me and my group -- and he owed me for the entire three weeks. When the club owner tried to wiggle out of that, I called the union and they came down and put a padlock on the club door.

Within five days, the club owner paid the union and they, in turn, paid me. And I never made that mistake again -- I made sure that the club owners or managers knew who I was and what type of group I had before they booked us.

By now, I was getting tired of the same routine. Besides, on the way home from Montreal, Canada, we ran off the road and I woke up at the bottom of a snowy ravine -- with all the instruments, including an organ, piled on top of me! That's when I made up my mind to quit -- the money that we were making was not enough for me to be risking my life.

But I couldn't quit right then -- we had too many commitments. One of them was back at Bertie's Hurricane Club in Pittsburgh, and you wouldn't believe what happened there. Because we had played at the club several times in the past, my jaw dropped when we drove up to the front of the club and I saw what was on the marquee:

"JOHN ERRISSON

Opening Tonight!"

You had better believe that I made them correct that marquee -- otherwise, we weren't going to be unloading our van. Ironically, that screw up marked the last time that I played at the Bertie's.

After our gig at Bertie's, we were scheduled to perform in 20 more jazz clubs around the U.S., but before we did those gigs, we had a gig at a tourist trap called The 40 Thieves in Hamilton, Bermuda. The 40 Thieves Club was the biggest club in Bermuda, and we had a wonderful two-week gig there. But, unfortunately, my personal life wasn't going that great.

When I was in Bermuda for those two weeks, I sometimes felt like "the spook that sat by the door." There was no shortage of beautiful white women who didn't mind sharing an evening -- and my bed -- with me, but it was a different story if I ran across them during the daytime. If I saw them on the beach or walking along Main Street, those women just turned their backs and wouldn't even acknowledge that I was there -- much less speak to me! So much for my thoughts that racism was a thing of the past (but, of course, this was still the 1960s).

When I returned to the U.S. to finish our gigs there, I started dating Karen again -- this time on a full-time basis. Every weekend when I was not working, I would fly to Rochester or Karen would drive her MGB to meet me wherever I was playing. We had a lot of fun as lovers, even when my travels took me out of the country.

Six months after leaving the island, I was back in Bermuda on an extended contract -- but without my band. Terry Brannan, the owner of The 40 Thieves Club, wanted to book only me -- he did not want to pay my band, since he had a house band that could back me. When I told Terry that I had to have at least my guitar player, Jimmy McLinton, he agreed and we sealed the deal.

When I played in Bermuda this time, the great Redd Foxx was the star of the show at The 40 Thieves Club. But, as fate would have it, I went on first. After they saw my show, people would leave -- the white tourists had come to Bermuda for island music, and I was able to give them just that; I could play calypso, reggae, jazz -- whatever they wanted.

After Redd talked to an empty house for three days, I asked Redd if he would mind if I closed the show. Redd, who did not like telling his jokes to an empty house, readily agreed, and we switched places.

Although that was the first time I had met Redd, he and I became the best of friends, and he began calling me "Mr. Bermuda." When his two-week gig was over and it was time for him to go back to the States, Redd offered me a job at his club in L.A. He said he could not pay me much but he would see that I got going because I was the greatest he had ever seen. He handed his card to me and insisted that I look him up whenever I got to Los Angeles.

I knew it would be some time before I would make it to L.A. -- I still had the rest of the year to go on my contract. I sure missed Redd, especially when the act that followed him was Rich Little. Well, the same thing happened to Rich that had happened to Redd -- both the tourists and islanders alike would catch my show and then leave. Like Redd, Rich didn't understand that the islanders were not much for comedians, and the white folks could see comedians on TV so they wanted an island experience and wouldn't sit through a comedy routine.

Rich's manager at the time, Gilbert "Gib" Kerr, was a very nice man, and he wanted to manage me (I guess he saw himself making money with me). But Rich would have no part of that. I think that Rich hated me for being good, because he told his manager that he would leave him if he took me on -- and this is after I ended up saving his ass like I did for Redd!

I should tell you that while I was in Bermuda Diana Ross and the Supremes were playing at a little club down the street from me. Unfortunately, I didn't get to see them because they were just there for a weekend and their show was over before mine was, but I would later have the privilege of meeting and performing with Diana, who is one of the most talented ladies in the business.

While I was living in Hamilton, Karen came over a couple of times, but after she would leave I would hook up with a girl named Gloria, who was from Bermuda. That Gloria was one beautiful girl -- she had very sharp features and beautiful teeth. I had a wonderful time with Gloria, except for one very painful incident.

You know, some people don't realize that black people can get a sunburn. In fact, I wasn't aware of the danger myself until the day that

Gloria and I swam across the sea to a small island. We made love, and it was such a workout that I fell asleep on top of her.

I was asleep long enough to get burned so badly that I could hardly put on a shirt (and I would pee like a snake for more than a week). Worst of all, the tide had gotten higher while we were on the island, so we had to swim even harder to get back to the beach where we started from -- and that salt water was kicking my ass all the way. By the way, Gloria only got a slight burn on her arms because I had sheltered her from the sun, but I will never forget that pain.

When my contract was up in Bermuda, I returned to New Jersey, where Tom Murray had booked me at the Fantasy Lounge in Trenton. I was back to the same old hassle, but this time I had over $70,000 on me - and I was looking for a new opportunity.

Opportunity soon came knocking. One night, a young man named Raymond "Ray" Taylor, who had just returned from serving in Vietnam, came into the club. After my show, he told me that he was a songwriter, and he would like to write some songs for me -- and that he and I should start our own record label. Although I had quite a lot of money and could afford to invest in such a venture, I told Ray that I would think about the idea for a couple of weeks.

True to his word, Ray brought some songs so I could give a listen. I did very little writing myself in those days, but I liked a few of Ray's songs, so we began our partnership. Because I was having such great success in the clubs, both of us believed that there would be a ready market for my music, so I put $55,000 into our company (Ray was the president and I was the vice president).

Not everyone was as confident as we were about our chances of making it in the music business. In fact, one of the old guys at a record-pressing plant told us that he had seen people lose their shirts trying to start their own label. But Ray believed in me and my talent so much that he had a comeback -- Berry Gordy of Motown had made it on his own, so why couldn't we? What Ray didn't think about was that Berry Gordy had an army of talented songwriters, but we kept the faith, naming our new label TrentTown (a nod to the city of Trenton, where we had met).

We finally recorded three songs -- "Champagne Cherie," "Don't Forget Your Auntie Levy" and "Get Me Car Started, Joe" -- in the same studio in New Jersey where I had recorded the *Brown Sugar* album with legendary jazz organist Freddie Roach. That had been my first studio session in America, but it certainly wouldn't be the last.

Ray and I decided on "Champagne Cherie" as our first single, and we put an instrumental on the B-side. Then the hard work began -- we went around to local radio stations and record stores, hoping to get some air play and make some sales. We were able to get some of the record stores to take a couple of singles on consignment, but we spent most of our time traveling the east coast, promoting the record to disc jockeys at local radio stations.

In those days, disc jockeys did not have their hands tied like they do today -- they had the freedom to use their discretion regarding the music they played, rather than having to stick to a format decided upon by the station manager or program director. So Ray and I were hoping that a major label, such as Motown, Columbia, Gateway or Mercury, would hear my music and offer a lucrative recording contract to us.

In Philadelphia, we met with the disc jockey of a white radio station. We had a good meeting with him -- and he even played the record on the air in front of us to see if it would fit his format.

As we were driving to another meeting, we switched on the station to hear the disc jockey that we had just left -- and, by damn, you would think we had paid him or something. We couldn't believe what we heard,

"Now, here is a new one from TrentTown Records -- and this young Bahamian is going to go places. Here's King Errisson with 'Champagne Cherie.'"

"See," Ray said excitedly. "I told you that you could sing. That guy thinks you sing like Frank Sinatra!"

It's funny, but I had never thought of myself as a singer -- I saw myself as a storyteller. But I must admit that the record sounded good -- it's amazing what you can do in a studio.

Flushed with our first taste of success, we drove to Detroit to visit Motown Records. The people there were not crazy about the record, but they told us that they would get back to us after they had listened some more. Little did I know that I was about to learn my biggest lesson in my career -- don't ever take your music to others and leave it with them.

Although Motown turned us down, by the next year, someone in the company had re-written our song -- changing the title from "Champagne Cherie" to "Mi Cherie Amor." And the rest, as they say, is history.

I'm not saying that Motown stole our song, but someone there sure wrote one just like it. Ray was really ticked off, but there was nothing we could do. Anyway, we had already approached another record company, Gateway Records, in Pittsburgh.

The company thought that the record was good -- and they offered us $35,000 for the one single and a contract for four years (with renewal options). I couldn't believe it when Ray said that was not enough, but he sure felt big as we drove to the next company.

"I told you we have a hit, so we can't take the first thing that comes along," Ray explained.

Our next stop was New York City, where we went to Columbia Records. The A&R (Artists and Repertoire) man there said that he liked the record -- it was good -- but he felt I needed more vocal training. He was willing to give us $50,000 and a five-year contract, provided I would take vocal lessons (which Columbia would pay for) for one year! He also said he would put us on salary for the length of the contract, because he felt that my voice would be in shape within a year.

I must admit that I agreed with the guy (I had no problem with taking singing lessons) -- so I fought with Ray for months because he didn't want to take the deal. I don't know what he expected us to get eventually, since he wouldn't go for this incredible offer!

To make matters worse, the rack jobbers who supplied our single to record stores wanted Ray to give them the record and let them run for us. But the rack jobbers wanted too big a piece of the pie, so, once again, Ray refused to make a deal.

The next week, all the little "mom and pop" stores pulled our record out of their bins because the rack jobbers told them to do so! Not only that, but the rack jobbers also had the power to pull the record from all the jukeboxes in clubs, as well!

Needless to say, I was getting more and more disgusted -- Ray was so hard-headed that we were losing all our (meaning MY) money. And I was getting tired of having to go along with his "say so" because he was the senior partner. It didn't take much for me to see myself headed to California to become an actor (remember, I already had a few bit parts in Japanese movies under my belt and I had taken drama lessons for a year in Canada, so I thought I was ready)!

But now I was broke, so I went back to the Fantasy Lounge for a week to make a couple of bucks. Fortunately, I was able to work in any of the clubs where I had worked before at a moment's notice, so Tommy had already booked me in Atlantic City after my gig at the Fantasy Lounge.

My closing night at the Fantasy Lounge, which happened to fall on my birthday, was a memorable one -- and not in a good way. Candy, the owner of the club, who was a beautiful, small black lady, was in love with my drummer, Rashied Ali, even though she was married to a big black man who was a judge. When Rashied wasn't able to make it that night, Candy thought that I fired him -- so she and her sister-in-law plotted to beat me up!

Since Candy's sister-in-law was the judge's sister, I made a big mistake that night when I got into a fight with her -- even though I acted in self-defense. The crap really hit the fan when I walked off the bandstand and put my foot up on a chair to pull up my socks (I was wearing some socks that had clearly seen their day, so after a set of drumming, singing and dancing, they were falling down).

As I was pulling those socks back up, the sister, who was as big, black and ugly as the judge, came over and pushed me down, screaming,

"Get your f**king foot off that chair!"

I got up off the floor and screamed back,

"What the f**k is wrong with you?"

Well, this woman started going on about my firing Rashied (which, of course, I had not done in the first place), so I answered,

"This is my group. If you want Rashied, then you should put your own group together."

Luckily, a friend of mine, a young white fellow by the name of Larry, had come to the show that night (Ray was there, too). As I turned my back and began walking away from that crazy woman, Larry shouted,

"Watch out, King!"

When I turned around to see why Larry had warned me, the judge's sister was coming toward me with a big metal tray. In fact, she was coming at me so fast that I all I had time to do was pick up a bar stool and whack her with it, knocking her down.

Well, someone called the police, and in no time two big, fat white cops were there. They picked me up like I was a sack of potatoes and tossed me into their van -- it was called a "meat wagon" in New Jersey -- and carted me off to jail.

That ride to the jail was very frightening. There were four other big black guys in the "meat wagon" already, and one of them was holding a piece of his ear in his hand! It turned out that he had gotten into a fight with the guy sitting next to him and the other guy had bitten part of his ear off!

As if that wasn't enough, another guy had just killed his girlfriend, so I was happy to hear that the fourth guy was just a thief. These were tough guys -- and not in a good way. And things didn't get much better after we finally got to the station, where I was booked and locked up.

There wasn't anything that anyone could do to help me at that hour, so I spent the rest of the night of my birthday in a holding cell with at least 15 other prisoners. Those guys were pissing and crapping in front of me all night, so I was thankful to be out of that hell the next morning -- even though I started the day off in court.

When my case was called, the judge asked how I would plea, and I answered, in my heavy Bahamian accent,

"Not guilty."

I then began telling the story of what had happened -- I told the judge that I was only defending myself when I held up the bar stool in front of my face to stop the woman from hitting me. I tried to make light of the situation by telling the judge that she came at me so fast that if she were in the jungle the breeze from her behind would blow the coconuts off the trees.

Well, the judge burst out laughing -- in fact, the entire courtroom was convulsed with laughter before the judge tried to restore order.

"Stop that laughter," he bellowed, before turning to me with as stern a warning as he could muster,

"Young man, this is not a comedy show, so let's stick to the facts."

Although he tried to hide it, it was all the judge could do to stop from smiling, but he was all business when he spoke to Candy. In fact, he told her he would shut down her club the next time he heard any complaints about it! He was tired of all the trouble the club was causing.

He then told me that I was free to go -- but to stay out of trouble. Believe me, I vowed to myself that I would never get into trouble again.

I finally arrived in Atlantic City, where I played at a place called the Wonder Garden. It was a very big club, and it was there that I met Kim Weston, who was one of the greatest singers I had ever heard.

Kim, who had signed with Motown in 1963, had hits for the label with "Take Me in Your Arms (Rock Me a Little While)" and "Helpless," but she became best known for "It Takes Two," her 1966 duet with Marvin Gaye. In 1967, Kim and her husband, William "Mickey" Stevenson, who was the former head of A&R for Motown (Mickey had also written and produced many of the labels big hits), left Motown to join MGM Records (Kim would later sue Motown over royalties).

Besides being a great singer, Kim was beautiful -- she was dark and smooth and had a Coca Cola shape. She was also tall, much taller than Mickey, in fact. But, speaking of tall, I had never seen a woman as tall as the one I met at the Wonder Garden.

This woman worked the door at the club in the evening, and I was mad for her. She never knew that, though, because I was afraid to approach her. When I had to pass this woman, I felt as if I were staring at her navel! She had to have been over seven feet tall, but she moved like a gazelle and was pretty as a picture.

Sometimes, I would hear some of the guys who were short (like I was) call her funny names, like "freak of nature." But I never thought she was a freak -- she was a thing of beauty. Every time I saw her, she took my breath away.

While I was at the Wonder Garden I had the chance to cross paths again with Sammy Davis, Jr. He and Lionel Hampton were playing at Club Harlem, which was right across the street, so I got to see both of them briefly.

After my gig at the Wonder Garden, I flew to Rochester to see Karen. She and I had talked just hours before I made that flight, and we had made plans for Karen to pick me up at the airport and go back to her house. When I got off the plane, however, I waited at the airport for an hour and a half. When I called her house several times, no one answered so I finally took a cab over to her house – only to find her drunk and spread out on the front room floor. I knew right then and there that we wouldn't make it together.

Karen was a hard drinker for a young girl, but so were her oldest sister and her brother. That was surprising to me because Karen came from such a distinguished family. Although her family was well-to-do, they were also racists. In fact, when she told her dad about me, she told him I was a Bahamian, thinking that would change his mind about her going out with me. Well, her dad told her that if I was black, I could never come to his house – Bahamian or not, I was still a nigger.

It was snowing cats and dogs, so I caught a cab from Karen's house and stayed in Rochester overnight. The next day, I left for New Jersey, where I spent a week in Newark getting my affairs in order in preparation for my trip west. I was finished with touring and the record scene -- I told Ray, my partner in the record business, that I was going to leave him because he was blowing too many deals, and I told Tommy that I was tired of doing my show. I gave the hearse to Jimmy McLinton, my guitar player, and the van to Tommy, and got ready to pursue my real dream -- becoming an actor.

At this time, I had very little money left -- at least none to talk about. In fact, after I packed up my drums, I had to send them by air freight because I couldn't afford to pay the overweight charges on them. Because I had so little money in my checkbook, I purchased a one-way ticket to Hollywood.

Chapter 14

L.A. Bound and Rebound

Despite being almost broke when I boarded the plane for L.A., I was one happy and confident guy. Not only had I wowed audiences all over the country with my playing, but I had also won the respect of many of the greats in music. I felt as if I could do anything because of the kind of exposure I had gotten -- and because of my friendships with some of the greatest jazz players in the world, including legendary alto saxophonist Julian "Cannonball" Adderley and his brother, Nat, as well as Joe Sample, Freddie Roach, and many others.

I met Cannonball, who would become my mentor, in 1967 at Bertie's Hurricane Club in Pittsburgh, where I was performing with six congas in a row (lined up like a piano) as well as playing a high hat cymbal with my left foot. Cannonball, a giant of a man, was in the audience one night, and, even though he was dressed in a dark blue suit that evening, he looked like a NFL linebacker as he came toward the bandstand to talk to me.

"Where did you learn to play like that? Six congas in a row! Man, you're giving yourself a hell of a workout every time you perform. Only a fool would work that hard – but you do know how to play them congas. And don't let anyone tell you different."

That exchange was the start of a long and lasting friendship. Cannonball was as intelligent as he was talented, and it was because of his remarkable insight that I would later recognize and be able to express how I felt about my music.

Miles Davis, who was as famous on the trumpet as Cannonball was on the sax, was another good friend. In fact, Miles was and still is one of the most talked about musicians in the world today. He and I used to have "lying contests" about which one of us was the most handsome (I always won hands down, of course).

Another great friend was George Benson. We often played at clubs around the corner from each other, and George and I would get together whenever we could to fill each other in on what was happening in our lives and catch up on trade gossip. My life and my career were richer because of my relationships with these wonderful, talented men who took the time to befriend me and offer invaluable advice on performing. I thank God for that because we didn't make much money back then.

Although I treasure the memories of the wonderful times I had in the company of these true music legends, I regret that my brother, Rodney, who was a wonderful saxophone player, wasn't there to share all the special moments with me. Rodney had decided he wanted to play the sax when he was a young boy, so I had bought a used one for him from a guy named Samson, who was from Jamaica. Samson taught Rodney to play, and my brother got so good that he put a little band together, and he, too, was successful in the nightclubs around Nassau at an early age.

When Rodney was only 18, he met a young girl named Joanne, who was 16 at the time. The two of them fell madly in love, although Rodney didn't know at the time that this girl was my daddy's first cousin's daughter. Rodney wanted to marry Joanne, but her love came with an ultimatum: it was either her or his music. If he wanted to marry her, Rodney would have to stop playing.

I didn't know quite what to think about that. After all, Joanne had met Rodney because he was playing the sax -- and then she asks him to give up what had attracted her to him! Even though I thought Rodney would be stupid to give up his playing, love did, indeed, win out over music, and some things do work out. Rodney and Joanne have been married about 50 years now, and they have ten children, many grandchildren and even some great-grandkids. Rodney runs my sister Maddie's business in Nassau, so he is successful as well as happy, but I can't help wondering how things would have turned out if he had joined my band and continued his career in music.

There was also another reason that I felt I could do just about anything. One night when I was playing at the Johnny Ellicott Grille in Buffalo, an old white waitress approached me and asked me if I knew I was a god. I was a little surprised by her words, but the request that followed was really a shocker,

"I have a grandson who is going blind -- in fact he is just about blind. He's nine years old. I have been watching you play. When you play, there are angels around you, and when you play, you're no longer here – I see you lifted from the stage and you go away. Only a man of God or a man with the blessings of God could do that. Would you pray for my grandson?"

Now there were times when I did feel like I was out of my skin -- and I had been told that many times by some of the old folks when I was growing up in Nassau. I was so engrossed with what I was doing that I seemed to become one with my drums and couldn't focus on anything else. But, up until now, I hadn't paid a lot of attention to that feeling. Over the years, however, I would learn that music is the greatest healing power – especially the drums, the first sounds of music (and the greatest of sounds).

This woman was so convinced that God would heal her grandson through me and my prayers that I couldn't help but agree to pray as she had asked. I'd never seen this kid, but I prayed for that boy every night for the next seven days that I played in that club. Every time I touched my drums, I prayed,

"Lord, let this kid see again."

I'll never forget what happened. On the second week, the woman walked into the club, crying tears of joy. She ran up to the bandstand, held out her hands to me (even though I was singing at the time), hugged me, and exclaimed,

"King, you did it! He can see again! It's a miracle -- and you are responsible for it."

I guess I shouldn't have been surprised – one night, just before the waitress shared the good news, I had a vision that the kid came to me and thanked me. I know that only God does those things – but for the rest of my stay at the club, that woman treated me like I was a god or some kind of high priest. Sometimes, it got to be too much, so I was very happy when that engagement ended. I heard from that old woman only once after that -- it was a few months later, and the boy still had his sight.

So when I boarded the plane for L.A., I was confident that doors would open for me in Hollywood. I was ready to take Hollywood by storm, and I looked the part – I had a bald head, and I was wearing a black mohair suit that had been custom made for me in Tokyo. I looked pretty sharp in that suit, if I do say so myself.

Although I was nearly penniless, I knew I was good – I just needed a chance to show my talent and I would make it. I had always believed in myself, but I can't believe I was so naïve. I would find out the hard way that you need more than talent to break into the music and acting scene in L.A. And it didn't take long for me to get my first lesson about the coldness that I would face there.

My seatmate on the flight was a beautiful black lady who had broken the ice as soon as we could see the lights of the city. I had never seen so many lights – so many that it frightened me. As the flight neared L.A., I started to cry to myself. For the first time, my confidence was shaken. I wondered if Redd had really meant what he said to me about working for him at his club.

"Where are you staying?" my seatmate asked.

"I really don't know. You see, I have never been here before."

"I wish you a lot of luck – L.A. is a big place."

Now, in the Bahamas, if someone asks where someone is staying and gets the same answer that I gave, a Bahamian would say, "O.K., you stay with me until you figure it out." But I guess that's only island people -- this woman just shook my hand and again said, "I wish you a lot of luck" as she left the plane.

It was 10:00 at night when I arrived in L.A. I walked over to a dilapidated yellow taxi and told the driver, an old white guy,

"Take me to the cheapest hotel you can find, man."

The cab driver took one look at me and asked,

"Why cheap, man? The way you look, you don't need no cheap hotel."

I shook my head and replied, "Man, just take me to the cheapest one you know."

"You sure?"

"Yes, sir," I replied emphatically.

To show you how embarrassed I was, when that old cabbie asked me how a sharp-looking dresser like me didn't have any money, I told him that I was a singer and an actor and that I had lost everything in a deal gone bad. I wish I could say that was the last time that I had to make excuses during my time in L.A., but, unfortunately, things would get even worse before they got better.

My downward slide began when the cabbie took me to a place called the Hotel Californian on the corner of 6th Street and Bonnie Brae. The hotel, which has also been called the Californian Hotel over the years, was originally opened as a luxury property in April of 1925. Built across the street from Westlake Park (now MacArthur Park), it had boasted a huge neon sign to distinguish it from the other upscale hotels in the area. Well, that neon sign was long gone before I got there – that night, my only clue to where I would be staying was the hotel's name carved into a stone on the wall.

And that was not the only thing that had changed. The once elegant hotels in the area were now run-down rooming houses occupied mostly by alcoholics, drug addicts, and struggling musicians and actors trying to find their big break (many of them would, indeed, go on to find success). And the famous MacArthur Park was now a hangout for drunks, drug addicts, and the homeless.

Since I checked in at night, I really didn't get a good look at the hotel or where it was located. But there was no mistaking the smell of stale alcohol, sweat, and urine that drifted from the park -- and into the hotel. The King was about to become a resident of Skid Row!

Coming from Nassau, where I almost always had a great life, I had never seen or even heard of a place like Skid Row, but all that mattered to me at the time was that the price was right -- my room, which was on the fourth floor of the five-story building, was only a dollar a night. Sadly, it wasn't long before I couldn't afford to pay even that small amount, and I started stealing food from food stands and liquor stores.

When I got 30 days behind on my rent, the manager put a plug in my door so I wouldn't be able to get back into the room. I was smart enough to go outside and jump up to pull down the steel ladder of the fire escape stairs, but there were times when I couldn't get in – I guess management had checked the room and locked the window that I had left open – so I slept on a cardboard box that I spread over the garbage.

They wouldn't let me sleep in the lobby, which was just as well – the garbage smelled better than that lobby! The lobby not only reeked of urine, but it also smelled like an open grave. It was always full of old, half-dead white people, so it wasn't a stretch to believe the rumor that the government sent old people and convicts to these dumps because it was cheaper for them to do that than to take care of them properly. During the time I was there, I saw only about a half a dozen blacks come and go, and they seemed to be in charge of the old white people.

On Christmas Day, I was standing on the outside of the hotel in the rain. It was a freezing cold rain, and the clothes that I was wearing weren't very warm, so I ran back into the hotel and took the elevator up to the fourth floor, where, of course, I saw the pin on the door. I went back down and asked the desk clerk what I had to do to get back inside, and he told me that I had to come up with six dollars.

I finally swallowed my pride and made a call to a girl named Pepper, who was the mother of my son, Vance (Vans), in Nassau. Pepper was one of the women I had left behind in Nassau, so I guess she had not forgiven me for deserting her. When I told her about my financial problem, Pepper replied that it was my f**king business; she said that I had gotten myself into that mess and now I should get myself out of it. Needless to say, I didn't talk to Pepper again for several years after we had that conversation.

I could have called my mother, but I didn't want her to know that I was on Skid Row – that would have killed her because I had always done so well and she was proud of me. Instead, I decided to call a couple of friends in Toronto, Canada, even though I didn't really want to tell them about my sorry condition.

First, I tried to call a friend named Gail. When I couldn't reach her, I called another friend, Beatrice, who was a president at Kodak Film at the time. I liked Beatrice a lot, but when I was 25, she was 60, so there was never going to be a love affair between us. Beatrice had gotten angry with me for leaving her for a younger woman, but she said she would send money right away. Since Beatrice had been so rude on the phone, I didn't expect anything, so I called another friend, who was also named Beatrice (I called her Bea).

I had met Bea, who owned a beauty parlor in Toronto, when she was dating a friend of mine, Richie Delamore (Richie was a famous Bahamian singer). Bea, who was a sweet woman, said, "No problem," and she was true to her word. In a matter of hours, there was $500 waiting for me at the Western Union office. And, shortly after that, another $500 arrived from Beatrice! I finally felt like the King again – I had a thousand dollars, so I caught up on my rent (and paid a few months' rent in advance) and paid off a pawn shop to get my Pentax camera and my tape recorder out of hock.

After taking care of the hotel and the pawn shop, I put aside some cash for a "rainy day," and I frequently traveled to Pico Boulevard, where many record distributors were located, trying to promote my single, "Champagne Cherie." I got lots of promises – and even some radio air play – but it was tough going. I guess it's the same everywhere – it's not what you know, but who you know, and I quickly learned that you had to know someone to get anywhere in L.A.

After having so many doors slammed in my face, I decided that maybe it would help if I got an agent. I put a resume together, and I also had clips from *Thunderball*, copies of *Drums of Nassau*, which had been a best-selling album in the Bahamas, and reviews from some of the plays I had done. I was ready to get an agent, but I wasn't going to settle for just any agent. I wanted to go with the big guys, so I called the William Morris Agency and was able to get an appointment with them.

What an experience that turned out to be! My appointment was for 2:00 p.m., so I decided to walk to the agency and then take the bus home to save some money. I started walking at about 8:00 in the morning and by the time I finished my nearly six-hour walk to Wilshire Boulevard my feet were hurting so bad that it felt like someone had beaten the bottoms of them.

I made it with 15 minutes to spare, and I was glad to have a few minutes to sit down to rest. I waited until the 2:00 appointment time, and then approached the secretary, who made a call to the agent. He was just in the next room, and I could clearly hear him say,

"Tell him I'm not in yet."

That really upset me, so I said to the girl,

"If he didn't want to see me, he should not have made the appointment."

Then I walked past her and kicked the door open. The agent, a big, fat, Jewish man, was sitting at his desk, and I practically bellowed at him,

"I have been walking for six hours to get here, and you say you're not in? You ARE Mr. Goldberg, aren't you?"

I'm sure my entrance surprised and unnerved him, but he managed to calmly say, "Yes, I am."

I threw my resume on his desk, and said, "Take a look," confident that he would be impressed. After all, I had toured with Sweet Richard, the Deacon, and my own jazz band, made a hit record album, and appeared in a blockbuster film.

After Goldberg looked it over, he surprised me by saying,

"You don't have a lot. What have you done here in L.A.?"

"Nothing," I admitted, wishing I had played at Redd's club before I wasted my time with this prick. "That is why I came to L.A. – to do something."

He handed my resume back to me and said,

"Come back when you have done something here in Hollywood."

What a rude son of a bitch! And I'm sure you can imagine how much I wanted to knock that chip off his shoulder.

"Man, when I have done something here, I will not need you," I defiantly answered.

I stormed out the door, vowing that I would never cross paths with that jerk again, but we would, indeed, come face to face a few years later. And this time, things were different.

In 1976, I was on my first world tour with Neil Diamond. We had already played to sell-out crowds at "trial shows" in northern California and Utah, and we began our "official" tour in Auckland, New Zealand. There was a big party to celebrate after the show, and there were a lot of people in attendance (including a gorgeous New Zealand model; she had seen me standing alone and came over to keep me company for the evening). But I couldn't believe my eyes when I saw that fat jerk agent across the room!

He walked over to me and exclaimed,

"Man, you're great! Do you remember me?"

"Of course," I replied (as if I could ever forget him).

I couldn't believe the next words out of his mouth,

"When you get back to L.A., please come to see me."

"You once told me to come back when I've done something in

L.A.," I replied. "Well, I've done something in there, and – like I told you back then – when I have done something in L.A. I won't need you. I will never come to see you."

I told him to go f***k a duck, turned my back on him, and walked back to the model, whose name was Susan. I'm sure that agent was kicking himself for giving me the brush-off when I had first come to see him. He could have made thousands of dollars off the "something" I had done after our first meeting -- sessions and concerts with the biggest names in music, a feature film, and now this gig with one of the hottest artists in the business.

As for me, I had a wonderful evening. Susan and I really hit it off, and we began a lasting friendship that night -- even after that agent and an attorney for the agency approached Susan during the few moments she wasn't by my side and told her that she should stay away from me because I was a nigger! Thankfully, Susan didn't listen to that bullshit; we would always be there for each other, and she was the inspiration for my song, "My Savior." In fact, when she was about to get married, Susan brought her future husband to L.A. to make sure I approved.

That was in the future, of course. When things didn't get any better for me in L.A. in those early days, I called my former partner, Ray Taylor, and told him about the difficulties I was facing. When he found out that I was in trouble, Ray, without my knowledge, called Karen, the nurse from Rochester. Karen immediately quit her job, got her affairs in order, and then made the long drive across the country to rescue me.

It was fortunate that I didn't know that Karen was coming; I did not want anyone to see me in the shape I was in. In fact, I was so ashamed of my condition, I had resorted to not only making excuses, but to outright lying.

One day, a young black boy came up to me and asked what a man who was as good looking as me – and such a sharp dresser – was doing at such a shoddy hotel. The boy, whose name was Chris, had come to L.A. from Bakersfield to look for his mother, who was a maid at another residential hotel just up the street.

I didn't want anyone -- not even this young boy -- to know how down and out I was, so I told Chris that I was a writer and that I was only there long enough to write a book on how people lived on Skid Row. It turned out that some old men at the hotel had put him up to asking me, because the young man turned to them and said,

"I told you so."

I could have been long gone from that dumpy place. Not only did I have Redd's card, but I also had the card of Rich Little's first manager,

Gib Kerr, who had been interested in managing me. But the last time I had seen them both, I was enjoying great success in Bermuda. My pride was holding me back from calling Redd, who had definitely seemed interested in hiring me those many months ago, and I was not going back to the two Beatrices for help; when they heard from me again, I wanted to be somebody. (Unfortunately, by the time anything great happened for me, I had lost contact with both of them. The first Beatrice, from Kodak, was a drunk, so it was just a matter of time for her. And when I tried to call Bea, her number was not in service. I don't know what happened to her, but losing touch with Bea put an end to my Canadian connections.)

You know, life could have been so much easier for me in so many ways in those early days in L.A. I could have called Redd before leaving New Jersey and had things set up for me before I reached L.A. -- or I could have gone back to Bea in Toronto if things hadn't worked out right away (she would have done anything for me). I did not want the people who loved me to worry about me – and I have always been a do-it-yourself kind of guy. I always wanted to be my own man (but I learned in a hurry that the U.S.A. is a team-player country).

My pride was my biggest obstacle – but that was about to change. One fateful day, I picked up the Bible that was in my room. On the first page that I turned to, I read the verse about destruction coming because of pride. Well, brother, I surely wanted to avoid being destroyed, so I finally called Redd's club.

A man answered the phone, and when I told him who I was, he immediately exclaimed,

"Mr. Bermuda! Where in the hell are you? We've been waiting for your call for months."

When I told him I was in L.A. and where I was staying, the man was puzzled.

"What in the hell are you doing there?"

"I don't have any money, and I didn't want to bother Redd until I could do better."

Well, in no time at all, that man was on the phone with Redd, who was performing at the Hacienda Hotel in Las Vegas at the time. And it wasn't more than a few minutes later that Redd placed a call to me at my hotel (I had to take his call in the lobby as there was no phone in my room).

Now, you know that my nickname was "the Fool" when I was a jockey, and both Cannonball Adderley and Redd Foxx called me "Fool," too – and this time, Redd had good reason to do so.

"You big dummy," Redd chided me, "I had everything set up

waiting for you. What in the hell are you doing on Skid Row?"

When I told Redd that I was broke, he said,

"I told you to call me the minute you got to L.A. I'm in Vegas tonight, but take a cab to my place and show those people what drumming is all about."

I told Redd that I didn't even have enough money for a cab and that I only had my bongos as my drums were still in storage.

"I don't give a shit," he replied, "Just go – I'll take care of the cab and we'll get your drums when I come back to L.A."

Redd was booked for another week in Vegas, but that Friday night I took a cab to his club. A man named Rudy was waiting for me at the door, and he shook my hand and paid the cabbie.

When I walked into Redd's club, I could not believe my eyes! The club was a mecca for up and coming stars, and you wouldn't believe the people who performed there; when I walked in, Lou Rawls was just ending his set and the house band was about to take the stage.

The band was called the Kurt Stuart Three. Kurt was the musical director for Julie London, and, since I had always loved her Western movies, I was thrilled to see her in the audience. When the band finished their song, Bill Cosby went up on the stage and started telling jokes. That was the kind of place Redd's club was – he had established this venue to provide an opportunity for his buddies to show off their talents to established stars and talent agents.

Everybody who was anybody in Hollywood came to see those rising stars -- Johnny Carson, Joey Bishop, Sammy Davis, Jr., Cannonball Adderley, Slappy White, and so many more could be seen in the audience. I wish I could remember everyone who was in the audience that night -- it was truly a wonderful experience to perform for that crowd.

Before I tell you about my life-changing experience at Redd's club, I want to tell you that I met Redd's father there that night. Redd, who had been born John Elroy Sanford in St. Louis, Missouri, had been raised by his mother and his grandmother after his father, an electrician, had left the family when Redd was only four years old. Redd and his dad had reconciled by this time, but another tragedy would again separate them.

Redd's father met an untimely end, accidentally killing himself with a shotgun that he kept on a shelf in a bedroom closet. One day, when he reached up for that gun, Redd's father lost his grip on it. He frantically tried to catch it before it hit the floor, but he wasn't fast enough -- the shotgun went off and blew him to pieces. The tragic accident was a huge blow to Redd.

That sad incident was in the future, of course. At this time, Redd was on top of the world…headlining in Vegas and operating his successful club in Los Angeles. You know, it's kind of ironic -- Redd gave his friends a "home" in L.A., but when he was in need later in his life, none of Redd's buddies came to help him. I wish that I had been able to help -- as you will see, I owed him a lot for what he did for me.

My unforgettable debut at the club started when Bill Cosby finished his set and announced:

"And now, ladies and gentlemen, this man is so bad that they named him after their country! For the first time in the U.S.A. -- Mr. Bermuda!"

Of course, that wasn't my first time performing in the U.S., but Bill's rousing introduction got everyone's attention. When I got up on the stage, I knew that I had to impress, especially since it was just me and my bongos -- no band, not even my congas -- and I did just that.

These people had never seen anything like my act in their lives, so I was determined to do something special for them. The first song that I performed was "Betty and Dupree." When I went into my next song, "Who's Gonna Be Your Man?," I wanted to sing directly to a woman for maximum effect, so I picked out one of the most gorgeous women in the audience. That woman was Martine Collette, an actress who had been a leading lady in several movies and also guest starred on several TV programs. I learned later that Martine was from South Africa, but all I noticed at that time was that she looked just like Ursula Andress, who was one of the stars I had seen in "Dr. No" (it turned out that Martine and Ursula were very good friends).

Well, I knew from the way that Martine responded to my song that I had struck gold. In fact, all the way through my set, which I ended with my signature song, "John Henry," there was applause from the audience -- except for one man. That man was looking at me as if he hated me!

When I walked off the stage, Johnny Carson asked me to come over to his table, so, I did, of course.

"You are good! In fact, you're great!"

"Thank you, sir" I responded.

"What are you going to do while you are here in L.A.?" Carson asked.

I was one cocky S.O.B, so I replied,

"Well, for one thing, I will be on your show."

"Will you?"

"Man, you can't let my kind of talent go unseen," I answered.

Now, Johnny was a very nice guy, but he never personally booked me on his show (I don't know if he even had anything to do with booking). But I would, indeed, appear on his show dozens of times, backing a number of different singers and musical groups.

A man that I met at Redd's club the following night would be instrumental in getting me on Johnny's show. That man -- the man who had glowered at me and not cracked a smile the previous night – was John Levy. John, a bassist who had backed such jazz greats as Billie Holiday and George Shearing, was now in the talent management business. When he opened John Levy Enterprises, Inc. in 1951, John became the first black personal manager in the pop and jazz music fields.

John had become successful in the business because no one knew he was black. Back in those days, there were two groups who had the power in Hollywood – the mafia and Jews. Because of his last name, everyone assumed he was Jewish, and, because most bookings were done over the telephone in those days, John was able to develop a roster that would eventually include some 85 stars (by the 1960s, he was managing George Shearing, Cannonball Adderley, Nancy Wilson, Joe Williams, Lou Rawls, Johnny Mathis, Ramsey Lewis, Etta James, Sarah Vaughan, Mariam Makeba, and many others).

After my set that second night, John came backstage to see me -- and he asked me if I would like to work for him!

"Are you sure?" I asked.

"Of course."

"Great! Call me anytime," I told him.

Wow -- here I had been performing for only two nights and I already had the number one jazz artist manager in the business interested in me! Yes, the King had arrived -- and my career (and my love life) would soon know no bounds!

Chapter 15

Women & Song

It was truly amazing how quickly things began happening for me after my debut at Redd's club. It was a thrill to see that so many people who had been in the audience on that first night came back to hear me on the second night -- and for my talents to be appreciated by one of the giants in the booking business. But I guess that my prowess on the bongos wasn't the only thing that impressed at least one member of the crowd.

On the second night that I performed, Martine Collette was once again in the audience, and she sent a note to me, requesting to meet me after the show. The note was delivered by an old Spanish waitress named Mavis, who made no secret of the fact that she wanted me to come home with HER! Wow, I almost felt like I was back in Nassau -- so many women were beginning to notice me.

I guess that was natural. I was a born showman, so I dressed the part. And, since I was lifting weights at the time, I had a big chest and arms.

Of course, I passed on Mavis' offer and met up with Martine that night. Martine was married to an old screenwriter then, and I guess she needed some passion in her life, because she sure wanted me. Martine's husband was out of town, so she drove me to her home on Fuller and Fountain in her beautiful red 1961 classic Cadillac convertible. I truly felt like a King in that car with a beautiful woman by my side.

After we made love, Martine drove me home, and she could not believe her eyes when she saw the Hotel Californian on Skid Row. She was so horrified that she not only offered to take me to a friend's apartment for the night, but she also promised that she would buy a place for me the very next day!

"Thank you very much, Martine," I said. "But I got myself into this mess and I will get myself out. Just continue to love me like you just did -- and buy a steak dinner for me once in a while. It won't be long before you are proud of me."

Martine kissed me and replied, "Mr. King Errisson, I love you – you are one of a kind. I'll see you at the club."

Yes, Martine had fallen for me -- so much so that the next time I saw her she had gotten an apartment on North Orange Drive and Franklin Avenue, just off Hollywood Boulevard, so we could be together; I wouldn't take her to Skid Row, of course, and she couldn't take me to her place when her husband was home. I spent several nights at the apartment with Martine after working at the club. After we made love, she would return to her home, which was just around the corner. I would stay the night in the apartment so she didn't have to drive me all the way across town to "Hotel Hell," and the next day, Martine would bring me back to my "holding cell" at Hotel Hell to get a change of clothes.

I really did want to get out of Hotel Hell, especially after an incident that really shook me up – an old man jumped to his death from his fifth floor window (that was the floor above me). I'll never forget the sight of him lying there on the pavement, his head burst open. But more than his body had been broken – his broken spirit had led to his tragic death. But, like I told Martine, I was determined to leave on my own – I knew I had talent to escape Hotel Hell.

One day, Martine brought me back to Skid Row early, so I told her I would take the bus to the club. I had plenty of time to take a nap, but my rest was interrupted by a knock at the door – a knock that would lead to the end of my beautiful relationship with Martine.

When I got up and went to the door, I very surprised to see my unexpected visitor – it was Karen! She had come to rescue me!

"Honey," she said, as she reached out to hug me, "Ray told me that you were not doing too well."

"At one time," I replied. "But not anymore."

"Well, baby, I came out to help you."

I thanked her, but I also told her that I had not called on her for help. I was still upset with her for standing me up when I went to visit her before leaving for California. And, I had also heard that she had been with another man before passing out drunk on her living room floor.

"Help me? You weren't even sober enough to see me when I came to tell you good-bye."

"Oh, Honey, I am very sorry," she said. "A doctor friend who had been my lover in college stopped over and we had a few drinks. But nothing else happened that night."

"Well, thanks anyway," I replied. "I'm fine. But I don't want you to see me in this kind of place."

"O.K., I will get a place for us so you can be the king again. Would it be O.K. with you to live with me?"

"We'll see," I answered. "In the meantime, why don't you just leave?"

Well, Karen had no intention of leaving. She hugged me and said, "Kiss me – a big, wet sloppy one. You sure you don't want me right now?"

The woman had come to get laid, and she did look hot, especially since she was wearing my favorite type of dress (I had brought dresses like that for her back when I was performing in Bermuda). When I pushed Karen onto the old raggedy-ass bed, I saw that she wasn't wearing any panties, so I started my job. Karen spent the rest of the day with me and drove me to work before going home.

It turned out that Karen had been in L.A. for some time; she was staying at her sister's house before finally coming to see me. Her sister was such a racist that she hated everything black – she wouldn't even wear black shoes. Her sister's husband, who was a pilot for American Airlines, wasn't a racist, but there was no way I would be welcomed in Karen's sister's home.

That night, Redd returned from Vegas. His club manager had already told him about the enthusiastic reception I was getting for my sets, so he was surprised to see that I had just brought my bongos to the club.

"Bermuda, where are your drums?"

After I reminded him that my congas were still being held by the airlines, Redd got up on stage to introduce me. When he got off the stage, I went up to play my bongos as usual. When I was finished, Redd, who was such a very special man, returned to the stage and said,

"Folks, you think he can play? Come back tomorrow night!"

Redd then told his club manager,

"Tomorrow you have his drums out of hock so these people can really see what he can do."

Just before Redd had introduced me, a woman in the audience got up to go to the ladies room. She was only gone for a minute, so when she returned, Redd asked,

"What the hell did you do? Spit?"

The woman, who was a German lady named Hilga, laughed. During her short time in the ladies' room, she had written a note to me, telling me that she wanted to get laid that night (she had also written her address and telephone number on the paper).

Now Hilga was a fine looking woman (she was a successful model), and I sure had no objections about accepting her invitation (those were tough times for me, so a good meal and a warm bed sounded very appealing). Besides, for some reason or other, Martine had not shown up; if Martine had been there, I would not have gone home with Hilga.

But, since I had "open range," I introduced myself to Hilga after I finished my set. I told her that I would love to go home with her, but she would have to wait for me until the end of the evening as I would need a ride to her place. A few hours later, I went with Hilga, who drove a 1968 Corvair (the cars with the engine in the back), to her home in the Silver Lake neighborhood in central L.A.

When we got to her place, Hilga made me feel so at home. She made a great late night dinner, which I enjoyed so much. I praised her for being such a good cook – not knowing that my meal had come from a box! I guess I was so hungry that anything would have tasted good that evening, but, believe it or not, I asked Hilga to make that dish several times in the few months that we dated (that's how stupid I was at the time).

After Hilga and I had a wonderful night together, she drove me home. Like Martine, Hilga was appalled that I was living on Skid Row and said she wanted to do something for me to get me out of Hotel Hell. Hilga didn't offer to get an apartment for me, but she made my life easier by offering her home as a comfortable place to spend the night (yes, I was juggling Martine and Hilga) and cooking for me.

The next day, Redd, true to his word, had gotten my drums out of hock – his club manager had gone to the airport, paid the storage fees, and brought my congas back to the club. They were set up for me on stage when I came into the club the next day, and my set with all my drums was the highlight of the night.

On the second night I performed with my congas, I had a back stage visitor – it was John Levy, who had said he wanted me to work with him. John wanted to talk to me about a young jazz singer he represented. Her name was Letta Mbulu, and she worked with Cannonball Adderley, David Axelrod, and Harry Belafonte after coming to the United States from her native South Africa in 1965. Letta, who married South African musical director and composer, Caiphus Semenya, was not only a great singer, but she was also a wonderful songwriter – penning songs that appeared on three of Miriam Makeba's albums. She was booked on *The Woody Woodbury Show*, and Levy wanted me to back her on the program. I had met Woody in Miami before I came to L.A., so I jumped at the opportunity.

As a side note, Hilga drove me to the set that day (my congas were crammed into her little car). Our relationship didn't last too long, however. One day, when we were driving down Sunset Boulevard, she saw a 1958 black two-door Jaguar for sale. The next day, she met with the seller, a six-foot, four-inch white boy named Joe, and bought that car. She also invited the seller over to dinner that evening (I am sure that dinner was from a box) – and by the next night, she was sleeping with him! They ended up becoming lovers, so that was the end for us.

I actually didn't mind going back to Skid Row – believe it or not, I had taken a liking to the rat's nest because nobody wanted to go to that dump (I had forbidden Karen to come back – I only saw her at the club, although I didn't see her for a few days after her first visit to Skid Row). Besides, I was on a mission to find success and nothing was going to sidetrack me.

The gig on *The Woody Woodbury Show* was the start of a lasting professional and personal relationship with John. This amazing man, who lived to be almost 100, became a great friend. We chatted often, and I was amazed that John remained so active in his later years. In fact, he was still driving in his late 90s, when I last spoke with him, and I joked that he would live to be 110.

"No, King, I'm tired," he replied, and he meant it -- John died just a few months later, just three months short of his 100th birthday.

A few nights after my appearance with Letta, I was working at the club when Karen, who had found a job in an old folks' home in Mission Viejo, stopped in with some surprising news. She couldn't stand the thought of me living in the rat's nest any longer, so she had found an apartment for us in the Baldwin Hills area. She had already gone to my hotel and told the desk clerk that she was my wife and needed to get into my room. After they let her in, she took all my belongings to the apartment before she came to the club to tell me what she had done!

Karen was one crazy woman, but what she did next was even crazier – she called or wrote to everyone she knew, telling her family and friends that we were married. She was receiving wedding gifts for months!

If I had been a smart man, I would have turned down Karen's offer and stayed with Martine -- she was one of the sweetest women I ever met as well as one of the most beautiful, and I loved staying in the apartment she had gotten for us. (I later learned that Martine had left her husband and hooked up with a black man she met at the Tournament of Roses parade in Pasadena. The guy was a drunk and had no teeth, so I couldn't understand why Martine, who was such a classy woman, was attracted to him).

At any rate, since I no longer had my room, I went home with Karen that night. The apartment was beautiful and clean, and, since I love to swim, I was happy to see the large pool in the courtyard.

During the time Karen and I lived together, I continued to perform at Redd's club – and started on the road to a successful career. It wasn't long after my television appearance with Letta that Cannonball Adderley asked me to back him when he appeared on *The Tonight Show Starring Johnny Carson*. I'll never forget walking onto that stage and hearing Johnny exclaim, "Damn! You're here!" It was a private joke between us for years – I would appear on the show with different performers four or five times a year, and, after introducing the guest, Johnny would always say, "And, of course, we've got King over there." So, although I wasn't the musical guest star, I was always mentioned – all because of the incident that night in Redd Foxx's club.

Besides backing Cannonball on television, I was also privileged to go on the road with Cannonball and his band several times over the next year. We didn't do extended tours; we would travel to a city or two and then return home to California. Our first gig together was at Baker's Keyboard Lounge, a famous jazz club in Detroit, the home of Motown, and we also played in other cities across the country, including St. Louis, as well as several gigs in California, including Berkeley and stops closer to home (the Playboy Club in L.A. and a big jazz club in Century City).

I can't tell you how much I loved that man, who was not only responsible for helping me to break into the "big time," but also explained to me what I couldn't have put into words about the talent I had. One day, he said to me, in a sort of professional voice,

"What you have to learn is that you are a jazz improviser. Which means that you are part composer. When you were surrounded by the great guys in your band, you were learning to play music – writing it, improvising it by imitating various models. Every composer in musical history has gone through the stage of writing pieces in the style of great musicians who were composers themselves. Think about Igor Stravinsky, Sir Edward Elgar, Bela Bartok, John Williams, and Duke Ellington. By imitating a particular composer, or improvising on his music, the learner assimilates the harmonic, melodic, and rhythmic language of the composer and he discovers how to project with reasonable accuracy what the composer would do were he given specific musical options to work on."

Cannonball's explanation was like a light bulb flashing in my mind. In a few words, he had described what I had learned to do. I never forgot what he told me on that day. He had not only given me a definition of my talent, but also a deep insight into the yearning that drove me to make musical rhythm on discarded tin cans when I was only four years old.

Cannonball also became a father figure as well as a mentor. I was on the road with him in 1968 when I received word that my father had been killed. Dad, who had walked the streets of Nassau as a drunk after my mother had left him and he had lost everything, had been stone cold sober on the day that he was struck and killed by an unlicensed driver who ran a red light. I felt an overwhelming sense of loss – just as I had felt when Paul Meeres had died – but Cannonball was there to comfort me…and he treated me like I was his own son.

During the time that Karen and I lived together, I was also studying drama – I had always dreamed of becoming a movie star, and L.A. was certainly the place to break into the business. First, I studied with a drama coach named Bob Doray (I think that is how you spell his name), who was a four-foot hunchback. Man, he was good – he started correcting my speech, and he thought I would be great. I stayed with him for about six months before moving over to a man named Phil Browning, who was also a great teacher.

The first play I did in L.A. was *Another Country*, an adaptation of a book by James Baldwin. The play went over pretty well, and my co-star, Janine Cline, and I both got good reviews. I thought I was pretty good (maybe even great), an opinion that was shared by one of the members of the audience – an old movie producer that Karen had brought to see me perform.

Karen and I were not getting along too well by this time, so she had started screwing around with this movie producer (she had met him in a supermarket parking lot). When I found out about her affair, Karen said that she had done it for us – she thought that her sleeping with the producer would help my career!

When she introduced the guy to me after the play, he told me that I was great – and that he would come back again to see me. I was flattered by his praise, but even more excited when the producer told me that he had four pictures in the works. I can't remember the names of all of them, but one of his films, *100 Rifles*, caught my interest in a hurry. I had always been particularly fond of Westerns, so you can imagine how I felt when he talked about making me the co-star of that film. I could picture myself as another Woody Strode, the black athlete-turned-actor who appeared in four of John Ford's films and helped to pave the way for black actors to be cast in non-traditional roles (Strode was nominated for a Golden Globe for Best Supporting Actor for playing a gladiator in the 1960 blockbuster, *Spartacus*, which starred Kirk Douglas).

After I talked with him, Karen took off with the producer and I went back home to our apartment. I believe that I could have enjoyed a successful acting career if I had been cast in any of the producer's films, especially *100 Rifles*. Unfortunately, the co-starring role of Lydecker in

100 Rifles (which was shot in Spain and released in 1969), would go to another black athlete-turned-actor, Jim Brown.

Later on, I found out that the producer had not hired me for that role – or considered me for any other roles – because of Karen. She and I were fighting all the time, so we finally parted ways. That's when the woman who had wanted to rescue me decided to destroy me instead. She went to the producer and persuaded him not to hire me – she said that I was no good, that I was unreliable, and other bullshit like that. And, unfortunately, the producer believed her.

But, although I was disappointed that I hadn't yet broken into films, opportunity was about to knock on my door – and my music career was about to soar. The day after I had talked with the producer, I was swimming in the pool when Karen came out on the patio, shouting that I had a very urgent phone call.

"King, some guy named Cannonball wants to talk to you right away." I jumped out of the pool and flew like a bird to the phone. I knew that the big man wouldn't be calling me at mid-day unless he had an important reason.

"What's happening?" I asked.

"Listen, Fool," he replied, "How long will it take you to get down here to Capitol Records? I want you to get these people straightened out on how to do my music."

I was on my way in five minutes! After I called for a cab, I jumped in the shower, rinsed off, and threw on some clothes (in those days, I didn't wear shirts – I usually wore only an open Levi's jeans jacket or a vest, like I did this day, to show off my big chest and arms). I lifted weights at the time, and, although I was small, I was built like Arnold Schwarzenegger (I had to be strong to carry my heavy conga rack). I grabbed my congas, hanging them across my back by their leather straps, and I was ready and waiting at the front of our building when the cab arrived.

I felt so proud to tell the cab driver to take me to the Capitol Records studio, and I was so excited that I would be working with Cannonball again. At the time, I had no idea of what I would be doing –

Cannonball had just said to get there quickly to help with his album. I did not know that the musicians for this session had spent an entire month trying to finish one track, "Lemadima," for Cannonball's album, *Accent on Africa*, for which he had written six of the eight songs ("Ndo Lima" was written by Joe Zawinul and "Up and At It" was composed by Wes Montgomery). I would later learn that three hours of studio musicians' time was the norm for recording one song, but about $150,000 had already been spent on that one track – and the song was still unrecorded - by the time Cannonball called me.

The session was being produced by noted producer and arranger David Axelrod, who was one of the hottest record producers in California at the time. After coming to Capitol Records in late 1963, he encouraged the label to promote their black artists. Axelrod worked with Lou Rawls, producing a succession of gold albums and singles, as well as with Cannonball; in fact, Axelrod had produced Cannonball's 1967 album, *Live at the Club*, which included the huge hit, "Mercy, Mercy, Mercy." Axelrod also produced some of Nat King Cole's records, and hit records for Nancy Wilson and for Joe Williams, who would become a good friend of mine.

Axelrod, who is credited with being one of the first producers to fuse jazz, rock, and R&B, worked with a select group of sessions musicians, including Carol Kaye on bass and Earl Palmer on drums.

Yeah, Axelrod was a big time guy – and he had never heard of me. In fact, Axelrod had initially turned down Cannonball's request to hire me. I could understand, of course – I had already learned that it is tough to break into Hollywood if you're not known. But, fortunately, Cannonball had stood up for me.

On the day he called, Cannonball had told Axelrod, "Look, I'm tired of spending so much time on this one track. I'll pay King Errisson. I'll pay King to come down here and fix this piece of music for us. He's the only one who can do it."

It is probably fortunate that I had no inkling that what would happen in the next hour or so would change my life – and finally bring the success that had been so elusive. Yes, King Errisson was about to break into the "big time." What would happen at that session would launch me into the stratosphere of such stars as the Beatles, George Benson, the Carpenters, Bobby Darin, Neil Diamond, Bob Dylan, the Jackson 5, Barry Manilow, Johnny Mathis, Diana Ross, Barbra Streisand, Barry White, and hundreds more greats.

Chapter 16

The Music Fixer

Unfortunately, that first studio session didn't start out so great for me -- I was so excited that I paid no attention to the red light that signified "Recording in Session" above the studio door. I knew that I had made a major goof when I threw the door open, and a voice shouted,

"Who is the ass who pushed the door open like that?"

"'Tis me, man," I replied.

"Me, man, who?" demanded the voice, which belonged to Axelrod. "Don't you know better than that?"

I was sorry I had interrupted the session, of course, and I immediately apologized,

"Man, I'm terribly sorry. I didn't see the light. 'Tis me, King Errisson."

Axelrod was not moved by either my apology or explanation. He had been reluctant about hiring me in the first place, so I'm sure he regretted going along with Cannonball when he formed his first impression of me. In fact, I could tell that everyone in the room – except Cannonball and his brother, Nat -- hated me. Cannonball never did anything without his brother, Nat, and they were the only ones who seemed happy to see me -- both of them smiled and Nat, who looked so small next to his giant of a brother, also waved at me.

There were probably 40 people in that studio that day. I had no idea that so many people were needed to make a record – and I certainly didn't expect to see so many white musicians, especially on a recording about Africa. All the string players were white except for one guy named Bill Henderson, and he might as well have been white – he was as fair-skinned as the white guys. Other white musicians included Max Bennett on bass and percussionist Emil Richards. Some of the black musicians were Earl Palmer on drums, David T. Walker and Arthur Wright on guitar, Harry "Sweets" Edison on trumpet, William "Buddy" Collette on tenor sax, and Joe Clayton on congas. Cannonball and his brother, Nat, of course, were black, as were the background singers, the Blossoms, who were very talented. Letta Mbulu was a guest singer with the group, and Letta's husband, Caiphus Semenya, conducted the background singers.

But, black or white, these were some of the finest musicians in the world, and I had not only walked into their session with too much authority, but my choice of attire also probably caused them to wonder, "Who is this freak?" I guess it is customary to show up at a session wearing a shirt (at the very least), so my entrance in my vest – with my big chest and arms prominently displayed – was an added surprise.

Axelrod told everybody to "take ten," and the studio people had me and my congas set up in a booth by the time the musicians returned to their seats after the break. Then Cannonball walked over to me and said,

"O.K., Fool, show them how it's done."

The session was conducted by "H.B." Barnum, a former child actor, pianist, and singer who had become a top studio arranger and producer (he worked with such artists as Count Basie, Aretha Franklin, Etta James, Lou Rawls, Frank Sinatra, and the Supremes). After joining Capitol Records in 1965, H.B. often teamed up with Axelrod to create an innovative jazz-funk sound that was often imitated.

Like Axelrod, H.B. was not impressed with me. In a condescending way, he asked, "You read music?"

"If it's on paper, I read it, man," I replied.

Still pissed off that I had interrupted the session, H.B. almost threw the score at me. I put the sheets on my music stand and looked them over. I must admit that I was not the greatest of readers, but I was glad that I had spent that year studying music in Las Vegas. I had to call their bluff -- I was an intruder, so I had to be good.

Fortunately, it was clear in a moment why the song was so complicated – there were so many time signatures and changes. I could certainly see why they had been working on this piece for a month without getting it right. No one – not the producer, not the conductor, not the band – understood what Cannonball was trying to achieve.

Axelrod, who still had not come out of his booth, asked,
"You ready?"
"Yes, man, I'm ready," I answered.

H.B. got up on his pedestal and started counting off the time signatures. I had not even seen or heard some of those time signatures before, and I didn't even try to play when H.B. started the song. After I listened for four bars, I heard the problem. The musicians continued to play, but I stopped – and did the unthinkable. I stopped the session again!

"Wait a minute, man. Wait one minute," I said.

Oh, did my interruption piss H.B. – and Axelrod – off yet again. H.B. threw his baton down and stepped off his pedestal and Axelrod came out of the control booth, bellowing,

"Who are you? You don't stop a session around here. I'm the

producer – I'll tell you when to wait!"

I did my best to calm things down.

"I am sorry, sir," I replied, "There's nothing to get upset about, man. But your guys are not playing the music right. I see what you're trying to do. Let me show you."

"You want to conduct? You do it!" H.B. shouted.

During this heated exchange, Cannonball was just standing against the glass of the recording booth -- when he was standing there with his folded arms resting on his belly, he looked like Buddha. After H.B. had challenged me, Cannonball again walked over to me and said,

"O.K, Fool, it's on you. Show them how it's done."

I went around to each musician, starting with the rhythm section. I told them what beat to play before moving on to Max Bennett, who was on the bass guitar.

"Mr. Bass Man, I want you to give me 'boom, de boom, de boom, boom, boom, de boom.'"

I then approached the drummer, Earl Palmer, who was one of the greatest drummers in the world. I pointed to his sheet music and explained, "I want you to just stay here."

Earl looked at the music and said, "Right on, bro."

My next stop was Joe Clayton, the guy playing congas for the session. I told him what beat to play – and not to change it.

"I want you to just give me a little of this…and don't move from it. I'll do the rest."

Then I went over to the guitar players, David T. Walker and Arthur Wright. Both of them were great players, but they did not read much music at that time, so I showed them what I wanted them to do before telling the string players and the horns,

"Just play what you've got written on the paper."

I then asked the musicians, "Now, are you all ready?"

When I knew that they finally understood how to make that song work, I am proud to say that I said to H.B.,

"You can start when you are ready, sir."

After H.B. counted off, we did the song in *one take*! Everyone played the way I told them to play, and we started and finished that track together – in one take! I looked over at Cannonball, and he just smiled -- his grin splitting his face in an "I told you so" expression. I had saved the day, but, even more importantly, I had made Cannonball proud of me. It was Cannonball who had instilled in me the confidence I would need to tackle the "big time," and I will be forever grateful to him. If Cannonball hadn't believed in me, I would never have been a part of that session, where I proved myself to some of the major players in the recording industry. In fact, I might not have even broken into sessions work in Hollywood if it hadn't been for Cannonball.

H.B. walked over to me and exclaimed,

"Bro, you're the best, man! Whenever I work, you work."

Axelrod was the next person to approach me – and he actually hugged me before echoing what H.B. had said!

"Whenever I work from now on, you'll be with me," he promised.

The musicians' contractor for the session was a man named Ben Barrett, a big white man who did the booking of the major sessions back then, and he was equally impressed. He walked up to me, held out his hand, and said,

"Where the hell have you been? I've never seen anything like this. I'm the boss of this town, and you'll be in on every session I do from now on. Give me your number."

Then the rest of the musicians crowded around me, exclaiming, "Thank God. We have been working on that damn song for a month."

I had never had so many white hugs in my life, and I was offered a job from everyone in that room who had the power to do so. And you know what? Those guys kept their word – it wasn't long before the new boy in town was making over $200,000 a year working with these people. The handful of people who were at that session changed my life forever.

We did just that one track that day, but after the session, Axelrod asked me if I could come back and overdub all the music that had already been recorded for the album. I did not know anything about overdubbing, but I agreed to his request anyway. The next morning, I was back in the studio; this time, there wasn't a crowd of people – it was just me, alone. It turned out that overdubbing was quite easy -- I put on my headphones and had a ball playing along with the tracks. In only two days, I was able to overdub the entire album.

That was quite a learning experience for me – but I consider all my sessions as my "college education." I learned so much from so many people in the early days. For example, there was Les Baxter, a former musician who turned to arranging and conducting (he did a lot of film scores -- mostly for horror films and teenage musicals -- for American International Pictures). Les taught me that I could play anything; when he had me for a session for one of his sound tracks, he showed me how to play instruments that I had never touched before! I guess I played them pretty well, too, because I was able to "fake" my expertise on those instruments in future sessions.

Some of my best teachers, though, were the other talented

sessions musicians. Whenever I had questions, they were always ready to help. There were never any bad answers, there was never any jealousy. Most of those musicians were doing two, three, or even four or more sessions a day, so we all wanted things to go smoothly so we could get to the next gig in plenty of time.

A good sessions musician would walk in and do his or her part (either singly or with a group, as was the case in my first session), and then he or she was finished with the project. In many cases, we didn't even know who the composer was or what song we were working on! It is also a (sad) fact that many of these talented musicians – especially the black ones – were not credited for their work or compensated properly. In most cases, backing musicians didn't share in any royalties; they were paid for the session and that was the end of that. The black musicians were happy that they were working and being paid, so they just accepted the status quo.

Before I tell you about what happened next in my career, I want to pay tribute to some of the sessions musicians who inspired me the most. Legendary drummer Earl Palmer was one of the first sessions musicians who impressed me. Man, that guy could play! By the time I met him, Earl, who had been born into a show business family in New Orleans, had played in the Dave Bartholomew Band, and he was a key player in New Orleans recording sessions (he can be heard on all of Fats Domino's big hits and most of Little Richard's hits, as well as on Lloyd Price's "Lawdy Miss Clawdy" and Smiley Lewis' hit, "I Hear You Knockin"). It was on Fats Domino's hit song, "The Fat Man," that Earl developed the backbeat that is so prevalent in rock and roll today.

There is a funny story about that backbeat that I'd like to share before I go on about Earl's accomplishments. In 1996, Cracker, an alternative rock band, released their third album, *The Golden Age*. One of the tracks, "I Hate My Generation," was featured in a music video that showed older people living life to the fullest; in the video, you can see footage of a gray-haired Earl rocking on the drums. When band leader David Lowery had asked Earl if he could keep up with the song, Earl gave him a look and answered, "I invented this shit." That was classic Earl – witty and wise as well as talented.

Earl had been a staple of the Hollywood recording scene since 1957, when he began working for Aladdin Records. He not only backed the top recording artists of the day, but he played on the scores of dozens of films and television shows. Earl kept a hectic schedule (15-hours days were not uncommon), and he sat in on 450 sessions in 1967 alone! His impressive credits include backing such recording stars as the Beach

Boys, Ray Charles, Bobby Darin, B.B. King, Frank Sinatra, Neil Young, and a host of others, so I felt fortunate to work with Earl on several projects.

Earl and I kept in touch with each other over the years, and it was in 2008 (forty years after we had first met) that I learned that Earl was seriously ill. I sent a card to his home in California and I was looking forward to visiting him, but, sadly, he died that September. With Earl's passing, I lost a great friend…and the world lost a great musician.

There are several other drummers that I love from those early days – they were all so helpful as well as extremely talented. There was James Gadson, who was featured on a long list of R&B recordings (his credits include backing Marvin Gaye, Herbie Hancock, Quincy Jones, B.B. King, Martha Reeves, and The Temptations, among others). Jim Gordon, one of the most prolific sessions drummers of the time, worked with me in The Incredible Bongo Band, so I'll tell his story later in this book. Ed Greene backed a number of performers, including Dizzy Gillespie, Johnny Mathis, Diana Ross, Steely Dan, and Three Dog Night. Paul Humphrey, who is known for his jazz, funk, and R&B rhythms, worked with such jazz greats as Charles Mingus, Blue Mitchell, and Wes Montgomery as well as pop artists ranging from Natalie Cole to Frank Zappa. Harvey Mason, a talented jazz drummer, is perhaps best known for his work with the contemporary jazz group, Fourplay, but he backed a number of recording artists over his four-decade career. Benny Parks, who has the greatest sense of rhythm, worked on several of my albums, including *The King Arrives* (1970) and *We Must Say Good-bye* (1973). Jeff Porcaro, the son of drummer and percussionist Joe Porcaro, worked on hundreds of albums by music's biggest stars from 1971-1992, and he is also known for co-founding the popular group, Toto. Ron Tutt is best known for recording and touring with two superstars, Elvis Presley and Neil Diamond, but he can also be heard on recordings by artists including The Carpenters, David Cassidy, Emmylou Harris, Billy Joel, Little Richard, and many others (Ron and I played together on Michael McDonald's first recording in L.A. – before Michael became a back-up vocalist for Steely Dan and then the lead singer for The Doobie Brothers). Spider Webb, whose real name is Kenneth "Kenny" Rice, worked with King Curtis and the Kingpins and Harry Belafonte's band, and his sessions credits include recordings by Herb Alpert and Aretha Franklin. Last, but certainly not least, there are two drummers, Dennis St. John and Washington Rucker, who were like brothers to me; I'll tell you more about them (and why I think so highly of them) in future chapters.

There were several drummers/percussionists that I admired. Ray

"Sticks" Cooper, who was from the U.K., backed a number of artists in the 1960s and 1970s, and he was also part of several groups, including The Traveling Wilburys. Sticks later toured with Sir Elton John, and he was featured in Elton's Million Dollar Piano shows at Caesar's Palace in Las Vegas. Alan Estes, the brother of percussionist Gene Estes, has nearly 170 recordings to his credit, backing such diverse artists as Ray Coniff, Neil Diamond, Nilsson, Barbra Streisand, and Frank Zappa. John Guerin can be heard on the recordings of such artists as The Animals, The Byrds (he was the group's drummer from July 1972-January 1973), Peggy Lee, Linda Ronstadt, and Frank Sinatra. Joe Porcaro recorded with a number of jazz and pop artists, including Natalie Cole, Stan Getz, Gladys Knight, Madonna, Pink Floyd, Frank Sinatra, and Sarah Vaughn. My favorite drummer/percussionist, though, was Vince Charles; I'll tell you more about this special man (and friend) later in this book.

Being a percussionist myself, I learned so much by observing and working with such talents as Jack Arnold, who played a variety of percussion instruments. He was in Louie Bellson's band, toured the world (at the request of President John F. Kennedy) with a small jazz combo, had a prolific studio career (working with Motown and pop artists), and recorded and toured with Percy Faith. Larry Bunker, who was a key figure in West Coast jazz, recorded with greats including Ella Fitzgerald, Dizzy Gillespie, Billie Holiday, and Peggy Lee. Gary Coleman spent 37 years as a sessions musician, backing several artists with whom I also worked, including Cannonball, Neil Diamond, Diana Ross, and Barry White. He can also be heard on the scores of dozens of television shows and feature films. Gene Estes who played percussion, vibraphone, drums, timpani, and tambourine was a top studio percussionist whose credits include recordings by The Beach Boys, Cher, Sam Cooke, Neil Diamond, Dean Martin, REO Speedwagon, Tina Turner, and Frank Zappa (he is listed as a member of the Mother's Auxiliary on Mothers of Distinction albums). Emil Richards also had a connection to Zappa – he was a member of Frank Zappa's Abnuceals Emuukha Electric Symphony Orchestra, recording several albums with the group, and he also played on Zappa's first solo album, *Lumpy Gravy*, which was released in 1967. Besides backing a number of recording artists (ranging from Blondie to Frank Sinatra), he can be heard on the soundtracks of hundreds of films.

I also worked with two talented black female percussionists. Bobbye Hall played on a number of Motown recordings (uncredited) before she came to Los Angeles, where she was one of the few female sessions musicians. Bobbye also toured with Bob Dylan in 1978 (Dylan compensated her handsomely to make up for the studio work she was missing) and Stevie Nicks (1982 and 1986). Sandra Crouch has to be the best of all time on the tambourine (she is the best that I have ever heard, anyway). In addition to her Motown sessions in the early 1970s, she recorded with Neil Diamond, Janis Joplin, Clydie King, Harvey Mandel, Mongo Santamaria, and Lalo Schifrin, and she was featured on several albums by her twin brother, Andraé Crouch, who passed away in 2015.

When it comes to guitar players, I was fortunate to work with the legendary David T. Walker. Like me, he played with Cannonball (*The Happy People*, 1970) and backed most of the great Motown artists (and, I am happy to say, he shared his talents on some of my solo projects). Richard Bennett has got to be one of the most versatile guitarists I have ever met; his long list of credits read like a "Who's Who" of country, pop, and rock stars. Richard, who is a genuinely nice guy, is also well known for recording and touring with Neil Diamond and with Mark Knopfler. And I can't forget Larry Carlton, a prolific sessions musician during the 1970s and early 1980s (he sometimes made up to 500 recordings a year)

There are also several bass guitarists that I have known and admired. Max Bennett, who was an excellent jazz musician, backed a number of prominent artists, including Joan Baez, Ella Fitzgerald, and Peggy Lee, and he can be heard on a number of records by The Monkees and The Partridge Family as well as on the soundtrack to the 1969 film, *Bullitt*. He later had several bands of his own: L.A. Express, led by Tom Scott, which included Joe Sample, Larry Carlton, and John Guerin; Freeway; and, Private Reserve. Darrell Clayborn, who played on my self-titled album in 1980, was also known for his work with Blue Mitchell, Eddie Kendricks, and The Friends of Distinction, among others. I was fortunate to have talented bassist Wayne Douglas play on two of my early albums, *We Must Say Good-bye* (1973) and *The Magic Man* (1976). James Jamerson was the uncredited bassist on most of Motown's hit records in the 1960s and early 1970s (he played on a record 30 No. 1 records and 70 top R&B hits). Reinie Press, who (like me) is perhaps best known for his work in Neil Diamond's band, was also a talented sessions musician, backing artists that included Joan Baez, David Cassidy, Percy Faith, and Art Garfunkel. Chuck Rainey, who began his career as a sessions musician in New York City before coming to L.A. in 1972, worked with Quincy Jones' big band, and he also backed such artists as Roberta Flack, Dizzy Gillespie, Lena Horne, Jackson Browne, Marlena Shaw, and Steely Dan. Bobby West can be heard on recordings by The Monkees, Dusty Springfield, and James Taylor, to name a few.

Three of my favorite keyboard players were Clarence McDonald, Don Randi, and Joe Sample. McDonald, who is featured on my album, *The King Arrives*, worked with a number of recording artists (Ray Charles, Ella Fitzgerald, Carole King, Barbra Streisand, and James Taylor, to name just a few), and he is also a talented composer and arranger. I love Randi, who was also a bandleader and songwriter as well as a sessions musician who backed a long list of recording artists. Sample, a pioneer in the use of electric keyboards in the 1960s, had a successful solo career as well as backing such performers as George Benson, Eric Clapton, Miles Davis, B.B. King, Steely Dan, and the Supremes.

When it comes to trumpet players, Freddie Hill is number one in my book. He was a fantastic jazz trumpeter, and I was so fortunate to have him play on my album, *The King Arrives*. There is also the legendary Freddie Hubbard, who worked with Wes Montgomery while still in his teens. Of course, I can't forget Nat Adderley, who began his career as a trumpet player but became a master on the cornet (Nat was largely responsible for the cornet becoming an accepted instrument in the jazz genre). Nat, who was a humble man, was content to work in Cannonball's shadow, but his credits include over 100 albums. He was also a songwriter; his "Work Song" became a jazz standard.

Notable saxophone players I have known and worked with – besides Cannonball, who was the greatest of them all -- include Buddy Collette, Bill Green, and Sonny Rollins. Collette, a fantastic jazz alto saxophone player, worked with several jazz greats and recorded with his own group, and he also became a noted music educator in L.A. Green, who also later recorded with his own jazz group, backed such greats as Louie Bellson, Tony Bennett, Nat King Cole, Ella Fitzgerald, Lionel Hampton, and Frank Sinatra. Rollins, a tenor saxophonist, backed all the jazz greats (Miles Davis, Dizzy Gillespie, Thelonious Monk, and Max Roach to name a few), and he is also known for writing such jazz standards as "St. Thomas," "Oleo," "Doxy," and "Airegin." I also met Eddie "Cleanhead" Vinson, and wish I had the opportunity to work with him; in the 1970s, Eddie worked blues and jazz sessions for such greats as Count Basie, Johnny Otis, and Buddy Tate.

Chapter 17

The Unsung Hero of Motown

After the word got out about my success as a "music fixer," I began getting dozens of calls from record producers or music contractors who wanted me to help them figure out how to make the timing jell on a troublesome track. I had gained an instant reputation for inter-playing the sounds of different instruments – brass, woods, strings, ivories, and drums – to make a melody come together with astonishing simplicity. I had been blessed with the ability to "hear" the completed version in my head, so I could orchestrate the different musical sounds into a composition that often exceeded the songwriter's original interpretation.

With my reputation cemented, I never had to worry about working in Hollywood – and I worked with most of the biggest stars in the business. Some of the artists I recorded with in the early years of my Hollywood career include (in alphabetical order) Teresa Brewer, Genie Brown, Severin Browne, Tim Buckley, Donald Byrd, Michael Edward Campbell, David Cassidy, Sean Cassidy, The Cate Brothers, Dennis Coffey, Compton & Batteau, The Friends of Distinction, Grant Green, Alexander Harvey, Freddie Hubbard, Bobbi Humphrey, Etta James, Eddie Kendricks, B.B. King, Lobo, Melissa Manchester, Ted Neeley, Flora Purim, Kenny Rankin, Lalo Schifrin, Seals & Crofts, Marlena Shaw, and the Ventures. In later years, I would work with such artists as the Bellamy Brothers, Blood, Sweat & Tears, Solomon Burke, David Clayton-Thomas, Giovanni, Quincy Jones, Danny O'Keefe, Carol Bayer Sager, Boz Scaggs, Jim Stafford, Ringo Starr, Swamp Dogg, Frankie Valli, Jackie Wilson, and many more.

It was such a pleasure to back so many talented performers, and I also recorded and performed with Neil Diamond, Tony Orlando and Dawn, and Barry White, as well as with Diana Ross and The Supremes (and Diana Ross when she went solo), and most of Motown's biggest artists. And, I can be heard on a number of hits, including "Feelings" by Morris Albert, Tom Jones' hit, "She's a Lady," "I Can See Clearly Now" by Johnny Nash, and several of Glen Campbell's most popular songs, including "By the Time I Get to Phoenix" and "Gentle on My Mind."

Early in 1969, my first full year as a sessions musician, I was thrilled when my friend, Sammy Davis, Jr., asked me to appear on an episode of *The Hollywood Palace* that he was hosting. When I got that gig, I knew I had "arrived."

The show aired on March 15, 1969, and it included a cute bit about "choreography" before Sammy showed off some "real" dancing with one of his incomparable tap dance routines. As he was finishing up, a drum beat was heard, and a curtain rose to reveal Louie Bellson, the talented jazz drummer who was married to Pearl Bailey. Sammy walked over to him and matched Louie's riff with his flying feet before another curtain rose, and Sammy "faced off" against Juan "Johnny" Mendoza, who played bongos on a number of Sammy's recordings and backed him at the Coconut Grove. Again, Sammy had no trouble duplicating the beat, so he walked over to the third drummer – a handsome "newcomer" standing behind four conga drums. (Three of the drums were black and one was white because someone had stolen one of my congas from the Hollywood Palladium, where I had just done a show with a group that recorded for CBS).

I must say I looked pretty sharp in my stage outfit, which included a shirt as well as a vest this time, but it wasn't my appearance that made the biggest impression on the audience. As he walked toward me, Sammy made a remark about knowing there would be a "brother" on the show (which got a laugh from the audience) before listening to my first riff. Sammy danced a couple of steps before asking me to play something from "home." When I complied, Sammy listened for a couple of seconds before waving his hands and walking away as if to say,

"I can't beat that. You win."

It was unheard of for Sammy to admit defeat in public, so, of course, the audience went wild as Sammy walked over to the last drummer, Jack Sperling. Jack was one versatile drummer – he had played with several big bands before becoming a studio and TV sessions musician – and he could play anything. Again, however, Sammy was able to match his beat before the four of us each played a beat separately and then a riff together to end the sketch.

That gig was extra special to me because two drummers that I admired, Max Roach and Shelly Manne, were also on the stage cheering us on (and Max's wife at the time -- beautiful jazz singer, songwriter, and actress Abbey Lincoln -- was also in the wings, as she also performed on the program). Not only were these heroes of mine impressed with my performance, but Sammy was also thrilled that I had been a big hit (that experience deepened the friendship between us).

At the time I appeared on *The Hollywood Palace* with him, Sammy was signed to the Motown label, and I, too, would become part of Motown's continued success. Over the next few years, I backed almost all of the great Motown artists, recording in both Detroit and in L.A. (as a member of Motown's West Coast Studio Band).   Some of the Motown greats I worked with include Lamont Dozier, The Four Tops, Marvin Gaye, The Jackson 5, The Marvelettes, Billy Preston, Martha Reeves, Smokey Robinson, Diana Ross and The Supremes (and Diana Ross when she went solo), and The Temptations, and I also played on Bobby Darin's first album for the label.

Before I share some of my Motown experiences, I want to tell you a little bit about my relationship with Berry Gordy and Ray Singleton. Berry and his second wife, Raymona "Ray" Mayberry Liles Gordy Singleton, were married in the spring of 1960 and divorced in 1964 after a tumultuous relationship. Despite Berry's womanizing during their marriage and Ray's bootlegging of 5,000 copies of Mary Wells' single, "My Girl," to keep an office of a Motown subsidiary open in New York City, the two remained on good terms after their divorce. In fact, Ray returned to Motown in 1968 and was very involved in the label's day-to-day activities when I met both of them.

I have to say that I love Berry – he was one of the few men in the business who was not afraid of me and my talent. When he saw me back Diana Ross and The Supremes at a show at the famous Coconut Grove nightclub in the Ambassador Hotel in Hollywood, he asked me to back the group on an upcoming road tour. It wasn't an extended tour – we played the Fontainebleau Hotel in Miami Beach, did more performances at the Coconut Grove, and performed the group's last two shows together at the Frontier Hotel in Las Vegas.

Berry also wanted to sign me up on the Motown label (he was the first one in Hollywood to offer a recording contract to me). He asked the A&R staff to sign me up, but, unfortunately, they did not like me – I was much too strong for them. A woman named Althea was in charge at that time, and that bitch didn't think I was good enough. She did nothing but find fault with my voice -- one of her complaints was that I sounded too "calypso" for the label; this was ironic because they had an American recording artist on their roster who was trying to sing calypso (and failing big time, I might add). But I guess Althea had a lot of power, because, in spite of Berry's urging, she refused to sign me. For years, no matter what I took to her (and I was writing a lot of good songs at the time), she never liked my material or the way I sang it, so I finally gave up on her and found other labels for my music.

But I continued to enjoy a great relationship with Berry. Sometimes, he would personally call me to sit in on a recording session, help with an arrangement, or go on the road with one of his artists. I'll never forget what happened on one of those tours to Miami Beach – I ran into Regina again!

It had been a long time since we had seen each other, but she seemed to be doing fine. But, after we exchanged hugs, Regina began to scold me – and not for the reason you might think.

"Why did you go and change your name?" she demanded.

"What are you talking about? I've never changed my name," I replied.

"Of course you did," she responded. "You called yourself Isaac Hayes."

"You have to be a dummy," I said. "I'm much better looking than Isaac Hayes, and I've never changed my name from King Errisson."

"Well, he stole your idea, then," she responded. "You're the only one who would dress like that."

"Yeah, but he's the one who became famous for doing so."

Isaac Hayes was a big star by this time (he was famous long before I was successful) – and he dressed much like I did early in my career; he wore flamboyant clothes and lots of gold jewelry…and he had a shaved head like mine. If you saw some of my old photos – especially the publicity photos from the late 1960s – it wouldn't be a stretch to think that Hayes had copied my style of dressing. But my nose is not as big as Isaac Hayes' nose, and I think that he is taller than me. Once I convinced Regina that I had never been known as Isaac Hayes, she and I had a big laugh over her mistaking him for me.

I also enjoyed working with Ray (I affectionately called her "Mrs. Music"). Ray, like Berry, had an unerring ear for talent, and, as I mentioned before, she was very involved in Motown business. In addition to being a bright, effective office manager, Ray was a fountain of creative energy – she wrote arrangements for songs, fine-tuned harmonies, and sometimes sang background vocals in addition to preparing professional lead sheets for copyrights and recording dates. She and I respected one another, and in her book, *Berry, Motown, and Me*, Ray called me the "unsung hero of Motown" (Berry also made mention of my contributions to the label in his autobiography, *To Be Loved: The Music, The Magic, Memories of Motown*).

I appreciated the praise I got from both of them, of course, but I truly was an "unsung hero." And the reality was that most of us backing musicians were unsung heroes – we were not credited for our work. I have already told you that Bobbye Hall worked on dozens of sessions for Motown and got no credit; the same thing happened to me.

One example is the first session that I did with the Jackson 5 (we were recording their debut album, *Diana Ross Presents The Jackson 5*, which would be released on December 18, 1969). Some of L.A.'s finest musicians were at that session: Joe Sample was on keyboards; David T. Walker was on guitar, with Arthur Wright on second guitar; Wilton Felder was playing bass; Harvey Mason was on drums; I was on the congas, of course; Sandra Crouch was on tambourine; and, Jerry Peters played piano. None of us got any credit for our work, which included my conga solo and help with the arrangements.

Although Diana Ross did not actually discover The Jackson 5, she introduced them to us that day – and she would introduce the group to national television audiences on *The Hollywood Palace* on October 18, 1969. The brothers – Jackie, Jermaine, Tito, Marlon, and Michael – were not only a cute bunch of guys, but they were very talented – and natural showmen. I remember Michael being quiet and shy (and also a little inquisitive), but he sure took control of the group (and the audience) when he performed.

That session was also memorable to me because I met the woman who was supposed to be the love of my life in the studio that day. Her name was Kattie, and she was a friend of Sandra Crouch. She was a beautiful Christian young lady (or at least she was at that time), and I was so smitten that I wanted to ask her out right there and then.

When I introduced myself to Kattie, however, she was very quiet; she hardly said a word – she just looked at me. I had no idea what she was thinking, so I decided to try once again to talk with her on my ten-minute break. Again, I got nowhere, so at the end of the session, I told her goodbye and said that I hoped to see her again.

I am happy to say that I not only had the opportunity to see Kattie again, but I that I would also work with the Jacksons many times. I wrote two songs, "Limbo Jelly" and "Zanadu," for their first TV special, and I played on all their music until the breakup of the group (I was never credited for either my playing or my songwriting, although I did receive royalties for my two songs for the TV special, which was produced at CBS-TV). I became friends with all of the Jacksons, but I was especially close to Jermaine; in fact, it was Jermaine who called me with the sad news about Michael's tragic death on June 25, 2009.

Besides working with Motown, I was also being regularly called by record producers and music contractors, so 1969, my first full year as a studio musician, was a busy one for me. At the end of the year, I backed Diana Ross and The Supremes at the Frontier Hotel in Las Vegas for one of their last appearances as a group. Although Diana had announced in November that she would be splitting from The Supremes, I backed them that December (as well as on January 14, 1970, when they made their final appearance – also at the Frontier Hotel – together). In fact, I was on the road with Diana Ross and The Supremes when Karen gave birth to our beautiful son, Kyle, on December 19, 1969. Since I was away, my friend and acting coach, Phil Browning, was there for Karen – and it was such a thrill to meet my handsome new son when I returned home.

Karen and I had gone our separate ways long before Kyle's birth, and I had moved in with a beautiful actress named Connie (she and I were doing a play together and she offered to take me in). I didn't need "rescuing" by now, of course – my career as a sessions musician was taking off – but I was still struggling to make it as an actor. Connie was a good actress, and she was very easy to work with, so I learned a lot from her – and from the acting workshops that we attended together.

Connie and I had only two problems – one was that Connie was being "kept" by some rich old white Jewish guy, and I'm sure that he was as unhappy about me being with Connie as Alan had been when I was with JMC back in Nassau. But Connie's sugar daddy was married and had kids so he couldn't say much – and when he came over from time to time, I would go out for a drive on the Boulevard. I don't think he was a good lay – Connie wanted to spend more time with me than him -- but she did what she had to do in order to keep paying her house rent and her tuition for acting school.

The other problem (for me, at least) was that Connie had three Chihuahua dogs (little rat looking dogs) that were jealous that I was with their mistress. Every time Connie and I would sleep together, those dogs would shit on the bed and pull the covers over it as soon as we left the house! In fact, anytime we would leave – to go to lunch or go to our acting workshops – the dogs would just destroy the place; we would always come home to a mess, and I still don't know how they did it -- they were so small. Those were some jealous dogs; I've been with girls with jealous dogs before, but those three took the cake.

Ironically, it wouldn't be the jealous "boyfriend" who broke up our relationship (although he was partially responsible) – it was Connie herself. One night, I was performing with Diana Ross, who had signed her solo contract in March and began recording solo in May of 1970, at the Coconut Grove. I had brought my other "leading lady," my acting partner Janine, who was a 5-foot, 10-inch beauty, to opening night, and she looked so stunning in her patchwork leather outfit that the photographers were all over her -- as if SHE were the star.

Before I tell you about our eventful opening night, I just want to say that if you have never seen one of Diana's shows, you are missing one beautiful performer. She is really something to watch on stage. And not only is Diana immensely talented, but she also shares a stage better than almost anyone I could name. Unlike some other performers, she wasn't intimidated by my talent or showmanship; I was featured in more shows with her than with any of the other big stars I backed. I believe it was because of the respect that we had for each, and I loved her so much for that.

Diana had no problem putting me right up front – right next to her – to share the spotlight; she also had no problem with me performing solo when she had to leave the stage to change costumes. Diana would have paid any amount of money to have me work with her, and I believe I would still be working with her if it hadn't been for her manager, Shelly Berger (but that's another story).

Since Diana wanted to keep me close to her, I set up my congas on the corner of the stage to her left. Unfortunately, I put my drums too close to the curtain, so when the curtain went up, two of my congas got caught in the material and sailed away into the air. The opening comedian that night was a guy named Albert Brooks, a very funny man who made the most of the moment, exclaiming, "Well, there go flying congas."

They had to bring the curtain back down so I could retrieve the "flying congas" and reposition them. When I walked out on the stage to do so, I heard a voice in the audience exclaim,

"Oh, my God, it's him. Him, my husband. We were never married, but we acted like were," the woman explained to the man accompanying her.

I turned around to look. The place was full of white folks, so I didn't pay much attention – I didn't think the woman could be talking about me. As I continued adjusting my drums, the woman continued,

"That's him! Only one man in the world walks that beautiful. That has to be King."

As I began to play, I looked out at the audience again. And there she sat – her mouth wide open -- Joan Marie. Amazed, I exclaimed, "That's my girl!"

After the show, a waiter brought a note to me. My hands were shaking as I read what JMC had written:

"Have you forgotten me so soon? This is your wife. I will be waiting to say 'hello' to you. I am here with my friend, Mark. Please come and say hello."

JMC had put her home address and telephone number at the bottom of the note, but, of course, I had to go out to see her after the show. I told Janine that I needed to go to meet an old friend who was in the audience, so she waited for me backstage. My heart was pumping hard and fast because I had no idea how I would act. But when I walked out, I was in for a big surprise.

JMC was a changed woman. She was no longer the gorgeous, petite, beautiful girl that I remembered – she was a butterball. She was still very, very beautiful, still gorgeous, but JMC had put on more weight than a sow pig.

"Yes, I've put on some weight since you last saw me," she said, probably reacting to my look of shock.

"That you have," I replied, not knowing what else to say.

JMC then introduced me to her escort, and I shook hands with him. So far, so good, but then JMC made a big mistake when she said,

"Well, you really did make it! I never thought I would see you come this far."

"What the hell do you mean by that? You thought I would curl up and die after you left me?"

"No, Honey, don't take it like that," she protested. "I didn't mean it like that. I was so proud to see you up there. I didn't say it right and I'm sorry for my choice of words. I always believed in you; you know that."

"Very well," I said. "I wish I had more time to talk, but I have a friend waiting for me in my dressing room. Let's get together another time to catch up."

I gave my phone number to JMC, shook hands with her and Mark, and said good-bye. Two days later, JMC called and invited me to come to her apartment in Redondo Beach so we could catch up. She shared the apartment with Mark, who was a big, fat young guy, and another fat, good-looking girl.

Mark, who was on his lunch break, was there at the time, but JMC and I were able to have a good talk.

"How did this happen?" I asked.

"Because you are all I wanted in life. When they took me away from you and you from me, I didn't want anyone else. To prove it, all I did was eat – I ate out of frustration. I ate and I ate and this is what happened to me."

When I left JMC that day, I was free – I was determined to never marry anyone again until I saw JMC. Unfortunately, my newfound freedom would cause me to become the marrying man – there would be many girls that I wanted to marry…and, it wouldn't be too much longer before I would actually take that big step.

In the meantime, JMC and I had an occasional date. One night, I made the mistake of taking her out to dinner at a place called the Hong Kong Bar. Unfortunately, the man who was supporting Connie was also there that evening. All I did was take JMC out to dinner, but by the time I got back to Connie's place, she had my suitcase packed -- her "boyfriend" had called her and told her where I was and that I was with another woman so that was the end of Connie and me. I didn't even have a chance to explain anything to her -- back in those days, girls like Connie got rid of you in a hurry if you messed with them. Connie left for Spain a year later and never returned to America.

One day, out of the blue, I got a personal call from Berry Gordy, so I went to his office at the Sunset Towers to see him. It turns out he wanted me to back one of the few white artists that the Motown label promoted. Her name was Chris Clark, a six-foot, platinum blonde white hippie from the San Francisco Bay area who had recorded a few soul songs with the label.

Chris had wanted to sing, so Berry had signed her up; I would have signed her up myself if I had his money (but not for singing). Berry was managing her (and he was also sweet-hearting her at the time – or so the story goes), so he asked me to do a favor for him and go with Chris to a gig at the Frontier Hotel in Las Vegas.

The previous year, Chris had released an album, *CC Rides Again*, on Motown's newly created rock label, Weed. The album failed commercially, but it went on to become a rare collectible since it was the only album released on that label. It didn't surprise me that it had failed – I didn't think that Chris could sing her way out of a paper bag.

"Please, King, go with her to the gig at the Frontier Hotel in Vegas because you'll make her look good. You always make everybody look good," Berry asked.

Although I was hesitant at first, I agreed because Berry was always nice to me – plus he was paying good money for me to back Chris for a month. I also must admit I am a bad man when it comes to playing my drums and doing my thing, so I thought there actually might be a chance to make her sound better.

Just before I was about to go to Vegas, I called JMC with an offer,

"I'm going to Vegas to work with this girl. Would you like to join me for a week?"

"Oh, yes," she replied, "But I would need a very special gown. You know that I like beautiful things, so I need a special gown in order to go with you."

"No problem," I said.

After JMC gave me an idea of what type of gown she wanted, I went to work. I bought the material and created a beautiful gown – I think the dress cost a few hundred dollars for me to make – and took it to her. She fell madly in love with the gown and said, "O.K., let's go."

So JMC and I went to Vegas, and we had the most wonderful time there for that week. She was still very beautiful, still very gracious, and people were falling all over her, even though she'd put on so much weight. When that woman got dressed up and went into any restaurant or nightclub, she walked like a gazelle, like a graceful gazelle. In spite of having gotten heavy, JMC still had that walk and that face -- you couldn't help but look at her. There was something very special about her.

I just wish I could say that my gig was going that well, although it was on that gig that I met a young wonderful jazz drummer who would become one of my best – and life-long – friends. His name was Washington Rucker, a tall, good-looking chap who reminded me of Calvin Lockhart, the famous Bahamian actor. Like me, Ruck, who was from Tulsa, Oklahoma, had come from humble beginnings (while my early instruments were empty cans and boxes, Ruck had made his music with a knife, a fork, and an old black skillet). Ruck and I also shared a natural sense of rhythm, we both played in our own unique way, and he was as arrogant as I was, so we hit it off right away.

I'm sure that Berry paid the hotel to let Chris sing there (she was so f**king bad). And, to top it off, her music conductor, a little white fellow named Deke Richards, was not that good either. It was going to be a long four weeks!

Determined to make Chris look good, Deke called rehearsals every day – we started at nine in the morning and worked until two in the afternoon. When I got my paycheck the second week, there was no money for the two weeks' rehearsals, so I asked Deke what was going on.

When he replied that nothing was going on, I asked for my rehearsal money – I always got paid for rehearsals, no matter who I rehearsed with (and Deke knew that). Not only had he not requested rehearsal pay for us, but Deke also had the nerve to say we didn't warrant it!

I was so pissed off that I told Ruck that I was going to do something about it, and when he heard my plan, Ruck said,

"If you do it, then I will follow you."

Now, I was right up at the front of the stage, just to Chris' right; I was her "shoulder," if you get my drift. After the band kicked off the opening number, I waited until we were halfway through the song – and then I started taking down my drums and Ruck followed suit. We had not let the other guys in on the stunt, so they were as surprised as Chris was.

Chris looked at me and asked,

"King, what's going on?"

"Ask your conductor," I replied.

"No, King. Whatever is wrong, we can fix it."

"See you, Chris," I responded as I took my drums off the stage with Ruck right behind me.

The best part was that this night there was a fairly good sized audience at the show. A shaken Chris turned to them and announced,

"Excuse me, ladies and gentlemen. We have a little misunderstanding here but we will be right back."

She ran backstage, where both she and Deke began begging me to return.

"I want my money," I told them. "And I want it before I go back on that f**king stage."

Would you believe that Deke ran to his room and came back with the checks for everybody's rehearsal pay – and a week's pay to boot! He was just a little piece of shit for trying to exert his power, but Ruck and I called him on it and we got what we wanted.

Our little rebellion didn't have any serious consequences for me – I was solid with Berry, who depended on me to make his artists look good – but Ruck didn't fare so well; he could never get any more work from Motown. Ruck was such a talented drummer, however, that he did go on to tour with Nancy Wilson, and he recorded with legendary blues shouter Big Joe Turner and did sessions for albums for The Beach Boys, Ray Charles, Dizzy Gillespie, Linda Hopkins, and Stevie Wonder. I also featured Ruck on my first L.A. studio album.

In a funny footnote to Chris' story, two years later she co-wrote the screenplay for Diana Ross' film, *Lady Sings the Blues* – and got nominated for an Academy Award for her work! Chris later became an executive for Motown Productions' film and TV division, so not being such a great singer worked out for her.

Chapter 18

The Ties That Bind

After I returned from the gig in Vegas with Chris, JMC and I remained friends, very close friends, but there was no lovemaking or any of that stuff, and both of us eventually moved on. JMC stayed in L.A. for a while but then decided to return to New York City. Before she left, I introduced JMC to Janine, my acting partner who had become my leading lady offstage as well as onstage. Janine, who was the only white girl I would have considered marrying, was beautiful and slim (the way I love my women), and she was as smart as she was talented. JMC, however, didn't like Janine, and she said something I will never forget,

"You are never going to find what you are looking for. Stop looking for me. I am still here -- I am still inside this fat body, which is fat because of you and Alan. But the woman you are looking for is dead."

Her words were true -- it was only her fat body that was keeping me away from her – and it was a terrible feeling to know that I was partly responsible for that. And, I WAS always looking for her and what we had. I compared every white woman I met to her – and, even though they were all beautiful, there was always something missing…that something I had only with JMC.

After JMC left L.A., we kept in touch with each other from time to time, but I didn't see her again until several years later, when I played at Madison Square Garden with Neil's band. Again, she warned me about another beautiful white woman I brought to meet her – and how I wish I had listened.

At this time, I was living in a rented house on Bronson Avenue in Hollywood. There wasn't much in the house at first, although I did have a bedroom set, but I enjoyed having a place of my own. As you might guess, I wasn't alone very much. It wasn't long before I was dating at least six different girls (two of them were famous). I didn't think about marriage to four of them because, although they were beautiful, they were white. One of them, Gabby, played around too much (just like Connie), so I would not take any chances with any of those girls.

My "main sweetheart" was a 5-foot, 11-inch black model named Michelle, but Janine was a close second. I loved Janine very much, but I changed my mind about asking her to marry me after I met her mother, who was a racist (in fact, neither of her parents approved of their beautiful daughter going out with a black man).

We continued to date, though, and maybe would still be together if it hadn't been for one fateful night. Janine and I were doing a play when a Japanese goddess walked into the playhouse. Chisako, who was from Tokyo, had just finished starring in her own film in Japan, and she had come to Hollywood to try to break into the "big time." At the end of the play, Chisako wiggled her way backstage, introduced herself to me, and told me how much she loved my performance. I was longing for a chance to practice my Japanese, and Chisako was impressed that our entire conversation was in her native language.

When I asked her if she was married, she said no -- that she lived alone.

"Good," I said, "so do I." I didn't mention that I was involved with several women, of course.

I asked Chisako if she would like to get some food, and, after she agreed, I told Janine I would see her later. That was quite alright with Janine because we never went home together anyway; even though we were lovers, we did not live together (Janine still lived with her parents in Sherman Oaks at this time). It was pretty late, so I took Chisako to dinner at a Denny's on Sunset Boulevard, where we talked some more and made plans to see each other again.

When I walked her to her car and kissed her, Chisako held me tight and asked,

"Do you really have to go now?"

"Not really," I replied, although I really wanted to go to Michelle. At that time, Michelle was sharing a big house on Highland Avenue with her family – her cousins, Paul Mooney, the black comedian and comedy writer (he wrote for Richard Pryor), and his wife, Yvonne. They were both wonderful people.

Well, Chisako was a party type, and she had heard that a club had just opened on Sunset and Fuller, not too far from the restaurant. The club, which was called the Citadel d'Haiti, was owned by Bernie Hamilton, an actor friend of mine (Bernie, the brother of jazz drummer Chico Hamilton, would later become well known for his role as Captain Dobey in the TV series, *Starsky and Hutch*).

Chisako and I went to the club in separate cars (she drove a 1969 Ford Mustang and I had a brand new 1970 Buick Opel GT). When we walked in, a reggae group from Jamaica was playing and Chisako pulled me straight to the dance floor. You'll never guess who else was on that floor – Michelle, the woman I had really wanted to be with, and actor Glynn Turman (the future husband of Aretha Franklin) were dancing up a storm; Richard Pryor was also there at the club with the two of them. Michelle and I were so surprised that we just stared at each other.

"What the hell?" I finally said to her. "It's a good thing this young lady wanted to go dancing because I was rushing to try to see you. Looks like everybody's out tonight, though."

"Yes," she replied, "and so are you."

Needless to say, that was the beginning of the end of my relationship with Michelle. There I was with this woman I had just met and there she was with two men I had always thought she was screwing. Both Richard and Glynn were friends of mine, but they were also close friends of Paul and Yvonne. I had seen both them at Paul's house, where Michelle was staying, many times – and I caught one or the other coming out of her bedroom on more than one occasion.

It still amazes me how nobody really gave a shit in those days. Back then – the days when flower children were screwing around whenever and wherever they felt like it (and with whomever they wanted to screw at the time) – people just seemed to go with the flow…as long as they got their own way. In a sense, I miss that time; maybe I wouldn't have had to experience the hurt and disrespect I suffered from a couple of my lovers if I had continued in that easy-going way of life.

Anyway, when we left the club that night, Chisako and I drove to my house on Bronson – which happened to be just around the corner from Chisako's place! She stayed for a few hours, and we made plans to meet for lunch before my 2:00 p.m. session with Bobby Darin (with Bob Rozario conducting) at the A&M studios the next day.

Over lunch, Chisako agreed to meet me after my play, which started at 8:00 p.m. that evening. In the meantime, I called Janine throughout the day, as I always did, and I also called Michelle that evening before I went to the playhouse.

"It sure was a surprise running into you last night – especially since you don't like clubs unless you are working," she told me.

"You couldn't have been more surprised than I was. I was on my way home to you, but I got sidetracked."

"Well, I can certainly see why," she replied. "If I were a man, that Japanese girl could sidetrack me any day. Did you have fun?"

"I might have if I hadn't found you out with the boys."

"You know those are friends," Michelle protested.

"You mean your friends."

"Am I ever gonna see you again?" she asked.

"The ball is in your court. If I get out of the session before 6:00, I will pick you up as usual."

Michelle agreed, but by the time I got to her place, someone had already picked her up. And the evening got worse -- Janine was very cold to me. She told me that she knew I went out with Chisako – and she could tell that Chisako was crazy about me.

When I told Janine that nothing had happened, she said, "Yeah, right," and walked off to get ready for the play. I had to do the same, but to this day I wonder why I never married Janine; I enjoyed her company so much. Janine was the sweetest girl in the world, and she played the guitar and wrote songs. And was she ever classy -- when Janine got dressed up and we went out together, you would swear she was Miss Hollywood.

Being with Chisako changed my mind about getting married, but, although she was my first choice, I wasn't very confident that a marriage would last. She hadn't been in L.A. for very long, and we had only known each other for two weeks, so I was worried that she would leave me once she got to know her way around…and discovered Chinatown.

But one day, I jokingly suggested,
"Let's get married for ten months."
"Why ten months?" Chisako asked.
"As soon as you find your way around town, you will leave me."
"Not if you buy an apartment for me," Chisako replied.

After I promised her that I would try to do that, we drove to Las Vegas to tie the knot. After we got married, we drove back to L.A. and I moved her and all her stuff into my house. The next day, Chisako left the house to do an errand. When she returned, she had a money order for $5,000 for me! When I asked her about the money, she said it was a dowry – that it was the custom for the bride to bring something to the marriage.

I have to say that, even though Chisako was legally the second Mrs. King Errisson, I would call our time together a relationship rather than a marriage, even though I had a great time during the few months we were together. It was only two weeks after our visit to Vegas that I got a call from Berry Gordy. He wanted me to go with Diana Ross for a gig at the Fontainebleau Hotel for a couple of weeks, and I took my new bride with me -- I was so proud of Chisako that I took her everywhere with me. Except for the few times that she had an interview with casting agents, she went to every recording session and TV taping with me. And, whenever I had time for leisure, we played tennis and went horseback riding and swimming.

On the rare times that I would take a road gig, Chisako also traveled with me. I didn't do that too often – I knew that L.A. was funny about studio musicians; usually, they forgot about you and hired someone else if you weren't around. Thank God, I was one of the lucky ones. Sometimes I would be gone for as long as a month and when I returned I would have a month's worth of overdubs to do. Yes, I was that good -- producers would actually hold the percussion work for me to do whenever I got back into town.

I never had to worry about work. When I was working with Diana in Vegas, I got up early in the morning, took a flight out to L.A., did as many as three sessions, and then flew back in time to take a shower before the show. It was wonderful being wanted.

But one night (exactly ten months after Chisako and I got married), I was on stage with Diana when my wife called and left a message. She asked the stage manager to tell me to call her the minute I got off. Now this had been one of the rare times when Chisako wanted to stay home – she had said she was not feeling well (at least that was her excuse).

When I called her back, she spoke to me in Japanese,

"Honey, you were right. I am leaving you."

"Why?" I asked, dumbfounded.

Chisako said that she had found a Chinese man with plenty of money, and he was going to buy an apartment building for her. It turned out that Chisako had become friends with another Japanese girl and they had started going to Chinatown together. That's where she met this guy – just as I had feared.

There was no fussing, no fighting on that call. When I asked her if she knew how much money we had in the joint account, she didn't say any amount – she just said there was "plenty."

Before we hung up, I asked her if she could wait until I came home and we could talk face to face.

"I couldn't leave if I saw you, so please don't come home."

Well, I certainly wanted to talk her out of it, so I took the early morning flight to L.A. But when I drove to my place, she was gone and the house was almost empty. Chisako had taken everything except an office desk that she had bought for me and there was a mattress on the floor. That was it – everything else was gone…except for my money. I still had lots of money -- Chisako had only taken the $5,000 that she had brought to our marriage as a dowry out of my account.

The next time I saw Chisako, she had called to invite me to her travel agency. Not only did her new guy buy a 20-unit apartment building for her, but he had also bought this travel agency – and moved Chisako into a big house in the Hollywood Hills. She begged me to keep our relationship quiet (she didn't want her new husband to know she had once been married to a black man).

I guess I could understand that. And, to be honest with you, I almost wanted to keep this relationship quiet myself. There is a lot more to this story, but I almost didn't say anything about it in the first place – like I said, it was more of a relationship than a marriage.

Amazingly, Janine was there waiting for me after Chisako and I broke our relationship off, and she and I started doing a lot of fun things together on weekends, including going to Zuma Beach in Malibu to run and swim. Janine was a fun girl, and I probably should have married her, but I did not want to be in a family that did not accept me. Janine used to say that I would marry HER, not her mother or father; she didn't care what they thought so why should I? But I always wanted to be a part of the family if I was moving into it, so I patiently waited for their acceptance.

Before I tell you more about what was going on in my career, I want to finish Janine's story. One night, after we did a play together, I promised her faithfully that I would come to her after I had gone home first. By now, Janine had turned 20, and she had moved into her own place. I could come and go as I pleased, as she had given a set of keys to me as soon as she had moved in.

Unfortunately, I had promised Janine that I would come home to her many times and had not shown up. This night, however, I used my key to open the front door and walked into her house. It was a good sized place, so she did not hear me until I got to the bedroom door.

I couldn't believe my eyes – Janine and a big black guy were in bed and were going at it pretty good. When she saw me, Janine pushed him off. I didn't know how long their affair had been going on, but I had only myself to blame – Janine was tired of me breaking my promises; why would she think I would come this night when I had left her alone so many times before?

"Hi, Honey," she finally managed to say.

When the guy turned over, I recognized him as boy I knew from the acting workshop. When he saw who had interrupted his good time, he stammered,

"Oh. Hi, King."

"You're not to talk to him," Janine scolded as she slapped him.

I don't know what Janine expected – maybe she thought I would kill the guy (or kill them both), but, of course, I didn't; I just turned and walked away from the door. Janine jumped out of the bed and followed me.

"Oh, Honey. I'm so sorry," she cried. "I'm so very sorry. I didn't think you would come over tonight."

"My Darling," I replied, "Go back to bed and finish f**king him."

"Honey, please don't leave me. This was the first time this happened and it will never happen again. Honey, please don't leave me," Janine begged.

I just kept walking and laughing, and, would you believe, Janine followed me straight to my car. She was stark naked, but she didn't give a shit!

"Honey, I will not leave you. Now please go back in the house and finish f**king that guy. I'm not working tomorrow, so let's have lunch and we'll talk then."

"You promise you won't leave me? Oh, my King, I love you and I am so very sorry."

"Honey, it's my fault," I reassured her before driving off. "I know you are only human."

When we met for lunch the next day, Janine was still apologizing. She said the guy had caught her at a weak moment and she had kicked him out when she got back in the house. She also said that the guy had no business saying "hi" to me, and she promised that I would never find her in bed with anyone again.

I took her at her word, and we got along great for a few months. Janine and I had such a great understanding; she was one of the few girls that I went with who was comfortable with our relationship. I was glad of that because I did enjoy being around her, but things were about to change.

One day, Janine and I went to an estate auction. By that time, she was taking night courses at UCLA (she was studying about gems), so she didn't want to stay long – but she did wait for just the right thing. Janine had seen a vase in a magazine, so she knew its value and waited for the item to go on the block. The bid opened at $500, and, since there were no other bidders, Janine won the vase.

We left right after she paid and picked it up, and as we drove home, she asked,

"Honey, do you know what we have here?"

"Yeah," I replied, still shocked that she would pay so much money for something that looked pretty ordinary to me, "A $500 antique flower vase."

"No," she replied. And she explained that the vase had some kind of funny name that I can't remember – and that she could sell it for

$35,000!

    We went for a quick lunch before I had to go for a session; I had her drop me off at the studios and arranged for her to come back for me at a certain time. When she returned to pick me up, Janine had the biggest smile on her face – sure enough, she had sold that vase on Rodeo Drive for $35,000…and she said she could have gotten more if she had pushed for it.

    "How much of the money would you like?" she asked.

    "Just buy a good steak dinner for me," I told her.

    We went out and had a great dinner before going home for some good sex. Janine was good in bed, and we did everything to each other. At one point, however, I hurt her. I don't know how it happened – maybe the thought of that big black man on top of her had made me lose control.

    "Honey, please don't. You are everything to me and you've never hurt me before. What's wrong – it seems like you're trying to kill me."

    "Oh, my darling," I replied, "I'm so sorry."

    "You should never hurt me," Janine said.

    Of course, I would never intentionally try to hurt her and I tried to make up for it. I stayed with her throughout the night to reassure her instead of going home, as I usually did. But I think that night was the beginning of the end for us.

    The next morning, I went to my place and she went to work and from work to UCLA for her studies. It wasn't long before she met a rich Arab who had just come from Iran to study and they became friends. I could see her slipping away slowly, and one night, while we were lying in bed, she told me that the guy wanted to marry her. If I wasn't going to marry her, she would marry him!

    I didn't know anything about the guy at the time, so I asked her if he was black or white and where he came from. When she told me, I warned,

    "You know, he only wants to marry you so he can get papers to stay in this country."

    "I don't care," Janine replied. "I am ready for marriage. Besides, the guy is loaded."

    I asked her to give me a little time to think it over – I would sleep on it. I guess I slept too long; two weeks later, they ran off and got married.

    When they returned from their honeymoon, Janine called me and invited me to her new house to meet her husband. I went, of course; after all, I was not angry at her. When I met the guy, I knew that he was just using Janine, but she was happy -- and her mother was elated.

"Looks like you lost that one!" her mother taunted.

"Yes, ma'am," I calmly replied, "Looks like it."

During my visit, Janine called me to her bedroom and told me how sorry she was, but she knew I would never marry her. She had to marry someone – she wanted children. I wish she had gotten pregnant by me, but I was still a playboy at heart and not ready to settle down.

That night, there was a big party in her house. It was a typical Hollywood party, and there was one guy there with more cocaine than you could imagine – pure cocaine, too.

"Janine told me you own a place on Pestell Beach on Acklins Island," he said.

"My people do," I replied. "Do you know Pestell?"

"Yes, that's where I fly my plane to drop off drugs for the local boys to pick up and take to Nassau."

I knew he was not lying because he knew the names of Chester's Bay, Hard Hill, Snug Corner, and Spring Point. It seems this guy got around the island.

Everybody was sniffing his cocaine and getting high that night, including me – it was the first time I had tried it, and I had a wonderful evening. Before I left, I kissed Janine, shook her husband's hand, and wished them both luck.

I didn't see Janine – and didn't even talk to her -- for a few years. By that time, she had what she wanted -- two beautiful girls. Boy, was I jealous; they could have been mine – as much as I loved my boys, I always wanted daughters.

Janine's marriage lasted a few years, but then the guy went back to Iran and brought his Iranian wife over. I started dating Janine again for a short while after her divorce, but the fire was out. I was busy with my travels, and Janine was busy with her kids and the gem store she had opened, so we didn't see much of each other. In fact, the last time I saw her was many years ago, when she put some diamonds into a pair of earrings for me. She was married to a Mexican guy and was doing great; she was a little on the heavy side, but still very pretty.

I really screwed that up big time. Janine was so in love with me, but I let her slip away. It seems that I have a knack for f**king up the people who love me the most. This was not the first time it happened, and, unfortunately, it would happen in both my personal and professional lives in the years to come.

Chapter 19

Milestones and the Incredible Bongo Band

In 1970, in addition to my studio work, I also released my first solo studio album since *Drums of Nassau* for Canyon Records, whose founder and president was Christian Waldemar "Wally" Roker, the former bass singer for the doo-wop group, The Heartbeats (Wally was also a fellow island boy – he had been born in the Virgin Islands). I recorded the album, *The King Arrives*, with a great lineup of talented musicians – David T. Walker and Calvin Keys on guitar, Wilton Felder and Bill Upchurch on bass, Clarence McDonald, Joe Sample, and Jymm Young on piano, Freddie Hill and Jack Walrath on trumpet, George Bohannon and Maurice Spears on trombone, Preston Love on saxes and piccolo flute, and Benny Parks and Washington Rucker, on drums. The album was praised for its conga-driven tracks, which included "Zola," "Samba D Jubilee," "Pwalyetta," "Yesterday is History," "Dracula," "Alone," "Dance After the Feast," and "Udaka," that fused funk, soul, jazz and Caribbean rhythms.

I sold the rights to the album to Canyon Records for $18,000, which was a tidy sum in those days, but I probably lost out on thousands of dollars in royalties -- *The King Arrives* was one of the first jazz albums to sell more than 150,000 copies! Sure, I always got a thrill when I tuned into a jazz radio station and heard my songs being played, but I sure wish I had known more about the recording business at the time.

Before you think that it was just the artist and/or the songwriter who got rich from those recordings, that wasn't the case. Although the record companies pay the costs for production and promotion, they get the lion's share of the pie. It wasn't until many years later, when I went to a function honoring Washington Rucker that I heard Frank Sinatra explain how the recording business worked. Superstars such as Frank, Diana Ross, Barbra Streisand, and Neil Diamond learned to demand huge advances (in the millions) against record sales because they had learned that royalty income was meager because of all the hidden charges the producers deducted from record sales. They also knew (as Frank said) that the best way to make money in this business was to tour, which is why so many recording stars and groups go out on the road so often.

Unfortunately, I had to learn that lesson the hard way. Many years later, I saw *The King Arrives* -- with a price tag of $75 – prominently displayed in the window of a record store on Crenshaw Boulevard in L.A. I was curious about the price, so I walked in and asked the elderly woman behind the counter why the album was so expensive.

"Let me tell you something, son," she replied, "I opened my store with only that album 20 years ago. It's made money for me, and that's the only copy left. Do you want to buy it? Buy it – or go."

Then she looked at me closely, and exclaimed, "My God, I recognize you from your picture! You're the King!"

That old lady's response – and learning that the album has sold for $100 or more in recent years -- made me realize that I had made a huge mistake in selling *The King Arrives* so cheaply. I also regret not having taken more control over my earlier recordings (which was something I did in later years, of course). But I was new at this game, and I actually did better than most.

Some of my memorable sessions from that year include the opportunity to work with Cannonball again. This time, I backed the Cannonball Adderly Quintet on *The Happy People*. We recorded the album in 1970, but it was not released until 1972.

Another session that would literally change my life, although I didn't know it at the time, also happened in 1970, when Herb Alpert of A&M Records called me to work on a song for Karen Carpenter of the popular brother/sister duo, The Carpenters. Herb had signed the two to his label in 1969 – after Karen and Richard had been rejected by every other major record label – and his faith in The Carpenters paid off; they were already well on the road to stardom when I went to that session at Herb's request.

In the studio, I reunited with the talented white drummer I had met when we were both working in the clubs in Atlanta. Like me, Dennis St. John had gone on to become a sought after sessions musician (in my opinion, he was one of the greatest drummers in the world – he could play any type of music), and he was also a talented arranger.

One particular song, however, had some difficult time changes, so Dennis asked me to help him with the beat. Now, Dennis was a great musician and I'm sure that he would have figured out the arrangement on his own, but he was extremely grateful to me -- and he promised that he would return the favor someday. I was happy that I could help him, just as I had helped a lot of other L.A. musicians (and I, too, had been helped along the way), so I certainly didn't think it was necessary to return the favor. But Dennis would follow through on his promise.

My third memorable experience that year, although I didn't know it at the time, would also lead to another connection with Dennis. As I told you, we studio musicians don't always know whose music we are playing – there was nothing secretive about it, our job was just to make a musical assignment come out in the best way possible.

I had worked on lots of songs written by composers whose names I didn't know, but at one session, I was really intrigued by the music I was playing, so I asked the music contractor, Hal Blaine, who was one of the greatest drummers in the world, about the composer of one particular piece. Hal told me that the composer of this song, which was titled "Sooliamon," was singer/songwriter Neil Diamond.

Now, I had heard of Neil, of course – he had many hit records by this time; in fact, I worked on some of his songs before this (not knowing that he was the songwriter) and always thought there was something special about them. But I had never actually worked with Neil before.

At the time, Neil's records were being produced by an Italian genius named Tom Catalano. During their long relationship, Neil and Catalano turned out some wonderful records. And this album, *Tap Root Manuscript*, which was released later in 1970, was no different; it included a number of hit singles, including the classic, "Cracklin' Rosie," which was arranged by Don Randi, the owner of The Baked Potato, the famed jazz club.

As usual, none of the studio musicians worked with Neil on any of the tracks. Catalano and Neil's understanding was that Catalano would take care of everything (musicians, singers, production), and then Neil would come to the studio to sing and play his guitar.

This album, which was Neil's sixth studio album, was considered a little "experimental;" since Paul Simon's *Graceland* was so popular, Neil wrote an extended piece called "The African Trilogy" for *Tap Root Manuscript*. "Sooliamon" was a part of the trilogy, and I would not only be a part of the recording session, but I would also be prominently featured when Neil performed the song publicly for the first time.

Before I tell you about that, something happened in 1970 that greatly impacted my personal life. I have told you that Diana Ross and I had a mutual respect for each other onstage, but we also had a wonderful chemistry offstage as well. We were always playing around – hugging each other cheek to cheek, kissing each other. In fact, there was gossip around Hollywood that we were sleeping together. Diana and I were never lovers – not that I would have minded that; the truth was that she and Berry Gordy had been in a secret relationship for many years before I met them. Yes, Diana was Gordy's woman, so you can imagine my surprise when I saw her around town with a white man.

If something was going on between Diana and Gordy, I sure didn't want to see her with a white man. One night, while I was at dinner with Diana, Berry, and a music executive named Robert Ellis Silberstein, I worked up my courage and playfully asked her to marry me.

"I'll get back to you on that," she joked back. We were always kidding around, but I was actually serious this time.

Well, she didn't get back to me -- in January of 1971, not too long after that exchange, I heard the stunning news that Diana had married Silberstein! I didn't know the reason right away, but it turns out that Diana was pregnant with Berry's child. In her autobiography, Ray Singleton, who was serving as sort of a personal assistant to Diana at the time, said she had been there when Diana made the call to Berry. Ray, who had been through the same thing herself – Berry hadn't divorced his first wife and married her until after their son, Kenny, was nearly a year old -- knew that Barry would not react well to Diana's ultimatum. When Berry refused to marry her, Diana, who was two months pregnant at the time, had married Silberstein.

Although everyone tried to keep up the ruse that Silberstein was the baby's father, it was pretty hard to keep the secret after Diana's daughter, Rhonda Suzanne Silberstein, was born in August of 1971. When I saw that baby, I knew there was no white in her (besides, she was the spitting image of Berry). There were also claims that the marriage was a "business arrangement," but Diana would have two daughters, Tracee Joy (born in 1972) and Chudney Lane (born in 1975), with Silberstein before the couple divorced in 1977 and Diana moved to New York City.

Although 1971 started off on a low note for me personally with the news about Diana's marriage, my career continued to soar. On January 10, 1971, Neil performed "Sooliamon," which we had recorded the year before, on *The Glen Campbell Goodtime Hour*. That performance was my first opportunity to actually perform with Neil, and it was a great experience. Neil performed on a pedestal that had four drummers, including me and Washington Rucker, in African dress beneath it. I was directly to his left, dressed in an impressive yellow costume, Ruck was next to me, and there were two drummers to Neil's right (one of them was an African drummer friend of mine named Lee La Shambu). I think I got some extra "face time" because I was a friend of Glen's (we had worked together as sessions musicians), and you can believe I flashed the biggest smile you've ever seen.

The performance also featured a beautiful African female and four male dancers, and it was so enthusiastically received that I think Neil's smile at the end was as big as mine had been earlier. That was the end of my participation in the show, but Neil also did a medley of some of his hits, including "Holly Holy," "I'm a Believer," and "Thank the Lord for the Nighttime," with Glen and one of his other guests, Linda Ronstadt (Liberace was also on that show).

Glen and I did get a chance to catch up after the show. I loved Glen – he was one of the handful of studio musicians who made it to the big time, and I can't think of anyone who deserved it more. He was a genuinely nice guy, but both of were so busy that I didn't see him again until several years later, when, ironically, I was playing in Neil's band. The tour included a stop in Scottsdale, Arizona, and Glen came backstage after the show to greet Neil and to tell me how great it was to see me again. The three of us chatted for a few minutes before Neil had to leave, but Glen and I continued to talk about the "old days" and his hours on the golf course, and the evening flew by far too quickly.

A month or so later, I was again backing Diana Ross at the Fontainebleu Hotel in Miami Beach, and we had a special guest in the audience. After the show, I walked up to Muhammad Ali and asked him if he remembered the island boy who had played the congas for him at his 20th birthday party at the Carver Hotel. Ali replied that he did, indeed – and he proceeded to hug me in his big arms like he did back when we first became friends.

After the show, Ali joined us – me, Diana, and Berry Gordy – at the bar, and we had a great time talking and laughing. Diana looked hot – she was beautiful and sexy, so everyone was after her.

During our conversation, I said to Ali,

"I wish I were as big as you are. Then, I'd call you a dirty name and you could give me a big pay day in the ring."

In those days, every one of his opponents got a pay day – people would flock to see Ali fight. So I jokingly started sparring with him.

Ali, who was smiling as he sparred with me, turned to Diana and said,

"You'd better send this boy to bed if you want a drummer tomorrow night."

"It's now 2:00 a.m.," I replied. "Maybe YOU had better get some rest or "Smokin' Joe" will beat you up."

Again, Ali predicted that he would win the fight in six rounds, but he was way off this time -- and I'm sure that Beaudine was sobbing his eyes out when Ali met Frazier on March 8, 1971 at Madison Square Garden in "The Fight of the Century." Ali's strategy was to make

Frazier "arm weary" from pummeling him, so he took a lot of hits (and ended up with a badly swollen jaw that would require x-rays at the hospital). The fight went 15 rounds and ended with a unanimous decision for Frazier, who not only gave Ali his first loss, but also took away his heavyweight championship title. The decision, by the way, was roundly booed by the crowd. Ali and Frazier met two more times – on January 28, 1974 for a non-title match that Ali won in a 12-round decision, and on October 1, 1975, when Ali won the "Thrilla in Manilla" by a TKO after the 14th round to regain the heavyweight championship.

I wouldn't see Ali until many years later, when I attended a function in his honor. Ali was already suffering from the ravages of Parkinson's Disease at this time, so he didn't recognize me when I walked up to him! And he still didn't seem to know who I was when I brought up incidents from the past to try to jog his memory. It made me very sad, but the next day Beaudine came to see me at the Bahamian restaurant I had opened, and he told me that Ali didn't know anyone anymore. It was a terrible feeling to know that I lost my friend long before his death on June 3, 2016, and I will always cherish the memories I have of the wonderful times we had together.

Later in March, I played on the session for what would become one of Neil's "signature songs," "I Am…I Said." Hal Blaine was once again in charge of that session, for which I played congas and the tambourine. Like we did before, the musicians did the session without Neil, so I didn't hear the lyrics until I was driving down Franklin Boulevard in Hollywood one day. The song just blew me away (and it remains one of my favorites), and I couldn't help thinking that if I didn't known better, I would think this man was black…or a white boy who had suffered a lot. When I told Neil about my thoughts sometime later, he thought that the story was touching – and said that he had, indeed, been through a lot.

That year, I also had my first session with one of my favorite performers, Barbra Streisand. Barbra was working on her *Stoney End* album, and I was able to "put my two cents in" regarding the arrangement on the title track (by this time, most people listened to my input). Both the album and the single were great successes, so Barbra had the utmost confidence in my work and we became great friends.

In 1971, I also had the pleasure of working with folk singer John Stewart on his fourth album, *The Lonesome Picker Rides Again.* John, who was a very nice guy, had been a member of The Kingston Trio from 1961-1967, and he was also the composer of several popular songs, including The Monkees' No. 1 hit, "Daydream Believer." The album was produced by John's younger brother, Mike Stewart, who was also a nice guy.

I teamed up with John and Mike again in 1972 for John's fifth studio album, *Sunstorm*. Mike did background vocals and handclaps on the album, and he also played acoustic guitar and shakers. As before, I had a great time working with both of the brothers, and I would continue to have a long association with Mike, who produced a lot of albums (his biggest success was Billy Joel's *Piano Man*). In fact, I did at least one session a week for Mike before we had a falling out that ended not only our working relationship but also our friendship (I'll tell you more about that in another chapter).

That year, I again heard from Dennis St. John, who had joined Neil Diamond's band in 1971. Dennis was indeed trying to return my favor, asking me to join the band for its upcoming Hot August Night concert at the Greek Theater. Neil's previous engagement there, which had begun on August 23, 1971, had run for seven nights; the 1972 version would include ten shows, beginning on August 18 (the performances were later released on Neil's 1972 album, *Hot August Night*). Unfortunately, I had other commitments at the time and had to turn down both the gig and Dennis' offer to join the band.

In 1972, I also decided to try to do a few gigs of my own. An old organ player friend of mine offered to find musicians for my band, and he also found a restaurant and bar where we could rehearse during the day. When I was driving to the first rehearsal, I noticed a young black man who was standing on a street corner. Both he and the rusty old steel drum that he was holding caught my attention, so I pulled the car over and asked him where he was going.

"I'm on my way to a rehearsal with a guy named King Errisson," he replied.

"Oh, I know him and how to get to that restaurant," I said. "Hop in and I'll take you."

I didn't tell Vince who I was, so it was a big surprise when he found out that he would be playing with me. I got the even bigger surprise, though – the guy was fantastic! I had never before – and haven't since – heard someone play those steel drums like Vince did.

I told you that I used to "fake" my way through some sessions – if they asked me if I could play steel drums, I said I could, of course. I guess that I played them adequately enough to get the job done, but all that changed when I met Vince. I never touched a steel drum again (except for playing them on my album, *L.A. Bound*, which was released in 1977); I made sure that Vince was called when someone needed steel drums on a recording.

Vince, who was born in St. Kitts, had first gained notice when he played at the Caribbean Pavilion at the New York World's Fair in 1964-1965, and he also played at Canada's Montreal Expo '67 before coming to Los Angeles to become a studio musician. I could certainly sympathize with Vince, who was an unknown with a lot of talent (as I had been), so I took him everywhere with me – and recommended him to anyone who needed a steel drum player. At one session, I suggested that Vince play the steel drums instead of me. That didn't go over well – they had hired me, after all – but I had an engineer friend of mine fix up two mics; Vince's would be "live" and my mic was not turned on.

Well, Vince did a fantastic job. The producers were enthused over how great the steel drums sounded, and they rushed over to congratulate me (in those days, everybody was always high so they paid very little attention to what was going on – they only knew it sounded good).

"It wasn't me," I responded. "It was my friend here, Vince Charles."

That session broke the ice for Vince, who would go on to record on albums by the Beach Boys, David Crosby, Crosby, Stills, Nash & Young, Neil Diamond, and Richard Greene. I was also fortunate to have him work on several of my albums, including *We Must Say Good-bye* (1973), *Errisson is King* (1981), and *Man* (1993).

I was especially happy to introduce Vince to Herb Alpert. Herb, who had disbanded his original Tijuana Brass Band in 1969 (although the group did an album together in 1971), was in the process of forming another group, which was billed as Herb Alpert and the T.J.B. Vince's sound and style was a perfect match for the new band, which made two albums and toured in 1973 and 1974.

Speaking of Herb Alpert, I thought he was one of my great friends in the music business, but he never gave me a record deal. Neither did another friend, Quincy Jones, who had joined the label in 1969 as a songwriter and producer as well as a recording artist). Quincy, who had been nominated for three Grammy Awards for his first three albums on the A&M label, called me for dozens of sessions when he needed percussion (and he also wrote a glowing introduction to *Learn to Play Like the King*, a book that I wrote about how to play the congas), but neither he nor Herb would sign me to the label. But they weren't the only ones – the list goes on and on – and I came to the conclusion that the studios want to keep certain people in the "right" place.

It is the same in every business, I guess. If you promote all the canners to managers, there is no one to can the fish; and that's all a studio musician is – a canner. If they gave recording contracts to all the great musicians, who would they get to make the music for them? I know that I'm better than some of the people I helped to make stars -- there's a lot of them, but, again, that's the way life goes.

Despite being an "unsung hero" behind recording stars, one of my sessions would play a major role in the evolution of a new, exciting genre of music. It began in 1972 with Michael Viner, who was in charge of Pride Records, a subsidiary of MGM Records. As the A&R man, Viner produced soundtracks for a number of American International Pictures, working with such stars as Frankie Avalon, Annette Funicello, Frank Sinatra, and Sammy Davis, Jr. In fact, Viner was largely responsible for Sammy's only chart-topping hit, "The Candy Man," which became one of Sammy's signature songs (despite Sammy's initial dislike for the song, which he thought was too saccharine).

"The Candy Man," which was also known as "The Candy Man Can," was written by Leslie Bricusse and Anthony Newley for the 1971 Paramount film, *Willy Wonky and the Chocolate Factory*. Viner and Mike Curb, who had merged his own record company with MGM Records in 1969 and was now the president of MGM Records/Verve Records, wooed Sammy away from Motown Records, signed him with MGM Records, and, along with Don Costa, Jimmy Bowen, Perry Botkin, Jr., and Isaac Hayes, produced Sammy's 1972 album, *Sammy Davis, Jr. Now*. The album included the Grammy Award-winning song, which Viner had handpicked for the project (and which featured The Mike Curb Congregation), and "The Candy Man" was also released as a single that year (the B-side was "I Want to Be Happy").

When Viner called me, he was working on a B-movie called *The Thing with Two Heads*. When the film, which starred Viner's friend and former roommate, Rosey Greer, and Ray Milland, was deemed by MGM management to need an additional chase scene, Viner needed to find appropriate music to heighten its dramatic effect.

The soundtrack to the film already included several songs from the 1950s and 1960s, including "A Prayer" by Jerry Butler, "Dip, Dip, I Got My Hands Full" by Billy Butler & Infinity, "Here I Am Again" and "May the Best Man Win" by Ollie Nightingale, "Fool's Paradise" and "I'm Truly Happy" by the Sylvers, "Take My Hand" by Sammy Davis, Jr., and "Oh Happy Day" by The Mike Curb Congregation. These tracks, all of which were from the MGM/Pride catalog, were done in a funk style, so Viner chose "Bongo Rock," a song co-written by Art Laboe and Preston Epps (who reached the Top 40 with the song in 1959), for the scene. His second selection was "Bongolia," which was also heavy on bongos, congas, rock drums, and bass, so it was a good complement to "Bongo Rock" for the chase scene footage.

"Bongolia" was composed on the spot in the studio by Jim Gordon and me. We were just jamming while waiting to record the track we came to do, and any fool listening to the song can tell it was a spontaneous moment. But whenever we played any kind of riff, Mike had the tape on record mode. Neither Jim nor I knew the song would be used in a movie – and we didn't get any credit for our work.

Viner called in a few of his favorite sessions musicians (including me to play the bongos) to record the two songs, and we were billed as The Incredible Bongo Band in the film credits and on the film's soundtrack LP. Viner realized that he had created something special, so he decided to release "Bongo Rock" and "Bongolia" as a single. There was no "real" Incredible Bongo Band – I was the featured musician and the acknowledged leader of the band, but numerous sessions musicians played on recordings attributed to the group. At various times, The Incredible Bongo Band included drummers Jim Gordon, Kat Hendrikse, and Ed Greene, percussionist Bobbye Hall, Joe Sample on piano, Mike Melvoin (keyboards), Robbie King (organ), Mike Deasy, Dean Parks, and David T. Walker on guitar, Jerry Scheff (bass), Wilton Felder (bass and saxophone), and Steve Douglas (saxophone and horns). Various "guest" musicians also played on some of our tracks.

This presented a real problem when it was time to design the sleeve and the promotional materials for the single. Viner assembled a fake band to appear in photographs and in publicity materials, and whenever the "band that never was" did a public performance, they faked it – they just played along with the tracks.

Although R&B DJs were receptive about playing the single, the record stopped selling when people saw the photograph of all the white guys in the band. Actually, that representation wasn't too far from the truth – most of the musicians who played with The Incredible Bongo Band were white (besides me, only David T. Walker, Wilton Felder, and Bobbye Hall, the talented female percussionist, were black). Viner and the record company remedied the situation by re-releasing the single in a plain white sleeve.

The single, especially the "Bongo Rock" A-side, was a minor hit in the U.S. but a big hit in Canada in 1973, so Viner set out to record more music with the "band" that year, using MGM recording facilities during "down-time" between other sessions. Our first album, which was titled *Bongo Rock* and credited to Michael Viner's Incredible Bongo

Band, was arranged and produced by Perry Botkin, Jr. and featured me, Jim Gordon, Steve Douglas, Jerry Scheff, Robbie King, and Mike Deasy. Tracks included "Bongo Rock," of course (although the song is listed as "Bongo Rock '73" on the track listing), and "Bongolia" from the film, as well as several covers ("In-A-Gadda-Da-Vida, "Raunchy '73," and a tune called "Apache"). The remaining tracks were "Let There Be Drums," "Last Bongo in Belgium," and "Dueling Bongos."

Although I was the featured player on these The Incredible Bongo Band recordings (as well as our second album, which I will tell you about later), Viner took all the credit. He not only took credit for putting the band together, but he also did not bother to correct a misconception that it was HIM playing the bongos on The Incredible Bongo Band recordings! I shouldn't have been surprised – Viner was always bragging, always boasting; in fact, he once claimed that he had produced Isaac Hayes' album, *Shaft* (the truth is that the album was released on Nashville-based Stax Records and Isaac was the composer, main vocalist, and producer).

In addition to not being properly credited for my work, I missed out when it came to compensation, too. I have to take the blame for that, though -- Viner had offered one percent of the royalties on the original recordings to me, but I (foolishly) turned his offer down. I was so busy – and biggity – at the time that I said, "Just pay me."

Well, Viner did just that. I got paid for those sessions, but little did I know that our recordings would take off and sell millions of copies (both when they were released and in the future). Since I had been paid already, I missed out on the royalties from those early releases as well as re-releases of our two LPs. But where I really missed out was with the unexpected – and continued – success and influence of "Apache."

"Apache" was written by English songwriter and composer Jerry Lordan, who was inspired by the 1954 American Western of the same name. The song was originally recorded by British guitarist Bert Weedon in early 1960, but it wasn't released until being covered by the British group, The Shadows, several months later. Although the song was No. 1 on UK singles charts for five weeks (and Weedon's version, which was released in the wake of the popularity of The Shadows' version, climbed to the No. 24 spot), audiences in the U.S. and Canada were introduced to the song by Danish jazz guitarist Jørgen Ingmann, whose cover reached No. 2 on the Billboard Hot 100 and No. 9 on the U.S. R&B chart (it was also a No. 1 hit on Canada's CHUM Chart) in 1961.

Other covers of "Apache" included Sonny James' vocal version in 1961 as well as instrumentals by such groups as The Ventures in 1962 and Allan and The Arrows in 1965. At the time it was first released, The

Ventures' version did not use congas; the band in those days consisted of co-founders Don Wilson (rhythm guitar) and Bob Bogle (bass guitar), Nokie Edwards (lead guitar), and Howie Johnson (drums). Several years later (around 1969 or 1970), The Ventures were recording under the United Artists label, and I was called to the label's recording studios to play congas on the song. It was such a great pleasure to work with the band, which still included Wilson and Bogle, but Gerry McGee was on lead guitar, Mel Taylor played drums, and John Durrill was on keyboards. I played "Apache" for the first time in that session; The Incredible Bongo Band's version wasn't released until 1973, and Viner told me that our cover of the song sold two million copies, topping the U.S. R&B charts.

"Apache" – specifically the long percussion break that features Jim Gordon and me – is still going strong. The song has been dubbed "the national anthem of hip-hop" due to its influence on the Bronx-born music genre known as hip-hop, and "Apache" has also been sampled countless times on rap and dance tracks.

Because I was one of the two key drummers on the break, I was featured on a 2006 Danish TV documentary (I discussed the making of the song and its later influence on hip hop), and in a 2012 documentary, *Sample This*, which was written and directed by my friend, Dan Forrer, who had spent years researching and creating the film. The documentary, which premiered at the British Film Institute in June of that year, was narrated by Gene Simmons of KISS fame, and included footage of Rosey Greer, Perry Botkin, Jr., Mike Curb, all the musicians (except Jim Gordon) who played on the *Bongo Rock* album, and a number of prominent hip-hop DJs, including Kool Herc, Grandmaster Caz, and Afrika Bambaaataa.

Chapter 20

Making Music with the Stars

In 1973, I also released my second solo L.A. studio album, *We Must Say Goodbye*. Since I was unable to get a deal with a major record company, I released the album on my own label, Kosons Records. I produced the album and wrote and arranged the eight tracks, which also included "Everyone Knows," "Life," "Pretty Pepper," "Mango Man," Yesterday is History," "People Got To Live a Better Way," and "King's Jam." I also sang on some of the tracks and, of course, played percussion on all of them.

The album also featured the talents of David T. Walker, Jose Corona, Mike Stuart, and Roy Gaines on guitar, Wayne Douglas and Wilton Welder on bass, Benny Parks and Harvey Mason on drums, and Vince Charles on the steel drums and marimba. The strings for the album were arranged by Jimmie Haskell, and featured the Sid Sharp String Players.

Since I was hoping that a major record label would pick the album up once they heard it, we pressed only a couple hundred copies. Because it wasn't picked up, the album has become quite a collector's item. I have seen it start at over $75, and it sold for over $125 in an online auction in 2014.

I also heard from Dennis St. John again in 1973. This time, he was working with a young country singer named Jim Stafford on his self-titled album, which would be released in 1974.

"You helped me out once, and now I'm hoping you'll help me again," he said. "Please, you've got to come with me to make me look good."

We drove to a studio in Torrance, California, where I suggested some changes to some troublesome passages in one of the songs, "Spiders and Snakes." The song, which was recorded the way I suggested, would go on to become a No. 3 single and sell over two million copies! It was a fun song, and I had a great time with Stafford and his manager and producer, Phil Gernhard, at the session. Both of them were very appreciative of my input, and I became close friends with both Jim and Phil.

Dennis was also appreciative, of course, so he again showed his gratitude by extending another invitation to join Neil's band for an upcoming world tour. Dennis told me that Neil, who had taken some time off from touring in 1972, was getting ready to go back on the road in 1974 and Dennis was assembling a group of talented musicians to back him. I told Dennis that I would think about it – I had a lot going on at the time, so it wouldn't be until the next year that I finally made a decision.

I also had another opportunity to work with Cannonball; we recorded his album, *Inside Straight*, and he was as pleased as I was over my success as a studio musician. Yes, life was going great – I had purchased a beautiful home in Beverly Hills, and reconnected with Kattie, the beautiful girl I had met during the Jackson 5 session. Kattie spent much of her time at my home with me, even though she had her own place. But, unfortunately, our "good life" wouldn't last too long.

I made one of the biggest mistakes I had ever made in my life when I returned home to Nassau in December of 1973 to spend the Christmas holidays with my family. Now, that may not sound like a big mistake, but my trip led to a fateful encounter with a woman from my past.

Before I tell you more about that, I'll tell you a little about Pepper and why she had been so spiteful to me when I needed her help when I first came to L.A. I had met Pepper when we were both youngsters in Nassau, and she grew up to be a beautiful woman. As you know, I have a weakness for beautiful women, but I was also adamant about not getting married. After Pepper gave birth to my big, beautiful son, Vans (Vance), on April 19, 1967, however, I promised that I would come back and marry her after I made it big. Was I ever sorry I had made that promise!

When I ran into Pepper on that trip home, I almost didn't recognize her; she was no longer the beautiful woman I remembered. Pepper had become a dope head, so she was skinny as a rail and had few or no teeth in her mouth, and, to top it off, she reeked of rum.

I felt sorry for Pepper, so I spent the evening with her – although all I remember of it was getting drunk (in fact, we both got very drunk). The next day, Pepper told me that we were married! I didn't believe it, and I still don't believe it as I have never seen any marriage certificate. But Pepper was convinced we were married (as so was my mother – she called me an ass), and she wanted to come back to L.A. with me! I told Pepper if that was the case I had made a big mistake – I had a beautiful woman waiting for me back in L.A., so Pepper would have to wait a few months for me to clear things up with Kattie.

That's how I ended up returning to Kattie as a married man. When I told her what happened, Kattie cried and packed her bags, but I convinced her to stay. I sure didn't want to be married to Pepper – and I didn't want to lose Kattie. I didn't think that Pepper would ever come to me looking like she did, but she was knocking on my door within a week! I couldn't believe my eyes when I opened the door and saw her there.

"Surprise!" she exclaimed.

"You got that right," I replied. "I thought you were supposed to wait for me to send a ticket."

"I couldn't stay away from my husband any longer," Pepper protested.

"Well, Kattie is in the bedroom," I told her, before I called for Kattie.

When Kattie came down, I introduced them, and I must say that Kattie was very strong at that point. She said "good-bye" to me and walked out the door, saying she was going home. She drove an old 1965 Chevrolet that you could hear a block away when she started it, so when I didn't hear it start for some time, I went out to look for her.

Sure enough, the car was still there, so I walked around the yard and then down the street, thinking that maybe she had gone for a walk. I came upon her lying in some bushes, so I sat down across from her and told her how sorry I was – and that it would not be long before she would have me all to herself.

Although my personal life was in shambles, 1974 would be a busy year for me professionally, including another project with Michael Viner. The first Incredible Bongo Band album wasn't the huge success that we had hoped it to be, but we followed it up in 1974 with *The Return of the Incredible Bongo Band*. This time, Viner had wanted to go to Vancouver, British Columbia, to record, and what a great time we had during the week we were in Canada! Our sessions were hot – Perry Botkin was again our producer (along with Viner), Steve Douglas, who was our Canadian coordinator, played horns, and there was also Jim Gordon on drums, me on congas, Jerry Scheff on bass, and Jim Horn on sax. Viner really knew how to produce a session; he treated everyone like kings, but why not? We made a lot of money for him.

The new LP featured some cover songs, including "Pipeline," "Wipeout," and "I Can't Get No Satisfaction," and it also included some of Viner's "corny" song selections ("When the Bed Breaks Down, I'll Meet You in the Spring," "Hang Down Your Head Tom Dooley, Your Tie's Caught in Your Zipper," and "Got the Sun in the Morning and the Daughter at Night"). Even though Viner made some strange song choices, he had the savvy to hire talented musicians and we always managed to make those songs work.

The cover of the second album, which was designed by Viner, featured him, me, Perry Botkin, Jr., and Jim Gordon. I must say that I looked rather handsome (although serious) in my red jacket and wide-brimmed hat – like those worn by the Mounties (Canadian Mounted Police) – but I don't think that any Mountie ever had a gold neckpiece like mine (it can clearly be seen in the cover photo)! That cover was one of the rare times that I received any recognition at all for my work with The Incredible Bongo Band.

During our trip, we ran into Ernie Watts, who had just bought a small island nearby. Ernie, who is one of the finest jazz saxophone players in the business, plays tenor, alto, and soprano sax as well as the flute, and he worked with a number of artists that I backed (like me, he had worked for Motown -- he can be heard on several of Marvin Gaye's albums from the 1970s). Since I was having such a great time, I decided to see if my charms would work on the girls in Vancouver, so one night, after our sessions were finished, I left my hotel to try my luck. And did I get lucky -- right away, I saw the prettiest blonde girl passing by, and I tried one of my favorite lines,

"Honey, are you always this pretty or did you expect to meet me?"

"Did you know I was coming for you?" she replied, much to my delight.

"Well, Darling, you found me," I answered, "So let's have dinner."

The blonde accepted, so we went to the hotel restaurant and had a wonderful dinner before going up to my room, where we made love all night. The next morning, she got up, took a shower, and thanked me for a great evening. Before she left, I asked her if I would see her again. She said she didn't know, but then she kissed me, told me again that she had a great time, and said she would try to see me later. Unfortunately, I never heard from her again and don't know what happened to her. I guess some women are like some men – one-night stands are enough for them. They have a good time, but then they move on.

That experience brought back memories of the girl who was sent to kill me after JMC had been taken away from me. This time, I didn't need to take the woman's pocketbook away from her to make sure she would not pull out a gun and shoot me, but I had great sex both times; of course, I was sorrier that I wouldn't see this girl than I was about not seeing the would-be assassin again.

I didn't have much time to dwell on my "loss" – that very morning I received some disturbing news. Keg Johnson, a friend of mine in L.A., placed a call to me at the hotel (of course, we didn't have cellphones in those days, so he had probably gotten information on where

I was staying from Viner or one of his people). Anyway, Keg had called with the news that he had found my "wife," Pepper, in my house, where she had tried to kill herself!

On the day Keg found Pepper, he hadn't known that I was out of town, so he came by to see me. When he got to the house, the front door was wide open and he could hear the dogs barking. When he noticed that my car wasn't there, he realized that I was away, so he went back into the house to try to find out why the door was open. He started looking around, and when he saw water coming down the stairs, he ran up to the bathroom – and found Pepper bleeding to death in the tub. He called the police before finding out where I was and making his call to me.

I told Keg that I would see Pepper when I came back; I was not about to lose work because of her bullshit. I was finished with Pepper -- six months after coming to L.A., she had stolen over $50,000 from me and sent it back to her dope buddies in Nassau. I was furious, of course, and went to the bank to ask them how they could let so much money be withdrawn from my account without my signature. When I threatened to sue them if I didn't get it back, they said I couldn't do that because this was America and the wife has the right to sign her husband's name. Of course, I closed my bank account right away!

Determined to protect myself, I had gotten a job for Pepper so she could start spending her own money. But that wasn't the last of Pepper's costly antics! One day when I went to Berkeley, California to record with Cannonball, I got a call from my publicist, who told me that she believed that Pepper was having an affair and I might want to check that out.

After two days in Berkeley, I got a call to do a TV show with Barry Manilow, so I left on an early flight to L.A. I snuck home that morning, and when I opened the door, I found Pepper with the other man. I beat the shit out of both of them – they both ended up in the hospital – so a warrant was issued for my arrest.

After the taping with Manilow, I flew back to Berkeley to finish my session with Cannonball – I was not about to turn myself in until I had finished my commitment to him. So it wasn't until two days later that I went to my lawyers to explain my problem and they accompanied me to the Beverly Hills police station, where I surrendered to the police.

After being fingerprinted, I was released on a $5,000 bail. It took three months for the case to be settled (at a cost to me of $70,000), and I couldn't believe what happened at that trial – you would have thought I had killed someone! All I had done was beat those two people like they stole something; and they did – they stole my pride. I only won the case because of the lone black on the jury. That woman was adamant that I was not guilty, so after the verdict was read I thanked her for freeing me, as those whites sure wanted to send me away.

The following month, however, the guy, who was a struggling actor, sued me for a million dollars, saying that I had caused him to lose a job in Japan. When my lawyer asked him how much money he made and what he expected to be paid for the supposed lost job, the guy said he was just getting started and had not been paid too much so far, but that he was going to be paid a lot for this job in Japan.

"How much is 'a lot'?" my lawyer asked.

"Maybe $10,000," the guy replied.

Well, before everything was over, Pepper took my side; when she said she was wrong, the guy lost all hope of getting big money from me – and of getting Pepper's help in finding a job. I believe I paid about $700 to patch his head up, as my lawyer, Gordon, said to offer something to keep him out of my life, but he didn't get another dime.

After the mess with the so-called actor, I just wanted Pepper to leave and go back to Nassau -- I certainly never wanted her to kill herself (although she had already tried to do so a couple of times because she was always seeking attention).

After I left Canada and got back home, I went straight to the Culver City Hospital, where I saw Pepper; she was lying in a bed and had tubes everywhere. The doctor said Pepper was on some kind of drugs – that she was on something and had been for a long time -- but they were having trouble finding out which ones. After she had been in the hospital for a week and they still had no answers, I told them that it was costing me money and they should just release her if she was able to go home. The doctor said there was nothing they could do for her, so I took Pepper, who had both wrists bandaged up and looked like shit, home.

Seeing the way she looked brought back memories of the first week that Pepper was in L.A. I spent $4,500 on her mouth then so she would look decent. Having a great looking mouth gave Pepper the confidence to speak to people…and she had the most beautiful way of speaking you will ever hear. People were also impressed by her intelligence – Pepper was very highly educated and had an IQ of 180, I think. Yes, she was smart, but she used her intelligence for all the wrong reasons.

Pepper stayed with me for a couple of months after getting out of the hospital but I finally couldn't stand the sight of her so I put her out and told her I would file for divorce (even though I still hadn't seen any marriage papers). She hung around L.A. for a while before leaving to return to Nassau.

Unfortunately, that was not the last I heard of Pepper. On the way home to Nassau, she made a stop in Miami, where she made friends with a banker. Would you believe that he let her cash one of my checks for $40,000? I couldn't believe that she would try to do that (or that they let her without checking the account first), but I told you that she was pretty smart, and she and her pretty new mouth must have poured on the charm. As luck would have it, I had learned my lesson after the first time she stole from me; I had closed that account and opened a new one.

One day, when I was taping the *Tony Orlando and Dawn* TV show, a police detective came to the CBS studios and waited for me to finish. He asked me if I knew Pepper, and I replied that I did – that she had been my wife for ten months. Next, I was asked if I had given her a check for $40,000.

"Hell, no," I replied.

The detective wanted to know if I knew where she was – and she should be happy that I didn't (I sure would have told them).

When I asked if she had gotten the money, I was told that she had withdrawn half of it and the check had bounced.

"Well, it should have. I closed down the account months ago."

"Would you help her to pay the money back?" the detective asked.

"Hell, no. Put the bitch in jail. If she cashed the check in Miami, then she should be in Miami."

The detective then left, but about a month later I got a call from Pepper's mother – she wanted me to help Pepper or she was going to jail. I told her that was too f**king bad – Pepper deserved being put in jail for what she did.

The next news that I got was that Pepper had been arrested, but I later heard that she was back in Nassau; I was told that someone in the Bahamian government had helped her out. That was a good thing for her – after all the crap that she had pulled on me, I would have let her rot in jail.

In a related development, Perry Botkin, Jr. deemed The Incredible Bongo Band a failure (despite the success of our albums), and he pulled the plug on Viner's "vanity project." That certainly didn't mean I was out of work -- 1974 was a good year for me. Still pursuing my dream of becoming a film actor, I hired Robert Ellenstein, a noted actor and drama coach, who came to my home in Beverly Hills to work with me. Ellenstein, who is perhaps best known for his role as henchman Licht in Alfred Hitchcock's 1959 spy thriller, *North by Northwest* (and, later, for playing the Federation President in *Star Trek IV: The Voyage Home*), was a great teacher. In fact, he taught theater for over 50 years, and Ellenstein also founded the Academy of Stage and Cinema Arts in L.A.

I learned a lot from Ellenstein, and I realized my dream of appearing on the big screen again that year, when I was cast in *Uptown Saturday Night*, which featured an all-black starring cast that included Sidney Poitier (who also directed), Bill Cosby, Harry Belafonte, Flip Wilson, Richard Pryor, and Calvin Lockhart. Sidney Poitier had cast fellow Bahamian actor Lockhart due to his similar charismatic style and intelligence, but I got cast for a very different reason.

My agent had sent my photo to the production people, and, as luck would have it, I was the spitting image of my Uncle Edward, who used to shoot dice in the streets with Sidney! And the part was that of a flamboyant gambler named Chicago – the nickname that Sidney had given to my uncle. When I was called to the production offices, I was told that a script would be sent to me, but I didn't hear from the production people again until I got a call to go to wardrobe. And I didn't get another call until I was told to report to the studio to film my scene!

I didn't know a thing about my scene, but I thought it would be easy to fake it, especially since it involved being in a casino. But several lines had been written for the part of Chicago, and when it was my turn to speak, I had no idea what to say! Sidney immediately stopped the filming. He was not too happy when he asked me why I had flubbed my lines, and he was astonished that I hadn't received a script. He had one brought over to me and I had ten minutes – ten minutes -- to learn my lines.

I thought I did O.K. – although I was unhappy that I hadn't had time to study the part and make the character my own. It turns out that someone on the production staff didn't like me –she thought I got my role simply because I was a Bahamian – so she hadn't sent the script. But I had a good time on the set – where I met (and charmed) a beautiful Jewish woman named Eloise who was in the editing department. It was Eloise who told me (as we were lying in bed after making love) that my speaking scenes were on the cutting room floor!

Was I ever disappointed! I can be seen at the tables in the nightclub scenes, but my name didn't appear in the credits as I had no speaking role! All was not lost – on the upside, I received $14,000 for that week's work and I met Eloise and many other nice people. But I still felt that a man of Sidney's stature should have done more for his countryman.

I never was cast as the leading man that I envisioned myself to be, but I did, in fact, appear in two later films -- *The Jazz Singer*, which starred Neil Diamond, in 1980 (that was just a small part – in the concert scenes and a fleeting glimpse in one of the recording studio shots), and *Tap*, with Sammy Davis, Jr., in 1989. Later in my career, I would also appear on the small screen as a guest star on *Fish*, which starred Abe Vigoda, and *The Watcher*, a series set in Las Vegas.

I also backed a number of musical guests on TV shows. Besides Carson's show, I appeared many times on *The Joey Bishop Show*, *The Mike Douglas Show*, *The Merv Griffin Show*, Burt Sugarman's *The Midnight Special*, and Don Cornelius' *Soul Train*. I was also seen on *The Real Don Steele* and several locally televised shows, including *Good Day LA* and *Good Day Arizona*.

My biggest TV success came after I did some records and albums with Tony Orlando, who asked me to go on the road with him and his back-up group, Dawn. The singing duo featured Joyce Vincent Wilson and Telma Hopkins, who had previously been a background singer for Motown (she was famous for shouting "Shut Your Mouth!" on Isaac Hayes' hit, "Theme from Shaft").

I fell in love with Telma, so I went with Tony to be close to her. Although Tony and I were supposed to be friends, he, like many guys who feel threatened by someone talented that they have to rely on, became resentful of me. This came out when I was featured on the group's TV variety show (aptly titled *Tony Orlando and Dawn*), which began in the summer of 1974 as a replacement for *The Sonny and Cher Comedy Hour*.

I stayed with Tony for a year – only because I loved Telma; I certainly wasn't getting any love from Tony. After several episodes of the show had aired, the writers had tried to persuade Tony to expand what I did – they wanted to actually feature me instead of keeping me in the background (I was in the pit with the band).

"King's been here all this time – let's put him in a sketch. Let's make him a bigger part of this thing."

They wrote some funny sketches that Telma and I could do together, with me backing up her voice on the drums. She was a great singer; in fact, I would say she was the best on the show.

But Tony wouldn't hear of it, "No, we don't need that. Take it out."

So the sketch would be removed on the day of the shooting – and then Tony had them rewrite it for HIM and Telma! That's when I realized that when it came down to who your friends really were, they were never those whose insecurities made them fearful for their own success. But I honored my commitment to Tony – even after I heard from Dennis St. John, who again offered me a spot in Neil's band.

I had already given a lot of thought to Dennis' previous offers. Although I had a great deal of admiration for Neil's talents as both a songwriter and a singer -- and was very flattered that Neil had considered adding me, especially since he had never employed a conga drum player in his band (although I had backed him on several of his recordings) -- I did have some reservations about Dennis' offer. First, Dennis had told me that Neil was afraid I would not be accepted in an all-white band, and Dennis had to convince Neil that things would be different in the 70s. Secondly, I was making very good money as a studio musician. Thirdly, I had made numerous, important contacts in Hollywood, and, as I have mentioned before, if a sessions musician is not around for an extended period of time, he or she is usually forgotten. And, last but not least, I still had an agreement with Tony Orlando and Dawn.

Signing on with Neil would mean turning my back on what I had built up over my years in L.A., so there was a lot at stake for me. I had to know if making a change would be worth my while.

"I'll need to be guaranteed at least $90,000 a year," I told Dennis.

"No problem," Dennis assured me.

I still wanted to "test the waters," so to speak, so I signed on for one tour. ONE TOUR! I went on the band's payroll that year, but the 1974 world tour was postponed. We did do a couple of rehearsals that year, and I backed Neil on *Serenade*, his second album for Columbia Records. The album, which was produced by Tom Catalano, would produce three hit singles – "Longfellow Serenade," "I've Been This Way Before," and "The Last Picasso" – and I consider it one of Neil's finest albums. The "icing on the cake" was having Vince Charles also involved with the project (you can hear his steel drums on "Reggae Strut"). And, I think that working with Catalano, who was a genius when it came to making great records, would later help me to become a better producer.

My fears about losing what I had built up were unfounded at the time – I continued to work with Tony Orlando and Dawn, and I was able to do my sessions and other work; in fact, there were times when I worked with Tony Orlando during the day and then backed Diana Ross at night! I just had to be available for recordings or rehearsals whenever Neil called (Dennis kept the band rehearsing for a couple of years, so when it was time to go on our first tour, we were more than ready). And, I was paid $750 every week until we finally went on tour in 1976.

Chapter 21

Headed for the Future

One great thing that resulted from my stint on *Tony Orlando and Dawn* was the opportunity to meet a wonderful, talented woman named Lisa. Lisa had been born into a show business family – her father, Alvino Rey, was a wonderful guitarist who had studied in Andres Segovia's master class, but he is perhaps best known for helping (along with Les Paul) to develop the electric guitar in the 1930s, and he also headed up his own big band. Lisa's mother, Luise King, was a member of the famous King Sisters, a singing group who made it big on radio and backed such stars as Frank Sinatra, Doris Day, and Johnny Mathis.

Lisa was a great singer, she played the harp and piano, and she wrote wonderful songs. She was also drop dead gorgeous, so you can believe that I made a pass at her. Lisa turned me down, saying that she was a Mormon, so she was not allowed to speak to blacks, much less sleep with them (she knew what I wanted). She also told me that they didn't even allow blacks in the church in Salt Lake City as there was a scripture that said blacks were of the devil!

One Sunday morning, we were recording and I took advantage of our break to approach her again. I was determined to break the ice, so I asked her if she had ever seen a black man pee! She said "no," of course, so I walked over to the table where the coffee pot was set up. Turning my back to her, I pretended to unzip my pants and get ready to do my business. At the same time, I pulled the lever on the coffee pot, causing coffee to drain down into the large wastebasket under the table. No one else was bothered by my prank, as they knew what a fool I was, but Lisa let out a big scream.

I wish you could have seen the look on her face, but I guess my little escapade worked – she agreed to let me take her out to dinner that evening! We had a wonderful time, and I learned more about the church's rules against blacks. According to their scriptures, there would come a time when blacks would be able to join the church and other church members would be allowed to associate with them. Lisa told me that if and when that day came she would find me because she loved me but couldn't do anything about it at the time we met.

We did reconnect a couple of years later; we enjoyed a warm friendship and wrote some wonderful music together. Lisa was a very special person, and I happy to say that she married a wonderful man (she is now Lisa Rey Butler) and has two talented sons (Win and Will formed the popular rock band, Arcade Fire). She continued in her career as a jazz harpist when her sons were growing up, and she is still a sought-after performer.

In 1974, I also heard from Barbra Streisand, who called me to perform on her album, *Butterfly*, which was being produced by her then-boyfriend, Jon Peters. The two had met when Peters designed a wig for Barbara for her film, *For Pete's Sake*. Peters not only became her boyfriend, but he also got increasingly involved in Barbra's career (when I met him, he fancied himself a record producer and arranger, and he later became a movie producer – although he didn't have much success in Hollywood after he and Barbra broke up). On the day I recorded, Jon, who didn't know shit from shinola, was strutting around as if he were in charge of everything.

The ten tracks on *Butterfly* included songs by a diverse group of writers -- Bob Marley ("Guava Jelly"), Paul Anka ("Jubilation"), David Bowie ("Life on Mars"), Buck Owens ("Crying Time"), and Paul Williams and Roger Nichols ("I Won't Last a Day Without You") – and Peters was credited as producer (as well as for art direction and design). John Bahler was the arranger for the vocals and horns, while Lee Holdridge was the arranger for the rest of the music.

I loved working with Barbra, but I must say that I also had some difficult sessions. One that stands out in my mind involved the incomparable Ray Charles. During my years as a sessions musician, I had always wanted to work with Ray, and one day I finally got my wish. When my service called to tell me that Ray wanted me to do a session with him, I was one happy guy – but, unfortunately, that session was not even close to a dream job.

Some of the greatest players in the studio business were in on that session -- Joe Sample, Wilton Felder, David T. Walker, Arthur Wright, and Paul Humphreys were some of the "heavyweights" who had been summoned. But none of us could please Ray that day -- and it seemed that I caught the most hell. There was nothing I could do "right," so I finally did the unthinkable -- I had a big argument with Ray.

I told Ray that I was playing what was on the sheet music, so I didn't understand what else he wanted. Ray was not happy that I had spoken up, but he played my part on the piano to show me just what he wanted from me. Now, Ray Charles was a genius and he heard and felt differently than others (I had experienced the same thing with another blind man who also played the piano). But, as much as I loved Ray and his music, I just could not feel where he was coming from, and I do my best work when I can "feel" the music.

I finally just played the music as it was written on the sheet, but, before I left, I told Ray,

"Ray, as long as you are a blind man, don't you ever f**king call me again."

"O.K., King," Ray replied. "If that's the way you feel."

When I walked out of the studio, our working relationship ended. True to his word, Ray never called me again, and he died before I ever got the chance to tell him how much I admired him and his music. That's the way life goes, I guess, but I sure miss him.

Despite (and, in a couple of cases, because of) my success, I had several encounters with jealous and downright rude people. As I have told you, Tony was jealous of me – although I was a regular performer on his show, he did his best to keep me down in the orchestra pit (and out of sight). But there was someone else, a typical rich, selfish black man who was so jealous that he was determined to keep me down. That man was Gene Page, a talented arranger who worked on more than 200 gold and platinum records. Gene had joined the ranks of record business elites after he arranged "You've Lost That Lovin' Feeling" for the Righteous Brothers, and he was an arranger on dozens of Motown hits as well as later arranging for Cher, Elton John, Barbra Streisand, Frankie Valli, Barry White (and his Love Unlimited Orchestra), and many others.

Of course, I had worked with Gene in the past, but I never dreamed he would be so jealous of my success. I had made so much money in the sessions business that I had not only bought my beautiful home in Beverly Hills, but I was also the proud owner of a brand new red Lotus Plus 2. One day, when I had a session at 10 a.m., I had some time to kill, so I was outside watering the garden while I waited for my butler, Reggie, to wipe down the car. Well, Gene just happened to be passing by at that time, and he nearly had a wreck when he saw me.

My session that day was with Morris Albert, a Brazilian singer (he was born Mauricio Alberto Kaisermann) who was recording a song called "Feelings." The song would go on to be a big hit, both as a single and as the title track of Albert's debut album, which was released in 1975. Before I tell you about the session, though, I want to mention the controversy surrounding the song. During the height of its popularity, Albert claimed sole credit for writing "Feelings" (and he was also the producer of the single). In 1981, however, he was sued by French songwriter Loulou Gasté, who testified that "Feelings" plagiarized the melody of his 1957 song, "Pour Toi." Albert lost the lawsuit, and the two are now co-credited with authorship.

It turned out that Gene was the arranger for the "Feelings" session – and the minute he had gotten to the studio he had told the entire crew of about 30 musicians about my success. When I walked in, he said,

"King, I didn't know you were so rich. You don't need to work."

And, believe it or not, that man didn't call me to do a session for him for many years – and, even then, it was not Gene himself who called. Barry White was doing an album, and he wanted me to be a part of it. In fact, Barry not only ordered Gene to call me, but he also threatened to cancel the session if Gene refused. Gene had to do as Barry requested, of course, but he refused to talk to me himself – he had a sister who was a music contractor, and he had her call me. I was so surprised when I heard from one of "Gene's people" that I asked her if she had the right number. She replied that Barry had requested me, which was the only reason she was calling.

After that session with Barry, I had an encounter with one of the rudest people I met in Hollywood. I had just left the studio when I saw Elvis Presley in the hallway. Elvis was one of the few major stars that I hadn't worked with (the other was Frank Sinatra, who didn't use a conga player, but Frank and I did meet a few years later at a function honoring Washington Rucker and I found him to be a very friendly and nice guy). I have always been a friendly guy, too – and I was an admirer of Elvis' music – so I walked over to say "hello" to him.

Wow, what a reaction I got.

"Get that nigger away from me," he shouted to his bodyguard.

I couldn't believe that he was so rude to me, but I guess I shouldn't have been so surprised. I had heard stories about his racism, but there were a lot of people who tried to downplay those rumors, pointing out how good he was to the blacks who worked for him. While it was true that he gave gifts of cars and cash to the blacks who were his hired servants, he did not consider blacks as his equals. In fact, Fats Domino once said that Elvis had told him that blacks were only good for shining his shoes!

There are going to be rude people in any business, and, unfortunately, I also experienced rudeness first hand from two seemingly likeable guys that I had admired for years. That incident happened when I attended a function at the Universal Hotel in Century City. I was thrilled to be at an event with so many famous people, and I was especially happy to see two of my heroes, singing cowboy and actor Roy Rogers and actor Glenn Ford, there. They were standing together, so I walked over to them with my hand outstretched to introduce myself and say "good evening." But neither one of them shook my hand, and when I began to say how happy I was to meet them, they both looked at me like I was a ghost and walked away without a word.

Fortunately, I encountered far more good people than rude ones during my Hollywood days. Most artists were respectful of me and my talents (after all, it was my job to make their music work and them look good), and I met many wonderful people. I have already told you that Glen Campbell was a genuinely nice guy (and a good friend), and singer and guitar player Trini Lopez also stands out as one of the nicest guys I have ever met in the business. Johnny Mathis also became one of my great friends. Johnny is one of the classiest men in the world, and I did dozens of sessions with him. Whenever we see each other, it's always a mutual hello and a big hug before we take time to catch up.

Of course, two of my favorite people were Cannonball and Nat, and I was thrilled to work with both of them in 1974 on Nat's album, *Double Exposure*, which was produced by Cannonball and David Axelrod. The album would be released on the Prestige label in 1975.

In April of 1975, I had the honor of working with Cannonball on what would be his last album – and, according to Nat, the work that Cannonball considered to be the most important project of his illustrious career. *Big Man: The Legend of John Henry* was a departure from Cannonball's familiar jazz albums – it was a musical play that included spoken parts and a chorus in addition to a wonderful score (Cannonball and Nate collaborated on the music).

Produced by Cannonball, Nat, and David Axelrod for Junat Productions, the two-LP album was recorded at Fantasy Studios, and featured several actors, who either spoke or sang their parts in character, the chorus, and a large number of musicians, including a string section. The cast included Joe Williams as John Henry (the steel-driving man), Randy Crawford as Carolina, Robert Guillaume as Jassawa, Judy Thomas as the Whore, and Lane Smith as "Sheriff, Bull Maree." The musicians (in addition to Cannonball, who was featured on the alto sax) included Allen DeRienzo, Oliver Mitchell, and Oscar Brashear on trumpet; Dick Hyde and George Bohanon on trombone; William Green, Jackie Kelso, Donald Menza, and Jay Migliori on reeds; Jimmy Jones on piano; Dawilli Gonga (the pseudonym of George Duke) on keyboards; Billy Fender and Don Peake on guitar; Carol Kaye and Walter Booker on bass; Roy McCurdy on drums; and, Airto Moreira and me on percussion.

I was thrilled to work on an album that was so special to Cannonball, and our time together was especially memorable because about four months later Cannonball was gone. He died on August 8, just four weeks after suffering a cerebral hemorrhage (stroke) – and just over a month shy of his 47th birthday. With his passing, the world lost an iconic figure in the jazz world – and I had lost a mentor, a great friend, and a father figure who meant the world to me.

Losing Cannonball was a huge blow to me – it affected me even more than losing Paul Meers or my father. Unlike Paul Meeres and my father, who were on downward spirals after suffering loss and disappointment before their deaths, Cannonball was "on top of the world" -- and just as innovative and creative as he had been throughout his career. How I wish he had lived to a ripe old age and continued to bless the world with his wonderful music. I still miss this wonderful musician and human being, and I will always treasure our friendship and the experiences we shared.

Fortunately, something happened in my life that helped to keep my mind off my loss. I realized one of my dreams – I finally got a record contract! It came about after I was called to do a session with Lonette McKee, a former child prodigy from Detroit (she was writing music and lyrics, playing keyboards, and singing at the age of seven, and she released her own regional pop/R&B hit when she was only 14). The year after our session, Lonette began her career as a film actress, playing her first role, Sister, in the 1976 film, *Sparkle*; several year later, she received a Tony Award nomination for her role as Julie in the Houston Grand Opera's production of *Show Boat*. Not only was Lonette one of the most talented woman in the business, but she was also one of the sweetest -- and Lonette was so gorgeous that I couldn't take my eyes off her.

The session was arranged and produced by the Detroit "soul team" of Dennis Coffey and Mike Theodore (Mike had known Lonette from the time she recorded her first hit). Dennis was a talented guitarist who had been a member of the Funk Brothers studio band and the Detroit Guitar Band, and Mike was a composer and producer who later made a couple of albums with his Mike Theodore Orchestra. The two men had worked together for Sussex Records before coming to Westbound Records, where Mike and Dennis were the co-producers of Dennis' 1974 album, *Instant Coffey*. I played the congas on that album, and, as it would turn out, Coffey would play guitar on my first album for the Westbound label.

After the session, Mike asked me if I had any music of my own that he could hear – he thought I could be a star! I almost shit! Although I had been a number one sessions musician for several years, no one had ever suggested that I could become a star. And now that I wasn't even looking, I suddenly got a bite!

I had written a lot of songs by then, so it only took a few days for me to get some music to Mike. That same week, Tony Orlando called, asking me to back him in Vegas (I took the gig as I was able to fly back to L.A. to do my sessions while working with him). In the space of two weeks, Mike called me with a record deal!

My first album for the Westbound label was *Magic Man*, which we recorded in 1975 in both L.A. and Detroit (the album was released in June of 1976). The tracks included "Conga Man," "Every Day's a Holiday," "Dance with Me," "The Magic Man," "Sleep Talk," "Back from the Dead," "Tight Rope," "Listen to the Music," and "Last Chance to Dance." I wrote "Back from the Dead" and "Last Chance to Dance," and Dennis, Mike, and I co-wrote "Conga Man" and "The Magic Man." I also wrote "Last Chance to Dance" (credited as Errisson) and "Every Day's a Holiday" (credited to Johnson, Pallman – nods to my birth name).

I worked with a great group of musicians, including Dennis and Bruce Nazarian on guitar; Chuck Rainey, Greg Coles, Henry Davis, and Wayne Douglas on bass; Jerry Peters, Patrice Rushen, Rudy Robinson, and Sylvester Rivers on keyboards; Ed Green, James Gadson, Lee Marcus, and Paul Humphrey on drums; Chuck Garnet and Frank Rosolino on horns; Robert Greenidge on steel drums (Vince was working with Herb Alpert at the time); and, Emile Richards and me on percussion. Sherrel Atwood and I sang lead vocals, and our background singers included Clyde King, Mara Bigelow, Merry Clayton, Prince Knewt, Shirley Matthews, Stephanie Sproule, the Gibson Family, and Vonetta Fields.

The album, which was again praised for my conga-driven tracks, was produced with a nod to the disco-style music that was becoming popular in the day, but it also features a funky backbeat and dense musical arrangements as well as female background vocals on many of the tracks. It is also known for its distinctive cover, which features me as some sort of voodoo priest surrounded by some very attractive (and handsome) followers.

I don't want to get ahead of myself, but in 1975 and 1976, Westbound was distributed through 20th Century Records, which was headed by Russ Regan. Russ was a veteran record executive who had started his career with Motown (his first project for the label was the Marvelettes' number one record, "Please, Mr. Postman," and he also promoted songs by Marvin Gaye, Smokey Robinson & The Miracles, The Supremes, The Temptations, and Stevie Wonder). He later was responsible for suggesting the name "The Beach Boys" for a L.A. group who had called themselves The Pendletons, and he was involved in promoting the careers of several superstars, including Elton John, Olivia Newton-John, and Barry White, as head of the UNI Records, 20th Century Records, and PolyGram Records labels. When he headed UNI, Russ was instrumental in launching the career of a newcomer named Neil Diamond.

As a side note, a former sessions musician named Barry White had also worked with Russ under the umbrellas of both UNI Records and 20th Century Records. Barry, who was promoting a girl group called Love Unlimited, had a friend named Paul Politi, who convinced businessman Larry Nunes to finance an album by Barry White and Love Unlimited. They took the record to Russ at UNI – and later moved to 20th Century Records with him. Of course, Russ took all the credit for discovering Barry, but it was his company, so I guess that's the way it goes in the music business.

Regan was a hands-on type of guy – everything had to be his way. When it was time to release my album, we had a "round table" to discuss which single should be promoted. The night before the release, we all agreed that "The Magic Man" should be the first single, but, when we listened to the radio the next day, we found out that Russ had gone behind our backs and picked the song that he liked the most. The song, "Every Day's a Holiday," did well, but it never made the Top 10 – and we all thought that "The Magic Man" would have gone to number one. Needless to say, we were all disappointed (I was so looking forward to hearing "The Magic Man" on the radio, but Russ had made the call; it was his company, after all).

They promoted the hell out of the album, but that single just wasn't strong enough. It was not R&B enough and not white enough, so there it was -- in the middle of the road. The album did make it to the Top 20 on the Billboard, Record World, and Cash Box charts (they were the top record reporting magazines in those days), but I can't help feeling that I would have become a big recording star IF we had released "The Magic Man" instead of Russ' choice. So it was back to the drawing board (I released another album, *L.A. Bound*, for the label in 1977).

In the summer of 1975, Neil was ready to begin our rehearsals for the upcoming world tour in earnest. It was then that I broke my agreement with Tony to honor my contract with Neil. Before I tell you about rehearsing as part of Neil's new band, I want to mention that my commitment to Neil resulted in the end of my friendship with Mike Stewart. One day, Mike called me to do a session for him, and I agreed. But, because I was unavailable (due to a rehearsal with Neil), I sent a substitute in my place instead. This was acceptable back in those days –

as long as you sent someone good to replace you, a studio musician was able to personally "opt out" without being in breach of the commitment.

Well, this didn't go over too well with Mike – he was furious. He told me that the guy I sent was the worst – and that nobody plays his music like I did. I know that I shouldn't have done that to Mike, but I had a lot riding on being available to work with Neil that day – including a world tour; I couldn't turn Neil down because of one session.

Unfortunately, Mike told me that he would never forgive me for letting him down – and that he would never in his life hire me again. Losing work is one thing (I had plenty of work), but that incident ended a beautiful friendship between Mike and me. He never did forgive me, and I never saw him again before his death on November 13, 2002. What is even sadder is that Mike did not die after "a long illness," as was reported; his son, Jamie, later acknowledged that his father's death was a suicide.

I rehearsed with Neil and the band for about six months on Soundstage F at Paramount Pictures Studios. Dennis had put together a group of fantastic musicians. The "new guys" included me, Doug Rhone on guitar, Tom Hensley on piano, Reinie Press on bass, and Reinie's wife, Linda, on vocals. Most of the rest of the band at that time had been with Neil since 1971 – Dennis on drums, Richard Bennett on guitar, and Emory Gordy, Jr. on guitars (he also played vibraphone, mandolin, bass, and percussion at various times); Alan Lindgren, who played keyboards (and was also a talented arranger and songwriter – he co-wrote several songs with Neil) had joined the band in 1970.

Incredibly, Neil thought that his fans might have forgotten him – although he had continued to record, he had taken time off from touring, so our world tour kicked off with some "trial shows" in northern California and Utah. All doubts that people had forgotten Neil were erased when the tickets to the two scheduled shows at the Sacramento Community Center (a 2,398-seat venue) sold out in minutes and a third show had to be added. After our performances there, which started on January 30, 1976, we traveled to Utah, where we played a show at the BYU Marriott Center (19,000 seats) on February 5. We then performed at the Utah State Spectrum in Logan the next day before finishing up at the Special Events Center in Salt Lake City on February 7.

I can't begin to tell you what a thrill it was to play in these venues packed with enthusiastic fans (I had never played for such large crowds before). It was clear that they loved Neil and his music, and they were very welcoming to us new band members (Neil would always introduce each one of us before we did our solos on his big hit, "Cherry, Cherry").

And, I suddenly found myself in the enviable position of having women flock to me, hoping that I could introduce them to Neil. Many of them were just using me, of course, so you better believe I used them back – some of those women were willing to do anything for a chance to meet their hero.

Playing in those trial shows was an amazing experience, and I couldn't imagine things getting any better. But was I wrong – less than a week later, on February 13, we began our "official" tour Down Under, playing two shows in New Zealand before moving on to Australia, where even more adoration – and adventures -- awaited.

Afterword

That first world tour – the one tour I agreed to join – took place 40 years ago, and what a ride I've had during those 40 years. I'll start by telling you about some of the highs and lows of that first touring gig with Neil. I have already told you about my experience in New Zealand with the agent from L.A., but I had a wonderful time when we played there (in Auckland at Western Springs on February 13, 1976 and at the Queen Elizabeth II Park in Christchurch two days later). The fans were warm and friendly – and I was genuinely happy to perform for them.

The Australian fans blew me away. They loved Neil, and he loved them back, and there was no end to the adoration they showered on Neil and his band (what was even more amazing to me was that fans from all over the world came to see us when we performed Down Under – I had never seen such loyalty, and I enjoyed meeting fans whom I would later encounter on our future travels). We opened with three shows at Festival Hall in Brisbane (beginning on February 18), before moving on to Sydney (three shows), Melbourne (three shows), Perth, and Adelaide; we then returned to Sydney for our final show on March 9.

Because of our popularity, beautiful women flocked to me (as in the U.S., many of them mistakenly thought that I would connect them with "their man"). I am ashamed to say that I took advantage of the situation, and I behaved pretty badly when we were in Australia. My worst escapade was throwing a teacher into a lake, but I truly didn't mean to cause problems. Being the only black in the group, I was lonely and bored. The white boys – even my friend, Dennis – always had something to do after the shows, so I was pretty much left on my own – except for those women.

It was pretty much the same when we came back to the U.S. Since Neil hadn't toured in some time, the venues were packed. One of the highlights for me was playing three shows at the Forest Hills Stadium in Queens, New York. Neil hadn't been there in four years, so we had some great crowds. It was especially memorable for me as I was able to reconnect with my son, Kyle, and he joined me for some of the stops on the tour (there is a video on youtube showing Kyle beating on a tambourine with a drumstick during one of our sound checks in Queens, and he was also with me in Las Vegas, where he attended Richard Bennett's wedding – along with Neil's son, Jesse).

Jesse, who was about the same age as Kyle, was like a son to me, and the two boys had a wonderful time together. Jesse had a lot of energy, and he was particularly fond of running up and down the stadium steps, leaving the security guard, a man we called "Fat Fred," sweating in his wake.

I also finally got to perform at The Greek Theatre in L.A., after having to turn the gig down twice before. We played eight shows there, beginning on September 13, 1976, and we ended that leg of the tour in Honolulu, where I had started my career with The Deacon.

Despite enjoying performing so much, there were a couple of downsides to my experiences on the tour. Since I was the only black in the group, I was often the butt of dressing room jokes -- and seemingly harmless (but expensive) pranks. Once, for instance, someone filled my $200 Thom McAn loafers with coffee (the experience reminded me of the indignities that my good friend, Sammy Davis, Jr., had suffered early in his life).

Even worse, I was the victim of what could have been a career-ending act of sabotage. One day, someone did the unthinkable – tiny bits of glass were spread on the heads of my congas! Long before I joined Neil's band, I had developed the habit of wiping my conga heads with my hand and using a towel to wipe my hands and my face. I found the glass when I wiped the drum heads with my hands, and then I wiped my hands off with the towel. Out of habit, I later wiped my face with that towel – and got splinters of glass in my eyeball! Fortunately, it was the last show of that tour; it ended at the Staples Center in L.A. so I was able to quickly get to a hospital to get the splinters removed.

I don't know whether it was an act of racism or simply jealousy, but I had my suspicions about who would have done such a despicable thing. I had no proof, but I went to Dennis and told him what had happened. Dennis, of course, was furious – he (and no one else in Neil's organization) was going to tolerate that type of behavior. Dennis got to the bottom of the incident, and two roadies ended up getting fired.

From that time on, I was always careful to check my drums, even though those culprits were long gone. In fact, I learned not to trust anyone in the band except Richard Bennett.

Before I move on, I also want to mention my disappointment that we never really did a "world tour" – we toured across the U.S. and Canada and went to Australia, New Zealand, and several countries in Europe. There are so many places that we didn't visit – including Asia (Neil has many fans in the Near East -- Japan, the Philippines, and Malaysia), South America, or many countries in Europe. We didn't visit Africa until 2011, when we performed in South Africa in Johannesburg (April 2), Durban (April 5), Port Elizabeth (April 8), and Cape Town

(April 11); I had a wonderful time in South Africa, and I would have loved to have visited the continent earlier (and often) to get in touch with my roots. And, we didn't even get to Mexico until we played in Mexico City on April 23, 2015. I would have loved to have gone back to Japan again – and would have loved to perform in other European countries, including Spain (which I love). People sometimes mention that to me – that they have had to travel to other countries to see Neil – but I am unable to give a reason why their home countries were bypassed.

The tour was exhilarating but exhausting; I had toured before, but never for such an extended time. I was also anxious to get back to my sessions work (I was getting very concerned that the sessions producers would forget about me). But I was a popular addition to Neil's band (I had made quite an impression on a number of fans), so he asked me what it would take to sign on again. When I told him I was lonely, he asked if there was another black musician I could recommend for the band. Of course, I jumped at the chance to suggest Vince Charles, and he joined us in 1977. We had a wonderful time together on the road – Vince loved everybody and everybody loved Vince, so we had some amazing adventures together.

Since there is so much more to my story, I am ending this first book here. It is impossible to fit everything into one volume, so in my next book, I will tell you about my favorite places on our tours, introduce you to special, lifelong friends and fans, and tell you more about my own career – including my solo albums, performances with my own bands, and guesting with other performers. I will also highlight some of my triumphs and failures, including a failed Bahamian restaurant and the end of my dream for a resort on Pestell Beach on Acklins Island.

And, of course, I can't leave out the women. You will meet wives number four to six as well as a number of other women who have enriched my life with their talents and their love. And, I will tell you more about my other "mistress," golf (I can't imagine telling my story without adding a few stories about my adventures on the links).

Thank you for joining me on this part of my journey. I hope you have enjoyed reading this book as much as I have enjoyed reliving some of the memories I have shared here. I am looking forward to taking you along for another trip down memory lane in the near future.

APPENDIX I
TIMELINE

1941	Errisson Pallaman Johnson (King) and sister, Aries Johnson, born in Nassau, New Providence, the Bahamas (October 29)
1946	Brother Rodney born (September)
1948	Sister Maddie born (December)
1955	Princess Margaret visits Bahamas
	Begins working at race track and is put out of school (age 14)
1956	Begins career as jockey (became leading jockey in Bahamas)
	Starts dancing limbo
1959	Brother Gerone Clark born (September)
1960	Ends career as jockey (age 19)
	Receives first formal instruction on bongos (teacher is John Chipman)
1961	Gig in Bimini; meets Sweet Richard
	Son Anton born (June)
	Begins performing with Sweet Richard in Miami
1962	Meets Cassius Clay (later Muhammad Ali) and plays for his 20th birthday party (January 17)
	Leaves Sweet Richard to tour Hawaii and Japan with The Deacon
	Brother Henry Shivers born (June)
	Paul Meeres killed by a car
1963	Tours "chitlin' circuit" in U.S. with The Deacon
	Solo show in Vegas after The Deacon is deported
	Moves to Miami, Florida
	Marries first wife, Regina
1964	Returns to Nassau; opens King Errisson's Chicken Shack
	Plays with own band at the Conch Shell Club
	Cast in the nightclub scene (at the Kiss Kiss Club) in *Thunderball*
1965	Meets JMC (March); Regina returns to U.S.
	Son Kenny born (July)
1966	Records first album, *Drums of Nassau*, with Lou Adams Orchestra
	Performs in clubs in Canada

1967	Tours U.S. with own jazz band
	Son Vance (Vans) born (April)
	Performs at The Forty Thieves in Bermuda (shares the stage with Redd Fox and, later, Rich Little) (September – 1968)
1968	Arrives in Los Angeles; lives on Skid Row
	Debut performance at Redd Foxx's club
	Break-through studio session with Cannonball Adderley (*Accent on Africa* album); gains instant reputation as a "music fixer"
	First performance with Cannonball Adderly in Detroit
	Father killed by car stolen by young man
1969	First full year as a studio musician
	Invited by Sammy Davis, Jr. to appear on *The Hollywood Palace* (March 15)
	Begins backing Motown artists
	Tours with Diana Ross and the Supremes
	Plays on first Jackson 5 single and album
	Son Kyle born (December 19)
1970	Backs Diana Ross at the Coconut Grove in Hollywood
	Reunites with JMC
	Backs Motown singer Chris Clark in Las Vegas; meets drummer Washington Rucker at gig
	First solo album, *The King Arrives,* released on Canyon Records in U.S.
	Backs the Cannonball Adderly Quartet on *The Happy People* (album not released until 1972)
	Session with Karen Carpenter; reunites with drummer Dennis St. John
	Records tracks for Neil Diamond's studio album, *Tap Root Manuscript*; "Sooliamon" among tracks recorded
1971	Performs "Sooliamon" with Neil Diamond on *The Glen Campbell Goodtime Hour* (January 10)
	Reunites with Muhammad Ali while backing Diana Ross in Miami Beach (March)
	Marries second wife, Chisako
	Studio session for Neil Diamond's "I Am…I Said."
1972	Own band organized; meets steel drummer Vince Charles on way to first rehearsal
	Request from drummer Dennis St. John to play with Neil Diamond's band for their second Hot August Night shows

	at the Greek Theatre; turns down gig due to other commitments
	Plays on The Incredible Bongo Band's first single, "Bongo Rock"/"Bongolia"
1973	The Incredible Bongo Band's first album released
	Arranges "Spiders and Snakes" for Jim Stafford's self-titled album at request of Dennis St. John, who again extends an invitation to join Neil Diamond's band
	Second studio album, *We Must Say Goodbye*, released on Kosons Records (King's label)
	Marries third wife, Pepper (December)
1974	The Incredible Bongo Band's second album released
	Appears in *Uptown Saturday Night* with Sidney Poitier and Bill Cosby
	Records and tours with Tony Orlando and Dawn; becomes regular performer on *Tony Orlando and Dawn* (TV variety show, summer replacement)
	Signs with Neil Diamond's band (tour postponed to 1976)
	Records tracks for Neil Diamond's album, *Serenade*
1975	Continues studio session work while under contract to Neil Diamond
	Plays on Cannonball Adderley's final album, *Big Man* (subtitled "The Legend of John Henry")
	Cannonball Adderley dies two weeks after suffering a stroke (August 8)
	Leaves Tony Orlando and Dawn to honor commitment to Neil Diamond
	Six months' rehearsals with Neil Diamond's band
	Records next studio album, *The Magic Man*, for Westbound Records (released in 1976)
1976	Start of Neil Diamond World Tour
	U.S. "test shows" – 1/30-Sacramento, CA (three shows); 2/5-Provo, UT; 2/6-Logan, UT; and, 2/7-Salt Lake City, UT
	"Official" World Tour begins 2/12 – Auckland, New Zealand

APPENDIX II
Credits with Other Recording Stars (includes congas, percussion, arranging, conducting, and songwriting)

A
Julian "Cannonball" Adderley, Nat Adderley, Toshiko Akiyoshi, Morris Albert, David Axelrod

B
The Bellamy Brothers, Blood, Sweat & Tears, Teresa Brewer, Genie Brown, James Brown, Severin Browne, Tim Buckley, Solomon Burke, Donald Byrd

C
C.J. & Company, Glen Campbell, Michael Edward Campbell, The Carpenters, David Cassidy, Sean Cassidy, The Cate Brothers, The Cats, Ray Charles, David Clayton-Thomas, Dennis Coffey, Compton & Batteau, Bill Cosby, Cut Chemist, Jimmy Cliff

D
Bobby Darin, Sammy Davis, Jr., Neil Diamond, Lamont Dozier, Dunn & Rubini

F
The Four Tops, The Friends of Distinction

G
Bobbie Gentry, Giovanni, Jim Gold, Grant Green

H
Janice Hall, Steve Harley & Cockney Rebel, Alexander Harvey, Donny Hathaway, Joe Herndon, Z.Z. Hill, Richard Groove Holmes & Ernie Watts, Jayson Hoover, Freddie Hubbard, Bobbi Humphrey, John Hurley, Willie Hutch

I
The Incredible Bongo Band

J
The Jackson 5, Jimmy Jackson, Etta James, Paul Jeffrey, Jim & Ginger, Quincy Jones

K
Eddie Kendricks, Albert King, B.B. King, John Klemmer, Charles Kynard

L
Glenn Leonard, Lobo, John Lucien

M
Melissa Manchester, Johnny Mathis, Michael McDonald, Melton, Levy & The Dey Brothers, Blue Mitchell, Essra Mohawk, Wes Montgomery

N
Johnny Nash, Ted Neely

O
Danny O'Keefe, Michael Omartian, The Originals, Tony Orlando and Dawn

P
Paul Parrish, Richard Perry, Billy Preston, Flora Purim, The Pyramids

R
Kenny Rankin, Martha Reeves, Lionel Richie, Johnny Rivers, Freddie Roach, Freddy Robinson, Diana Ross (solo), Diana Ross and The Supremes

S
Gary St. Clair, Buffy St. Marie, Lara Saint Paul, Boz Scaggs, Lalo Schifrin, Seals & Crofts, Seanor & Koss, Doc Severinsen, Marlena Shaw, Bobby Sherman, Johnny "Hammond" Smith, O.C. Smith, Soul Mokossa, Spider, Jim Stafford, Ringo Starr, The Staehely Brothers, John Stewart, Barbra Streisand, Swamp Dogg, Foster Sylvers

T
The Temptations, Triple S Connection, Stanley Turrentine

V
Frankie Valli, The Ventures, Michael Viner

W
Wendy Waldman, T-Bone Walker, Johnny Guitar Watson, Barry White, Jay White, Michael White, Hank Williams, Jr., Joe Williams, Lenny Williams, Jimmy Witherspoon

and

Compilation Albums by Various Artists, Original soundtrack, *Ted & Venus* (1992)

APPENDIX III

SOLO ALBUMS & MUSIC

1966	*Drums of Nassau* (with Lou Adams Orchestra)	Bahamian Rhythms Limited
1970	*The King Arrives*	Canyon Records
1973	*We Must Say Good-Bye*	Kosons Records
1976	*The Magic Man*	Westbound Records
1977	*L.A. Bound*	Westbound Records
1980	*King Errisson*	Erisong Records
1981	*35 Carat Lady*	Erisong Records
1984	*Hoosier Girls*	Shatter Records
1986	*I Am Somebody*	Atomic Records
1987	*Together*	Acklins Records Macola
1991	*Global Music*	Erisong Records Ichiban Records
1993	*Man*	Erisong Records Ichiban Records
1996	*Natural Feeling*	Acklins Records
2000	*Pouring Reign*	Acklins Records
2006	*Nice*	Acklins Records
2009	*Conga Serenade*	Acklins Records
2013	*In My Secret Life*	Wolf Entertainment
	Reggae Lover	Wolf Entertainment
2014	*Can't Get Enough* (retitled *Guava Duff*)	Acklins Records
2016	*Ain't No Cure for Love*	Tabitha Records

APPENDIX IV

THE MOTOWN WEST COAST STUDIO BAND

Keyboards – Larry Knechtel, Clarence McDonald, Don Randi, Mike Rubini, Joe Sample

Guitars – Adolph Green, Weldon T. Parks, Louie Shelton, Thomas Tedesco, David T. Walker, Arthur Wright

Bass -- James Jamerson (session), Ron Brown, Wilton Felder, Carol Kaye, Bill Pitman

Drums – Ed Greene, Paul Humphreys, Earl Palmer, Gene Pello

Percussion – Joe Clayton, Gary Coleman, Sandra Crouch, **King Errisson**, Bobbye (Hall) Porter, Emil Richards, Jerry Steinholtz

Arrangers – Gil Ashley, James Carmichael, William Goldstein, Gene Page, Arthur Wright

APPENDIX V
KING ERRISSON CONTACT INFORMATION

OFFICIAL WEBSITE: kingerrisson.com
Welcoming message; News; Biography; The Work (Albums, CD Shopping Cart, Film); Contact info; Media; Friends

FACEBOOK:
Main Page: www.facebook.com/king.errisson (photo with Neil Diamond current profile photo)
Alternate Page: www.facebook.com/errisson.king (photo with drums current profile photo)

TWITTER: www.twitter.com@Kingerrisson (search for account with purple background with white oval; other accounts are not currently in use)

RECORD LABEL: Acklins Records
Acklins Records/Erisong Productions, Inc.
P.O. Box 752501
Las Vegas, NV 89136-2501
(702) 516-2097; (702) 516-4642
Office Hours: Mon. – Fri., 9:00 a.m. – 5:00 p.m. (Pacific Time)

Disclaimer: All information is correct as of this writing; if pages cannot be found at these addresses, please use a search engine to access the current information.

Made in the USA
San Bernardino, CA
07 March 2017